Looking Backward Moving Forward

ASHLAND

The Garland City Of The Inland Seas

Edited By
Jane S. Smith & Michael J. Goc

New Past Press Inc.   Friendship   Wisconsin 53934

Looking Back-Moving Forward
Ashland, The Garland City of the Inland Seas

Copyright, 1987 Ashland Centennial Task Force (City of Ashland) & The New Past Press, Inc.

All rights reserved.

Dust Jacket Art: Connie Cogger, Washburn, Wisconsin
Dust Jacket Design: Sandhill Studio, Green Lake, Wisconsin
Page Design, Typesetting, Publishing Services: New Past Press Inc., Friendship, Wisconsin
Printing: F. A. Weber, Park Falls, Wisconsin

Printed in the United States of America

Smith Jane S. & Goc Michael J.
Looking Back—Moving Forward, Ashland The Garland City of the Inland Seas
Illustrated by Connie Cogger, Donna Lanni, Eleanore Gengelbach

ISBN 0-938627-02-3

Table of Contents

Dedication--To the People of Ashland

Beginnings	9
Serving the People	19
Maintaining Law and Order	30
Battling Blazes, Saving Lives	32
By Rail, Water, Road and Air	38
Optimists and Opportunists	48
Communications	66
The Medical Center of the North	70
A Center of Learning	76
The Ashland Chronicle	85
Of Faiths Diverse	95
Ashland's Most Honorable	108
The Faces of Ashland	111
Places for Gathering	126
Welcoming Sights	131
The Competitive Spirit	138
Creative Expressions	146
Fellowship and Service	155
Boy Scout Anniversary	167
Bibliography	168
Bird's-Eye View of Ashland	46-47

Acknowledgements

The making of this book was a bit like the making of Ashland itself. A lot happened very quickly. The volunteers who researched and wrote it compressed what is normally a year's work into approximately three months. Many will remember the winter of 1986-87 not as the year of unusually warm weather, but as the Winter-of-the-Book. They had very little time to enjoy the weather and they deserve the first thank you.

Thanks should also go to those who supplied information and assistance in other forms: photographers, typists, and family members; those who filled out organization questionnaires and collected church and family histories.

A special thank you is owed the artists whose original drawings enhance both the cover and inside of this book.

The archives of the Ashland Historical Society and the exhibits of the Ashland Museum were an invaluable source of information. We must also thank the Boards of both organizations for patiently acquiring the material out of which the book is fashioned. Along those same lines, thanks is owed to the many Ashlanders who have supported the Historical Society and Museum over the years. Their support is the root and branch upon which this book has blossomed.

Work on the book has spurred a lot of interest. Many Ashlanders have produced books, letters, photos and artifacts—even a bottle of crushed bed bugs once used as a moth deterrent—that will permanently enrich the record of the city's past.

While thanks should go to all the researchers, writers and donors, responsibility for errors does not. That is accepted and apologized for by the editors. Ashland has a great past. We had a great time telling its story.

April 1, 1987
Jane S. Smith   Michael J. Goc

The Ashland Centennial Committee would like to take this opportunity to thank all of the businesses, organizations, foundations and individuals who financially contributed to the centennial project in order to help make it a success. However, at the time this historical document went to press, we had not received all of the contributions and we felt it inappropriate to publish a partial list of the donors.

We gratefully acknowledge your support! Without it, the entire concept of "Celebrating 100" would have been impossible to put together and carry to a successful conclusion. Once again, the Ashland Centennial Committee sincerely thanks all of you for aiding us in making "Celebrating 100" a reality.

James Junker

James Junker, Chairperson
Ashland Centennial Committee

Section Researchers and Authors

Beginnings; City Builders; By Rail, Water, Road and Air	Jane Smith
Serving the People	Carol Larson
Optimists and Opportunists	Joyce Dierauer
A Center of Learning	Dave Pauli, Caroline Sandin, Astrid Berthiaume, Malcolm McLean
Libraries	Ellen Kasulis
The Faces of Ashland; Places for Gathering	Sue McCue
The Medical Center of the North	Dr. Carol Blum, Theresa Sandor
The Competitive Spirit	Pat Flynn
Welcoming Sights	Ruth Goetz
Battling Blazes, Saving Lives	Karen Morzenti
Maintaining Law and Order	Gordon Gilbertson
Creative Expressions	Donna Lanni
The Ashland Chronicle; Communications	John B. Chapple
Fellowship and Service	Jan Kupczyk, Carol Pauli, Kay Roffers
John B. Chapple; Boy Scout Anniversary	Joseph Gerwood

Artists
Connie Cogger
Eleanore Gengelbach
Donna Lanni

Photographers
Gib Westman
Bill McRae
Joseph Gerwood
Edith Merila

Thomas Smedley
Robert Fromholtz
Bob Stadler
Rick Olivo

Warren Nelson
Betty Ferris
Don Chase
Jim Melin

Other Contributors

Irv Brittig
Howard Pearson
James S. "Monk" Monroe
Bob Blaskowski
Bev Blaskowski
Emeline Hagen
Art Johnson
Ralph McVic
Florence Brenseke
Paul VanPernis
Mildred Swanson
Peter Leciejewski
Tony Leciejewski
John Kirklewski
Connie Junker
Jerry Giese
Sue Theno
Bob Soine

Mary Jane Doss
Don Kupczyk
Fred Tidstrom
Mary Roguski
Avis Olson
Anita Pray
Madeline Garnich
Keith Dallenbach
Larry Wisner
Ann Moran
Harold "Hudda" Martin
Floyd Hovarter
Walt Kingum
Virginia Burtness
Don Straw
Muriel Weimar
Marjorie Trogan
Inez Beesley

Grace Sexton
Irene Berg
Wilma Housko
Dale Kupczyk
Cora Johnson
John Kontny
Roger Larson
Evelyn Lutz Durocher
Wayne Lordes
Joe Hunt
Dennis Olby
Ashland Daily Press
Ashland Historical Society
Bayfield Historical Society
Mellen Historical Society

Typists
Sue Hnath
Michelle Larson
Karyn Carnahan
Patti Ekstrom
Marlene Ronning
Kathy Holevatz

Greetings

Dear Friends and Neighbors:

Welcome to Ashland's Centennial Celebration—Looking Back, Moving Forward.

One hundred years ago the residents of four separate settlements along Chequamegon Bay—Ashland, Bay City, Whittlesey and Parishville—banded together to form a new city. They chose the name *Ashland* after the Kentucky home of that great and beloved American statesman, Henry Clay.

In its beginnings, Ashland was a bustling, rough and brawling town. Its waterfront was lined with saw mills, ore docks and cargo terminals. Smoke spewed from numerous industrial smokestacks. Lawlessness and political corruption were not all that uncommon. Life surely must have been interesting in those times, if not altogether healthy.

The big timber having been cut and ore having run out, Ashland went through decades of decline. Thankfully, that decline has now stopped.

Ashland today is a vibrant and growing community. Our pride is back. We look toward the future with optimism.

The turnaround in Ashland during the past year is nothing short of a miracle. Our industrial and retail sectors have expanded greatly. The downtown is getting a facelift. The new Hotel Chequamegon is one of the finest hotels in the Midwest. The new marina, the RV Park, Bayview Park and the Waterfront Trail will add greatly to our recreational potential. The restoration of the old Soo Line Depot will be a magnet to the community. Parks and streets are being improved, trees are being planted and homes are going up. Cultural opportunities are expanding.

My thanks to the Centennial Committee for organizing all the events of our celebration and for compiling this outstanding record of our history. As you read these pages, I'm sure that you will have a greater appreciation of our colorful history.

We've come a long way from our humble beginnings. Let us honor the past and serve the future as we celebrate one hundred years of progress.

God Bless You.

Sincerely,

Mayor Daniel O. Theno

Introduction

Providence must have smiled on the Chequamegon. By geologic chance, the region evolved replete with natural resources in the ground, dense forests abundant with game and beauty, clear streams full of fish and, above all, the best fresh water harbor in the world.

Four flags have flown over the area: Spanish, French, English and American. It was part of the original Northwest Territory and was contained inside the borders of three states. Eight different Indian nations lived on the Bay. Then came the first white explorers, missionaries, and fur traders. They were followed by the Yankees who platted and developed the lands, the railroaders, shippers, loggers, entrepreneurs and settlers.

The people who came envisioned something special here. They were optimists and opportunists, people of stubborn courage who braved harsh winters and primitive conditions to build a civilized life. They valued hard work, honest dealing with their neighbors, decent homes for their families, good schools for their children and an opportunity to enjoy all those things which these lands can provide.

Other cities have come and gone, but Ashland is still here. It has enjoyed boom times and endured tough times, yet somehow always landed on its feet. This book is a humble attempt to do justice to the story of Ashland's past; to recall for present and future generations the spirit and enterprise that built the community that still prides itself as The Garland City of the Inland Seas. Ashland has much of which to be proud. The builders of the past left a legacy of optimism and energy pointing to a future that can be brighter and more exciting than anything that has gone before. Ashland began with boom. Maybe the biggest and best boom is yet to come.

Beginnings

"There's something that one of these days is gonna be gone and people won't know what it was all about and yet, it's part of our past."
Alan Cate

The one hundred years of Ashland's corporate history are a mere speck of geologic time. The forces that formed the particular patch of earth that the city now occupies began to shape its future billions of years ago.

The Ashland region was once an island in a vast ancient sea. Minerals washing down into the water laid down 25,000 feet of sediment that fused into what is called Chequamegon brownstone. Volcanoes spewed molten rock from beneath the surface and laid the foundations for the mineral wealth of the Trap, Copper and Penokee Ranges. Ice Age glaciers cut across the land many times, carving the bed of Lake Superior, Chequamegon Bay and thousands of inland lakes and streams. The deep harbor that has played such an important part in Ashland's story is a legacy of these icy rivers. Erosion, the force of wind and weather and time, wore away softer rock, and left the hard spine of the Penokees for men to contend with. This ridge of rock is a geologic fact of life and has had a most important influence on the history of Ashland.

The Penokees formed a barrier that determined how Ashland would develop. Rivers that might have flowed north to Superior instead ran south and logs that might have been shipped to mills in Ashland instead went down the St. Croix, Namekagon, and Chippewa Rivers to build cities there. The railroad on which Ashland's foundation depended was delayed for years while engineers worked to penetrate the ridge north of Mellen. The iron ore that made Ashland a port of worldwide significance was embedded in these hills. Much of Ashland's history was determined by the forces that made the earth long before any human arrived on the shore of the bay.

About the time Columbus arrived in the New World, the Chippewa people came to the long, narrow, sandy strip of land they called *Sha-ga-waun-ik-ong*. This term has been translated in several ways. It is either

This fanciful drawing from an 1800s promotional booklet published by the Wisconsin Central portrays a busy Chequamegon Bay lined with bustling communities.

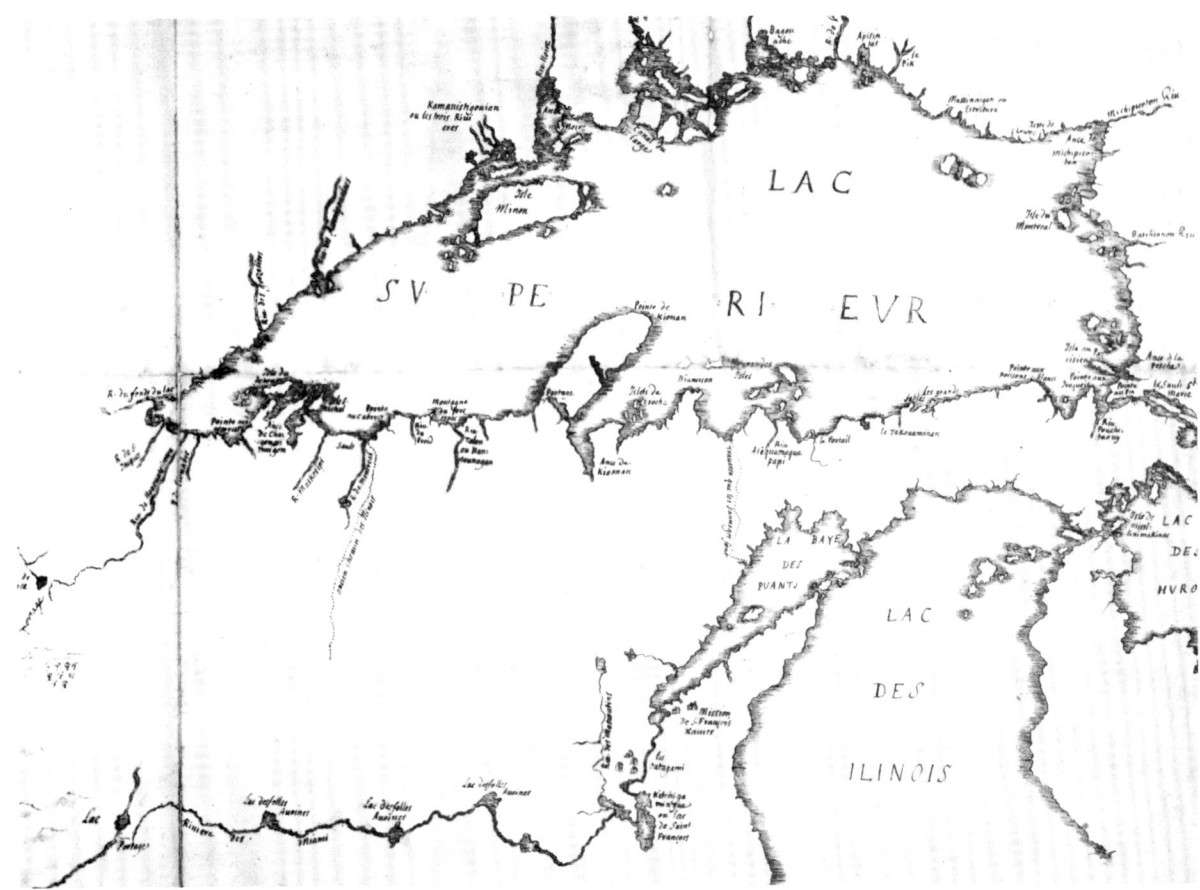

Chequamegon Bay is identified on this 1659 French map of Lakes Superior and Michigan. The Fox-Wisconsin River waterway is to the south. The Brule-St. Croix River route to the Mississippi is to the west of the Bay.

"lowlands," or the "needle." It may also be "the region of shallow water," where "there are large extended breakers." Each version is descriptive and suitably accurate.

The Chippewa stayed on Chequamegon Point for about a century before leaving it, first to settle on Madeline Island and then to move to the Sault region. In the years that followed, the Chippewa came and went to and from the Ashland area. Their travels were dictated by the necessities of hunting and gathering, by their long years of war with the Sioux, and, after 1659, the fur trade.

The two French fur traders Pierre d'Esprit, le Sieur Radisson, and Medard Chouart, le Sieur des Groseilliers, were the first white men of record to visit Chequamegon. They arrived in 1659 and built what has been called the first white dwelling place in Wisconsin. Radisson described it as a triangular, "fort of stakes" with a gate facing the water for quick escape from any "murtherers" who might try to kill the two men and with "a long cord tyed with some small bells, wch were sentereys."

The Chippewa were anything but hostile to the newcomers. They so heartily welcomed the Frenchmen that Radisson wrote, "We were Cesars, being nobody to contradict us...those poor miserable(s) thought themselves happy to carry our equipage, for...we should give them a brasse ring, or an awle..."

The mainland whose surface Radisson and Groseilliers barely scratched, abounded with moose, bear, elk, deer and buffalo but the beaver was the most valuable animal. Millions of pelts ultimately worth millions of dollars were shipped out of the Chequamegon trading post at La Pointe on Madeline Island. By the time the French lost their North American territory in 1761, Chequamegon was one of the most valuable posts in a fur trade empire that included all of the Great Lakes-St. Lawrence River Valley, and the Ohio and Mississippi Valleys as well.

Although it was fabulously lucrative for some, the fur trade was not the only reason Frenchmen came to Chequamegon. Only five years after Radisson and Groseillers hauled the equivalent of a small fortune in furs out of the Bay, Father Claude Allouez arrived. He was a Jesuit missionary and he brought the first word of Christianity to Wisconsin's shores. When Allouez landed at Chequamegon, he found a large Indian settlement consisting of Chippewa and other tribes. He saw it as, "Chagouamigong, for which we have so long looked forward. It is a beautiful bay, at the

bottom of which is situated the great village of the savages who there plant their fields of Indian corn, and lead a stationary life."

Allouez built a chapel dedicated to the Holy Spirit not far from Radisson's and Groseillier's stockade and remained at the Bay until 1669. Father Jacques Marquette then came to "La Pointe du Saint Esprit," but he and the Chippewa were soon forced to flee to the Sault by invading Sioux warriors. Conflict between the two tribes would continue for another century and it forced both missioners and traders to shift their activities off the mainland to the safer premises of Madeline Island.

The transfer of Wisconsin from France to Great Britain in 1763 made little change at Chequamegon Bay. Furs now went to wily Scots factors instead of friendly *habitants* from Montreal. In order to insure the smooth and lucrative flow of fur to London, King George's government favored the Great Lakes tribes by prohibiting the westward expansion of its thirteen colonies on the Atlantic Coast. This policy was one of the unredressed grievances mentioned in the American Declaration of Independence. When the American rebellion succeeded on the battlefield, the treaty negotiators—Thomas Jefferson, John Adams, John Jay and Benjamin Franklin—insisted on American possession of the Great Lakes region as a condition for peace.

American control of Wisconsin meant the end of Indian life as it had evolved since the fur trade began. After the War of 1812, the British transferred the trade to the Yankees, and Chequamegon fur helped to build the fortune of the first American millionaire, John Jacob Astor. Unlike their European predecessors, the Americans were interested in more than fur or souls. They wanted land for settlement and pursued a policy of Indian removal. In 1843, the Chippewa were forced to cede their land in Wisconsin and the Chequamegon region was open for settlement.

In the early 1850s, Colonel Charles Whittlesey conducted a geological survey of northern Wisconsin. He learned the Chippewa name for iron, *Pewabic*, and used it to name the hills traversing central Ashland County. Either Whittlesey's penmanship or the eyesight of a printer in Madison was faulty, for the name appeared on the survey map as Penokee and has so remained.

Whittlesey had better luck writing to his brother Asaph in Ohio. The railroads were due to arrive at Chequamegon shortly, the hills inland were loaded with exploitable ore and timber, Charles told Asaph, so why not move the family to the Bay? Asaph said, why not indeed? He then joined his wife Lucy and two daughters on a steamer and traveled up Lakes Erie, Huron and Superior to La Pointe. They arrived with a few household goods and twenty-five cents of pocket money.

On July 5, 1854, Asaph Whittlesey and another Ohioan named George Kilborn set out from La Pointe to explore the head of Chequamegon Bay. They landed on the

Much worn down by the effects of nature, the monument at the mouth of Fish Creek and Lake Superior still stands. The inscription, though difficult to decipher, reads: "The First House Built By White Men in Wisconsin was erected near this spot by Radisson and Groseilliers in the fall of 1658." The monument was erected by the Old Settlers Club in 1929.

beach and walked up to what is now the intersection of Front Street and Beaser Avenue. Whittlesey later reported that, "As I stepped ashore, Mr. Kilborn exclaimed, 'Here is the place for the big city' and handing me the ax added, 'I want you to have the honor of cutting the first tree in the way of settlement upon the town-site.'"

The tree became one of the foundation logs in the first American building in Ashland, which Whittlesey erected on what is now Lot 2, Block 105 (on the Bay side of what is now 18th Avenue West and Front Street). The cabin measured ten feet by fourteen, had one door facing south and one window facing the Bay. Lucy and daughter Eugenia joined Asaph in August and they prepared to winter in their new home. The nearest neighbors were eleven miles away, with no connecting trail. The Whittlesey's had only the thick woods and the cold blue lake for company. Asaph was understandably concerned about his wife. He wrote, "Mrs. Whittlesey's surroundings were much in contrast with her former life, and so absolutely were we shut in by the dense forest that there was but one way to look out, and that was to look up."

In September the steamer *Sam Ward* brought a load of visitors from the island, but they didn't stop Whittlesey from building two more cabins before winter set in. One of these was a two story building twenty by thirty feet, the first permanent home in Ashland. It was located on what is now the corner of Beaser Avenue and Front Street.

Civilization quickly followed the Whittleseys to Ashland. The first community dance was held in their house. The Reverend L.H. Wheeler preached the first sermon and the first Independence Day was observed there. It was the location of the first post office, and the polling place for county offices. Sunday school was conducted on the premises, but that didn't stop Henry Cross from becoming Ashland's first Yankee murderer when he dispatched Robert Boyd in January of 1858.

The first Yankee child born in Ashland was Katherine Goeltz Ellis, whose father, Conrad Goeltz, built the fourth house in town. She later recalled, "The Ashland of long ago, as I remember it, was a vast wilderness with its main street simply an Indian trail leading from a great water front to a greater forest beyond. Here and there along side this trail, now Beaser Avenue, was an occasional clearing just large enough to permit of a log cabin or claim shanty . . ."

G.L. Brunschweiler surveyed and platted the original 280-acre site of Ashland in 1854. When the plat was registered at the Superior land office in late 1856, it was recorded that Asaph Whittlesey and George Kilborn each owned one-eighth and Martin Beaser owned three-fourths.

Beaser was a New York native and a shrewd pioneer developer. He made sure the town was platted, built the first dock and store in the village and the fifth house. He also petitioned Washington to establish a post office in the town he dubbed "Ashland" in honor of the home of Senator Henry Clay of Kentucky.

Clay was one of the most prominent political leaders of his day. He ran for President and lost twice, but was mentioned as a candidate in virtually every national election from 1820 to 1850. He belonged to the Whig party which held positions akin to what a conservative Democrat or moderate Republican might espouse today. He is remembered as the "Great Compromiser" who in 1820 and 1850, found peaceful

In this 1800s bird's-eye-view, the Ashland skyline is dominated by the Old Chequamegon Hotel. Wisconsin Central tracks run out into the Bay on dock at left.

The celebrated portrait of Ashland founder Asaph Whittlesey dressed in his traveling clothes. He snowshoed to Chippewa Falls to catch the train to take his seat in the Wisconsin Legislature. (Inset) Whittlesey in more conventional garb.

A good horse and buckboard were essential equipment for a frontier doctor like Edwin Ellis. He was the first of many medical men to have an impact on Ashland well beyond the bounds of his profession.

political solutions to the crises of a nation divided over the issue of slavery. After Clay died in 1852, no more peaceable solutions came forth and the United States slipped into Civil War.

The post office department in Washington turned down Martin Beaser's petition to name his town Ashland since another developer in Richland County had already claimed the title for his village. For six years then, until the Richland County Ashland became a ghost town, mail for Chequamegon Bay was addressed to the post office of Whittlesey. When the other Ashland failed, the post master accepted Beaser's claim to the title, and in June of 1860 the name Ashland was officially affixed to the settlement on Chequamegon Bay.

Just as word of potential mineral wealth in Ashland brought Whittlesey, Kilborn and Beaser to town, it also brought an enterprising capitalist and medical doctor from St. Paul named Edwin Ellis. In company with Cyrus A. Rollins, Ellis traveled through the wilderness to Superior then, guided by mail carrier Baptiste Gauden, mushed a dogsled to La Pointe. They walked across Chequamegon Bay on snowshoes, waited for spring in a shanty owned by Lusk, Prentice and Company and were more than favorably impressed with the place.

In June of 1855, Ellis was in Dubuque, Iowa, urging General Warner Lewis, Surveyor General of the northwest region, to plat and divide the land around Chequamegon Bay. Lewis dispatched an engineer named Augustus Barber to the Bay and he platted out the community of "Bay City" which Ellis recorded on behalf of the stock company that had dispatched him to Chequamegon in the first place. Bay City survived until the recession of 1857 killed development in the area. By 1860, Bay City was a ghost town. Part of the original plat was restored in 1870 as the Ellis division of Ashland.

While Ellis platted, Samuel Vaughn pre-empted. He moved south from Bayfield in 1856 to claim ownership of 160 acres along the Bay. He voiced the optimistic sentiment that brought all these pioneer developers to the new town when he said, "From the natural location of Ashland, it would become a place of importance."

The early 1850s were years in which frontier Wisconsin was taken up by what can be called "railroad fever." Land speculators and town developers schemed and dreamed, wheeled and dealed to bring the puffing locomotives and iron tracks to their prospective cities. If they succeeded, towns grew and prospered. When they failed, empty buildings and deserted streets mocked their dreams.

By 1857, the first Ashland pioneers had been joined by other optimists and their families. Myron Tompkins, Lawrence Farley, Charles Hamlet, Anthony Fisher, Frederick Bauman, Austin Corser, John Corser, M.H. Mandelbaum, Henry Drixler, Captain J.D. Angus, John Beck, A.W. Burt, A.J. Barkley, John Donaldson, Andrew Scoobie, J.P. Haskell all settled by the Bay. As their names indicate most of these pioneers were Yankees who hailed from New England, New York, Ohio or the British Isles. The melting pot had yet to cook in Ashland because the ingredients were absent. The ethnic diversity that so characterized the city by the end of the nineteenth century had yet to appear in 1857.

Recession came instead. It was followed by the Civil War, in which the energies of the nation were turned away from the frontier. In the late 1850s, every railroad in Wisconsin declared bankruptcy and all hope of any line reaching the Bay disappeared. So did the population of Ashland. The Whittleseys moved to Bayfield, the Beasers to Ontonagon, Dr. Ellis to Odanah. The rest dispersed to other towns that looked more promising. The first census of newly-formed Ashland county found 513 people in 1860. By 1865, 256 remained to be counted, with 211 in 1870.

The township government, called Bayport and consisting of all the mainland portions of what was then La Pointe County, was organized in 1856. It lasted ten years, then dissolved for lack of people. After the Ashland post office was accepted by the federal government in 1860, the same name was transferred to a new county assembled from portions of La Pointe County. At its first

The long-awaited first train from the south passed the White River trestle in 1877. It connected Ashland to Milwaukee, Chicago and points beyond and triggered the north country's first boom.

annual meeting in November of 1860, the county board authorized the payment of $314.70 of bills and noted that the assessed value of lots in Bay City was $1.04 and $2.08 in Ashland. The board also took action symbolic of the times. The village of Bay City was dissolved due to lack of population.

Martin Roehm, his wife and their children William, John and Lucy hung on in Ashland. They occupied the abandoned Beaser house on Front Street from 1863 to 1869, sole occupants of an empty town. By the end of the 1860s Wisconsin's railroads had reorganized and consolidated. The Wisconsin Central, forerunner of the Soo Line, was pushing tracks north through the center of the state with first Bayfield, then Ashland as its goal.

When word of the railroad's renewed interest in Ashland spread, former settlers returned and new ones came to the Bay. In 1871, Ashland County felt optimistic enough to issue $200,000 in bonds to help the Wisconsin Central build its rail line through the county. Aid from local, state and federal governments to railroads was common on the frontier. Cities routinely donated land for right-of-way, depots and railyards. They floated bonds, solicited donations from businesses, even encouraged farmers to put up their land as collateral for railroad financing. The railroads that developed pioneer communities like Ashland were the product of a partnership between government and business.

Encouraged by Ashland County's bond issue, the Wisconsin Central sent a colony of workmen to the Bay. Their chore was to cut through the timber, bridge the rivers, and fill the marshes for a rail line south to the Penokee Gap near Mellen. Sam S. Fifield, who was Chairman of the Town of Supervisors described the situation aptly when he wrote:

> Picture if you can, the planting of twelve hundred people among the pine trees on the townsite, the bringing order out of chaos, organizing a local government for the protection of the people, the making of the necessary improvements, the opening of streets building of bridges, stores, hotels, saloons, shops, homes, docks, warehouses, rushing business day and night before the coming of winter . . . from a thousand to thirteen hundred men were engaged in the tremendous task of clearing a track through the forest and building a railroad.

Railroad construction sparked a colossal boom in Ashland. The community that had an assessed value of barely three dollars in 1860 mustered nearly a quarter-million dollars of improvements in 1872 alone. The atmosphere of the frontier town, full of possibilities and hopes, dreamers and schemers was outlined

Looking east from the old log bridge over Fish Creek circa 1890. Ashland is in the background.

by Sam Fifield when he described Ashland as, "...an organization of society out of rough, strange human element, a mixed population rapidly brought together of rough railroad builders, a camp following of bad men and bad women, sprinkled with a goodly number of brave and true pioneers, who came to make for themselves new homes."

Ashland was on a roll in the summer of 1872. By winter the city was out of the game. A national recession occurred again and railroad construction halted. Twelve hundred railroad workers were stranded in the tiny village on the Bay. The rail line petered out in the wilderness south of town and the Bay was locked in ice. The only way to get out was to walk, and even then the only possible destination was an equally isolated and less than attractive Duluth.

In December railroad management told its man in Ashland, Captain W.W. Rich, to pay off the working men and send them out of town. They had been idling in a camp on the edge of town since construction halted in late fall and demanded that Rich and the railroad give them "pay to date" rather than to the day work actually stopped. The mood grew ugly and Rich was forced to protect himself and the paymaster by drawing his revolver.

He escaped to Ashland and alerted Town Chairman Sam Fifield. Fifield ordered all saloons closed and saloonkeepers seemed to comply by locking their front doors. They then began a booming business out of back entrances, and angry railroad workers took over the town.

Fifield and other Ashlanders sent a plea for help to Nelson Boutin, Sheriff of both Ashland and Bayfield counties. He rode into town at midnight on New Year's with a posse dubbed Company D of the Bayfield Rifles under the command of Robert D. Pike. They marched up from the ice and occupied McElroy's Hall at the corner of Vaughn Avenue and Front Street. Sheriff Boutin shut down all of Ashland's saloons and mounted armed guards from one end of Second Street to the other. The railroad men sobered up, dallied in their camp for about ten days, then set off on the long chilly walk to Duluth. Calm returned to Ashland once again, the calm of hard times.

Spring brought new hope and new money to the Wisconsin Central. Work on the Ashland route resumed and pushed south from the White River to the Penokee Gap. A thirty mile long "pig-tail" route curled through the forest from Ashland but stopped dead in the hills a good fifty-six miles short of the northern terminus of the Wisconsin Central at Chippewa Station.

The "pig-tail" route boomed, however, and illustrates the power of a rail line to stimulate development. Sawmills set up along the tracks and shipped regular carloads of lumber to Ashland. A daily passenger train from the Bay was hard-pressed to handle the human traffic of loggers, settlers, and entrepreneurs ready to penetrate the northern wilderness. The port of Ashland developed and grew as a shipper of timber, while the city itself had its pick of lumber for building materials.

Still, the break in the rail line slowed progress. The Wisconsin Central, slow to recover from the mid-1870s recession, was in danger of losing its federal land grant unless it completed the line to Ashland. Finally, in

1877, the money was raised and track laid through the Penokees.

Asaph Whittlesey, who had waited more than twenty years for it, drove the last spike. He later said:

> I had the honor of driving the last spike, which took place at Chippewa Station, amid the shoutings of a large assemblage of people, including laborers upon the road, and in a few moments thereafter, the first train from Milwaukee passed over the road on the way to Ashland, amid great rejoicing and demonstration of joy over the victory. At Ashland also, the excitement became intense, and though it was late on a Saturday evening when our train reached the town, the illumination of the place brought to view a field of faces crazy with excitement over the event they were celebrating.

Ashland was now connected by rail with the rest of the United States. The north coast of Wisconsin and the hinterland to the south were now about twenty hours away from Milwaukee. Loggers and sawmill owners would now clear away the virgin timber. Miners would scrape away the hard rock of the Penokees for iron. Settlers would occupy the stumpland and take crops out of the grudging northern soil. And Ashland, with its optimists and opportunists, was on top of it all.

Martin Roehm and his family stayed in Ashland during the 1860s when all the other settlers abandoned it.

D.G. Sampson (center) and his crew of surveyors. They laid out some of Ashland's first plats with transit, stakes and chains. Present streets and lot lines owe their location to this work.

Edwin Ellis, 1824-1908

Born in 1824, Edwin Ellis spent nearly all of his first thirty years in his native state of Maine. He moved to St. Paul in 1854 and became associated with a syndicate of developers who had their eyes on Chequamegon Bay.

It was as their representative that he came to Ashland during the winter of 1855-56 and entered by pre-emption the plat of Bay City. He moved his family there and built a one story log cabin on the bay shore east of Bay City Creek.

The Ellis family left Bay City when the depression of 1859 and the outbreak of the Civil War postponed an expected rail line to the Bay. Ellis ran a drugstore and worked as a doctor for a copper mine in Ontonogan until 1872 when railroad fever struck Chequamegon Bay again.

Unlike many other of Ashland's first prominent men, Ellis did not amass great wealth. Instead he donated property worth thousands of dollars for depots, docks, school sites, industry and churches. He also gave generously to many causes and led a fund-raising drive that netted $30,000 and brought the North Wisconsin Academy to Ashland. A prominent Mason, he also served as president of the school board and the First National Bank. Thomas Bardon described him as "...judge, doctor, merchant and general businessman. At the same time, he took part in all public affairs in everything that helped to build up and advance the interests of the City of Ashland."

The country was never very far from downtown. A man leads a cow down Third Street circa 1895. Picket fences around homes were intended to keep stray livestock out of yards.

Dr. J. M. Dodd, Sr.

Dr. J.M. Dodd was one of Ashland's most popular mayors. He led the city through the rough Depression years of 1933-39, yet another medical man and civic leader.

Serving the People

"All that district of country in the County of Ashland, hereinafter described, shall remain a city by the name of Ashland . . ."
Wisconsin Legislature, March 25, 1887.

Rapid growth of the settlement on Chequamegon Bay following the extension of the Wisconsin Central Line in 1877 created a need for a local city government. The township government organized in 1860 and the county had laid the groundwork for the city. Elementary police and fire protection, water and sewer lines, election and recording officers were in place by the time the City of Ashland drew its first official breath. Nevertheless, the concentration of people here and the obvious permanence of the settlement led the Wisconsin legislature to draw up a charter for "a municipal corporation by the name of the City of Ashland." The city's official birthday is March 25, 1887, the day the legislature approved the charter.

Ashland's first municipal election took place only a few weeks after the charter was granted. The campaign was enlivened by competition among Democrat John H. Knight, Republican William R. Durfee and Knights of Labor candidate John McCarty. The Knights of Labor made up the largest national labor union of its day. That it could field a candidate in rapidly industrializing Ashland gives testimony to the power of labor in the new city.

Knight won the election and so did aldermen George Nelson, W.F. Shea, R.A. Kennedy, Duncan McRae, and B.S. Sparks. The aldermen were joined by five supervisors—F.X. Shotmueller, W.D. Clark, H.F. Higby, B.G. Armstrong and G.W. Harrison—to form the first city council. At its first meeting on April 19, the council elected W.F. Shea president and set about organizing the city government, a task that would require daily meetings for several weeks. At these first meetings the outline of Ashland's government was filled in. Examining the subjects discussed then serves as a handy guide to the following century of city government.

Annual salaries for city administrators were set with the clerk and street commissioner each earning $800, the attorney and auditor $750 each, the assessor $500, and the physician $200. Policemen topped the list at $900. The mayor served without salary while the treasurer was encouraged in his work by a commission of one per cent "for his collecting all sums, aside from taxes."

Ordinance Number One prescribed the fire limits and an ordinance passed later established the fire department. Other early laws governed shows, circuses and theaters. Peddlers and hawkers were licensed as were saloons, billiard parlors, bowling alleys and shooting galleries. Rights of way for street railways, easements for railroad tracks, and rules prohibiting interference with legitimate street traffic were outlined and passed.

The condition of Ashland's streets were of immediate concern. "Second and Third Street are in a condition unfit for travel," read the Minutes of the first meeting of the Committee on Streets and Bridges, "and the board recommends that as soon as practicable said streets be plowed and crowned and the gutters on either side of the said streets be kept clear for the free flow of water."

Side streets seem to have been in worse shape. P.J. Dullanty claimed and was paid $200 from the General Fund to make up for the loss of his horse in what must have been a cavernous mud hole on Ellis Avenue. Upon reflection, the Council discounted the claim and instructed the city attorney to get the $200 back from Dullanty. There is no record of whether he succeeded.

An early experiment with streets paved with boards was declared a failure when the planks sank into the ooze beneath and prevented it from drying. Another experiment using cedar blocks to cover the mud also failed. Eventually, it was decided that the only way to keep Second Street dry was to raise the grade six-to-eight feet. In the process, the first story of many of Ashland's oldest buildings was buried.

In time Ashland's streets were graveled and graded with slag from the blast furnace often used for fill. A roller was drawn by a horse over the material and the weight to compact it consisted of as many children as could be rounded up to sit in the wagon for a day. The automobile brought about the end of the gravel roadway. Second Street was first paved with bricks in the 1920s. The distinctive rattle of traffic on a honeycomb of brick sounded on Second Street for another sixty years.

Until the advent of auto travel, snow

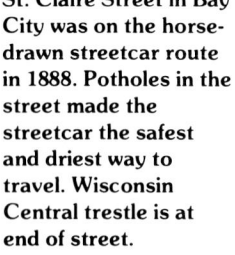

St. Claire Street in Bay City was on the horse-drawn streetcar route in 1888. Potholes in the street made the streetcar the safest and driest way to travel. Wisconsin Central trestle is at end of street.

removal from streets was hardly necessary. Horse-drawn sleighs could travel faster on packed snow than wagons could on the roads. Ashland's first plowing of snow from its streets took place when the streetcar company mounted a plow to clear a path for itself down the center of Second Street. That was the price of progress.

A Health Department was also established at one of the first Council meetings and given broad power "to examine into and consider all measures necessary for the public health . . ." These measures included ordering vaccinations, quarantine and medical care to stop the spread of disease. The health officer was also empowered to enforce basic sanitary laws controlling the disposal of wastes and garbage and mandatory connection to the city sewer system. This was an important chore in a time when outhouses were common and farm animals were kept in backyards.

The city police force wasn't organized until July of 1887 and a cloud immediately fell over the conduct of the first Captain, August Swartz. He was suspected of taking bribes to wink at illegal activities in Ashland's red-light district. The committee appointed to investigate Swartz exonerated him, finding "no proper or reliable evidence to support these charges." The Swartz controversy was part of a larger dispute between Mayor Knight and Councilman George Harrison that made up Ashland's first major political rivalry. The two men vied for control of city government in its first years and used appointments to city jobs as a means of gaining power.

Knight won re-election in the spring of 1888 but resigned the following November for business and health reasons. In a long and meticulously written resignation speech Knight railed against "that class of people who make their living by the commission of crimes or in occupations which are outlawed . . . there are four or five places, not including houses of prostitution, that are rendezvous of these evil doers where plunder is divided."

The mayor had ordered the captain of police to enforce laws against gambling and prostitution in Ashland. Apparently, while Knight was away from the city for several months, a few city councilmen convinced the captain to ignore the order. Although he urged the council to hire "skilled detectives" to investigate the evil doers, Knight himself left city government to them and pursued his own fortune.

Laws governing public morals were regularly placed on the books. An early ordinance

Ashland's first city seal featured a dock and a sawmill perched on the edge of a pine forest.

The Lakeshore Art Association commissioned Connie Chase to draw a new city seal in 1987.

John H. Knight, 1836-1903

Delaware-born John Knight was admitted to the bar in 1860. The following spring, Abraham Lincoln made his first call for volunteers for the Civil War and Knight enlisted. He saw action in many battles, was wounded several times but left the army with a colonel's commission. By the time the war ended in 1865, Knight's health was very poor. After Ulysses S. Grant's election to the Presidency in 1868, Knight was named agent to the Lake Superior Chippewa. He sought the post in the belief that the northern climate would improve his health.

It must have worked, for shortly after arriving in Bayfield in 1869, Knight resigned his government post. By 1878 he had moved to Ashland and was at the center of business activity.

He organized the Superior Lumber Company and was involved in the Ashland National Bank, First National Bank, Ashland Brownstone Company, the street railway and the blast furnace. He was also the local attorney for the Wisconsin Central and the first mayor of Ashland. He is probably best known for constructing the Knight Hotel.

Knight once campaigned for the state legislature's appointment to the United States Senate and hoped to gain the support of powerful veteran's organizations. He visited a veterans home in Milwaukee commanded by a Colonel Arthur MacArthur who had a son named Douglas. The Colonel, who had spent twenty-eight years in the army without a promotion, was reportedly discouraging his son from entering the military. The story is told that Knight promised to help young Douglas gain appointment to West Point if the elder MacArthur would support Knight's Senate campaign. Knight never entered the Senate, but before he withdrew from the campaign he reportedly made sure that his opponent would use his influence with Milwaukee Congressman Theobold Otjen to appoint Douglas MacArthur to West Point. Since young MacArthur registered a near perfect score on an exam Otjen used to sort out applicants, it is unlikely that he needed the aid of a political deal to begin his military career. The Knight story does make a good yarn, though.

An Ashland street crew in the 1890s. The street roller was only as effective as the number of kids weighing it down.

prohibited gambling and houses of "ill-name or ill-fame." Another law prohibited the sale of obscene and indecent books. An ordinance of 1901 stated, "It shall hereafter be unlawful for any women or company of women to enter or be in any saloon . . . for the purpose of giving a vocal or instrumental entertainment of any kind either musical or otherwise."

In 1889, the city council and the police were again at odds, this time over the issue of prizefighting. Ashland and its iron-range-neighbor Hurley were both two-fisted towns out of step with the prevailing sentiment against prizefighting in Wisconsin. Captain of Police John O'Brien was connected with some sort of fight scandal in Ashland and an investigating committee recommended his resignation or dismissal.

With all the furor about morals of both males and females in Ashland's first days as a city, it is interesting to note that the council meeting discussing Captain O'Brien's involvement in boxing was well attended by women. Females in the council room constituted a new experience for one alderman who moved "that they be heard now." Mrs. Bancroft responded for the group and said, "We came here because we felt we had the right to come. We have nothing special before the meeting of council tonight. We came to listen to their works."

Subsequent city records show no involvement of women in city politics for

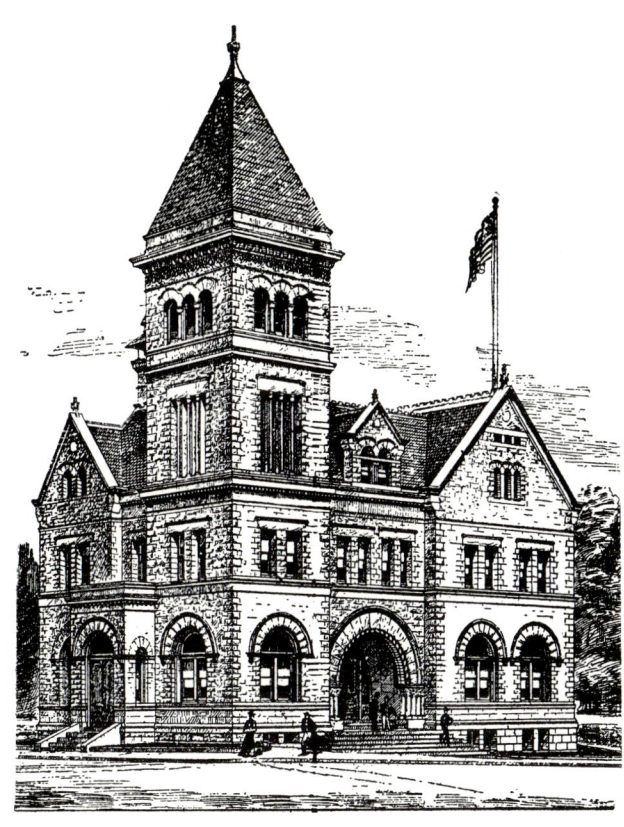

The current City Hall was renovated in 1975-76. Having served as federal government building, post office, and vocational school, the Hall is listed on the National Register of Historic Places.

The first Ashland High School building became the City Hall after the Ellis Avenue High School was built in 1904.

Larry's TV at 101 E. Second Street now occupies the building that served as Ashland's first City Hall. City offices were on the second floor, the post office below.

23

Dr. George W. Harrison, 1850-1905

George Harrison was born at Oldham, Lancashire, England, but migrated with his mother to Fall River, Wisconsin, in 1864. There, he divided his time between agriculture and teaching for a few years before entering Rush Medical College in Chicago where he received his degree in 1880. He set up his medical practice in Ashland and was involved in many state, national and international medical societies.

He was one of the incorporators of the Ashland National Bank and a director for many years. He was president and general manager of the Ashland Light, Power and Street Railway Company, which he helped organize. He also had interests in timber and mining lands and was a major stockholder in the West Range Iron Mining Company, which developed properties near Ashland.

Harrison was a prominent Republican and possessed considerable influence at the local and state level. He served as chairman of the town board before Ashland was incorporated and as the city's second mayor.

Following Page

Deer were first brought to Prentice Park by Park Commissioner Charles Maslowski in 1928. When a new buck was needed, men live-trapped an animal in the Barrens. Glenn Larson (here) tended the animals in the 1960s.

many years. In 1954, the year Ashland celebrated the centennial of white settlement, Marjorie Lockard took her seat as the first woman on the Ashland City Council. In 1976, Mary Bailey made an unsuccessful attempt for the mayor's office, the first and only woman to run for that position.

The city inherited its first debt of $26,000 from the Town of Ashland in return for the services the town had organized prior to incorporation and took over town assets of $7,000. The first major source of revenue for the new city was not the property tax, but liquor license fees. Ashland's first financial report of May, 1887, showed the city had collected over $26,000, nearly all of it from $500 fees from fifty-one saloons. A month later eight more $500 licenses were sold. From its very first days Ashland's municipal budget, like that of many other Wisconsin communities, was based on saloon license fees. Taxing saloons was much more politically palatable than taxing property, and municipalities were grateful when the legislature granted them the power to charge fees as high as $500. Saloon fees gave a city a stable tax base and helped many begin municipal life. By comparison, the property tax was only a minor source of income, but one that would gain importance with the passing of time.

One asset the city acquired from the Town of Ashland was the waterworks. The system was privately owned with local residents as stockholders, and the first city council granted the company a fifty-year lease on Ashland's water system. In 1891, when Ashland's boom seemed limitless, a Boston firm named Wheeler and Parks purchased the company. They made regular improvements, adding fourteen miles of water mains and tapping fresh water directly from the Bay. When the original lease to the private water company was about to expire in 1936, the city established the Ashland Water Works Commission which continues to run the system under guidelines set by state statute and the Public Service Commission. In 1949, Ashland became one of the first small cities in Wisconsin to fluoridate its water.

The formation of city parks was another subject taken up at the first city council meeting. A year later Ashland could boast of Beaser Park, Chequamegon Hotel Park, Ellis Park, Fuller Park and Prentice Park. By the time the city was founded, the idea of public parks as a mark of civilization and civic pride was widely accepted and Ashland was no exception. In addition Ashland, although a rough-and-ready industrial town, was also pursuing tourists. The fresh water of the Bay and the springs in Prentice Park were touted for their healthfulness while the abundance of city parks enhanced the atmosphere for visitors.

In the early 1900s Ashland had an Outdoor Art League, whose purpose was to make the city more beautiful by making it greener. The League planted flowering shrubs and trees in the center of Ellis Avenue, making it a colorful boulevard stretching across the city and transforming Ashland into *The Garland City of the Inland Seas*.

Lake Park was laid out at about this same time with plans calling for its extension from Ellis Avenue all the way to Sixth Avenue West. The original plans were never executed beyond building Memorial Park and its bandshell, but recent efforts with funds provided by various grants and the work of the Wisconsin Conservation Corps have revitalized the lakeshore.

Of the five original parks, only Fuller Park has been completely lost. Beaser Park remains adjacent to Beaser School. Hotel Chequamegon Park has become the grounds of the county courthouse. Ellis Park has lost space to school and fire house construction. Prentice Park, with its "remarkable Ashland Mineral Springs" is still well maintained with walking paths, campsites and an enclosed deer yard.

Maslowski Beach, named after one of Ashland's early police chiefs and park commissioners, affords excellent summer swimming under the watchful eyes of trained lifeguards. Mini-parks are located throughout the city. Since 1975, the city has received nearly $500,000 in outside funding for parks and lakeshore development.

Sunset Park, at the end of Prentice Avenue, has a boat launch, swimming beach, and twenty-six unit recreational vehicle facility. Individual sites come equipped with electricity, running water, cooking grills and picnic tables.

Lake Park was recently sold to Bretting Manufacturing Co. to make room for their expanding business. Funds from the sale were combined with Coastal Management and DNR grants and WCC labor to purchase and develop lakefront property in the east end with its spectacular view. Bay View Park promises to be one of Ashland's finest parks.

Ashland's first welfare budget amounted to $20 appropriated for what was called Poor Relief. Money was paid directly to grocery stores, wood and coal merchants, doctors, hospitals and pharmacies after they submitted bills for services rendered to the indigent. The Poor Commission approved applications for relief from adults and oversaw the welfare of abandoned or orphaned children, the elderly incapable of fending for themselves and the mentally handicapped. Relief was a local responsibility that city and county taxpayers shared with little state or federal aid until the Great Depression.

The close of lumbering, slowdowns in the mines, the agricultural depression of the 1920s and the Great Depression of the 1930s greatly increased the need for poor relief in Ashland. In 1931, Mayor Michael Dillon asked the council for up to twelve thousand dollars for relief. That same year nearly 3,000 homeless

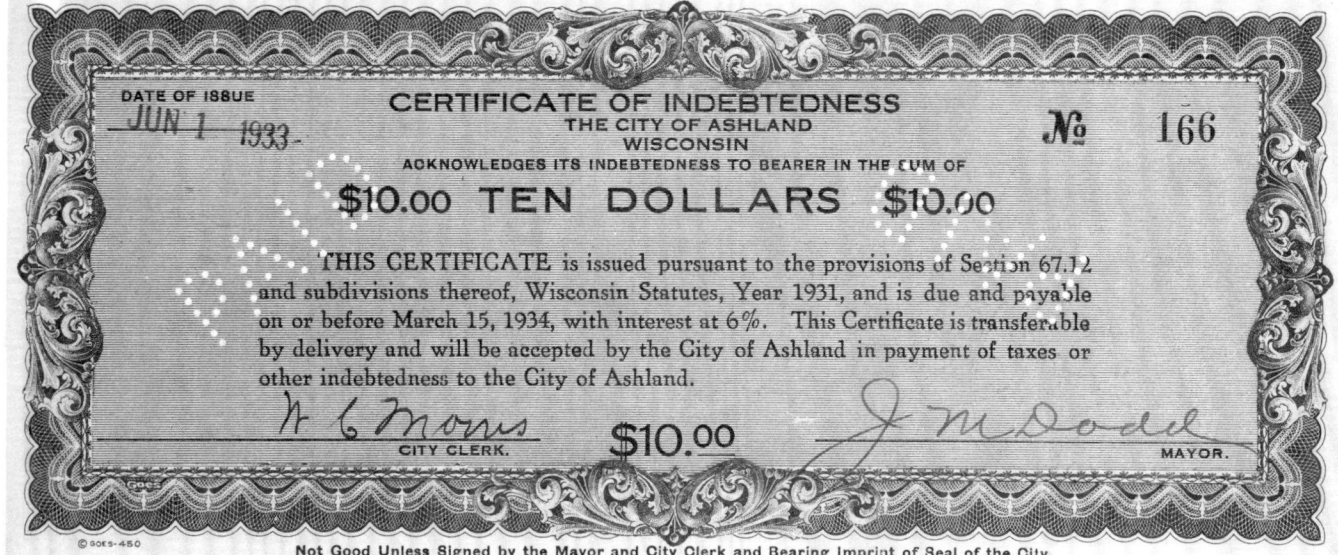

After the banks closed and cash disappeared in 1933, the city issued scrip to pay employees. Mayor Dodd signed 5,000 of these notes in one day to make them legal tender.

women and children were given temporary lodging in City Hall. Men went to the hobo jungle on the lake shore, where they stayed until all hope of finding work in Ashland was exhausted and they hopped a train out of town.

The city council was also obliged to extend the payment of property taxes without penalty. In November of 1932, a resolution "providing that any taxpayer, who, upon investigation, shall be found to be unable to pay taxes on account of unemployment, shall be given work and that the money so earned be applied in whole or in part for the payment of his taxes" failed to pass. Instead, the Council approved the issuance of certificates of indebtedness for property taxes.

With little property tax money coming into the treasury the city could hardly pay its own bills. City employees were paid in scrip that was redeemable for goods at local stores. The city guaranteed the debt and slowly paid it off. The last Depression scrip bill of $138 was written off in 1951.

After 1933 and the coming of Franklin Roosevelt's New Deal, responsibility for relief was taken off city taxpayers. Public works projects in Ashland included the bandshell, airport improvement, highway and conservation work that made jobs for thousands.

One project that could have been completed in the 1930s was not. Starting in the late 1920s the Wisconsin Board of Health had been warning Ashland to stop dumping untreated sewerage into Chequamegon Bay. In 1938, with the aid of federal funds, the city could have built a treatment plant for $83,500, but the option was voted down at a referendum. Raw sewerage continued to pollute the Bay until 1951, when the state threatened to fine the city $250 for every day the effluent continued to run. Two years later the city completed construction of a modern treatment plant for approximately two million dollars.

The form of city government has changed over the years. Originally composed of a mayor, a five member board of aldermen, and a five member board of supervisors, the government was elected every year. Annual elections turned every spring into a job-hunting season for those in search of city employment. "Every mayor had to reward his

Second Street was still paved with bricks in 1952. Lake Superior District Power Building still had its round tower and the Central Block with its tall, steep roof still stood.

The bricks that first paved Second Street in 1922 were torn up in 1980.

henchmen and he needed the affirmative vote of a majority of the city council to confirm his appointments," wrote historian Guy Burnham. "The question of municipal economy, matters of real business importance were subsidiary apparently to who should hold the appointive offices."

In 1899, mayoral and aldermanic terms were increased to two years and the patronage fever broke out half as often as before. In 1912, after the Progressive Movement had reached its height in Wisconsin and across the country, voters adopted the commission form of government. By this system a powerful two-member commission and a weak mayor ran the city. The reform was intended to encourage rational city administration without politics, favoritism and corruption. It lasted until 1918, when the voters rejected the commission by a vote of 1469 to 455. The mayor and the aldermen came back and stayed for three decades.

The reformist fad swept through Ashland once again in 1948 when the city adopted the council-manager form of government. The intention was to place the affairs of the city in the hands of professionally trained non-political officials. Five council members were elected at-large. They chose one of their own as council president to preside at meetings and also hired a manager to administer the city. The council-manager plan survived two referendum votes to abolish it. A third vote was successful and the city returned to the mayor-council plan in 1955. Two years later a proposal to return to it was defeated at the polls. The mayor-council form of government remains, as it has for most of Ashland's history, the government of choice.

Throughout the 1950s and 60s government in Ashland presided over a city facing serious economic decline. Of necessity, city leaders did their best to maintain services and rally flagging civic spirit. Of particular note were the revitalization efforts during the Mayor Hub Perrin administration of the late 1960s when an extensive street improvement program was undertaken. In 1975, the city began to pursue and was awarded a series of state and federal grants that made the next decade a period of renovation and revival.

Renovation began with $300,000 from the state that transformed the vacant former post office building into the present City Hall. Other grants razed dilapidated or rehabilitated houses; improved parks and streets; funded programs for the Treatment Center Halfway House, the New Horizons Developmental Workshop, the Youth Center, and the New Day Shelter for Battered Women. Perhaps the most memorable project occurred between 1981-83 when the brick surface of Second Street was paved over. Since 1985, federal and state grants totaling $1,154,000 have helped fund the construction of a new city marina that points out a new direction for Ashland's future. The waterfront that once bustled with sawmills, locomotives and ore carriers, will become the home of pleasure boats and the base for a new tourist-centered economy. In total, the city received nearly $5.5 million in grant money between 1975 and 1985.

In its Centennial year the City of Ashland employs eighty-six people. The operational budget is $4,134,256 with a debt service of $727,605 and $100,000 for the street improvement plan. For these services the city levies $1.8 million after revenues. Based on an assessed value of $138,091,820, the total levy is 37.66 and after state credit is 32.39. Twenty percent of the total tax levy is for city operations.

The government chartered by the state in 1887 has changed and developed with the city it serves. The process will undoubtedly continue into Ashland's second century.

Restoration of the old Soo Line Depot began in early 1987. Refurbishment of the building is symbolic of Ashland's Centennial spirit - honoring the past to serve the future.

Mayors

John H. Knight, 1887-88
George W. Harrison, 1888-89
H.H. Beaser, 1889-90
Lewis C. Wilmarth, 1890-91
William W. O'Keefe, 1891-92; 1893-94
W.R. Durfee, 1892-93
F.F. Hubbell, 1894-95
C.M.E. McClintock, 1895-96
Thomas Bardon, 1896-1901
Burt Williams, 1901-09
John Joyce, 1909-10
W.C. Knowles (Acting), 1910-11
J.M. Dodd, 1911-13; 1933-39
Clarence Dennis, 1913-19
Frank S. Dhooge, 1919-23
Charles Bloss, 1923-27
Michael E. Dillon, 1927-33
Gus F. Johnson, 1939-45
Harry F. Van Guilder, 1945-48
Leo Martel (Acting City Manager), 1948
Joseph A. Warren (City Manager), 1948-51
Harlow R. Richardson, 1951-55
James O'Leary, 1955-56
Mark Movrich, 1956-58
Harry Simon, 1958-66
Hubert L. Perrin, 1966-70
Roger W. Hanson, 1970-74
Arnold Koehler, 1974-76
Bruce A. Hendrickson, 1976-78
Stephen F. Zohimsky, 1978-80
Edward G. Wagner, 1980-84
James S. Monroe, 1984-86
Daniel O. Theno, 1986-

Durocher Dock & Dredge Co. began construction of the new Ashland Marina in fall 1986. Pleasure boats will once again tie up in downtown Ashland.

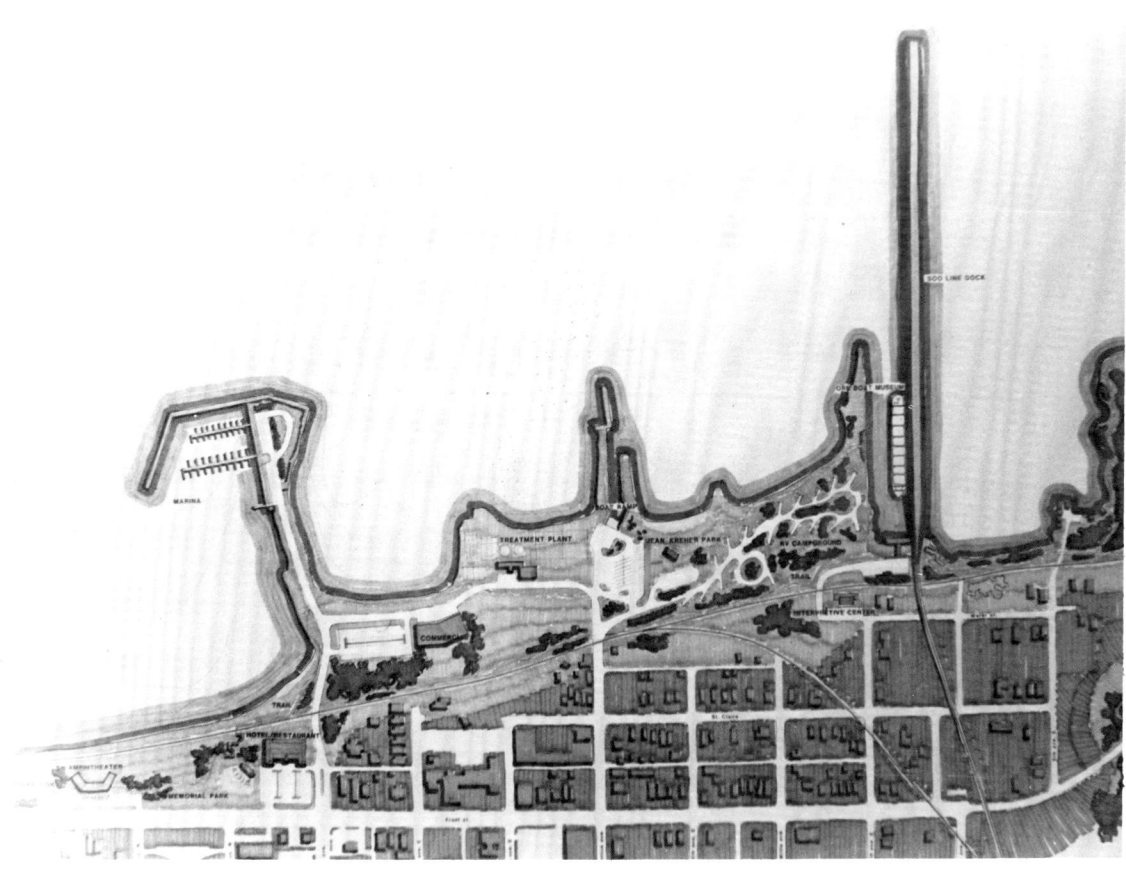

Ashland's 1985 Waterfront Development Plan. It includes the marina at left, Sunset Park with a boat launch and RV campgrounds and the old Soo Line dock. The plan was drawn by Fred Gould of Northwest Regional Planning Commission.

Maintaining Law and Order

"We didn't believe in riding those fellows on the handle bars."
Police Sergeant "Ole" Ecklo

The Ashland Police Force in 1937. (l to r, front) Joseph Kegel, Alvin Biesemeir, Chief Clarence Overdahl, Lyle Tolliver, Arthur Ruha. (back) Arvid Johnson, John Kirklewski, Sgt. Louis Mateofsky, Terry Lindquist.

One of the first acts of Mayor Knight and the first city council in April of 1887 was to appoint John Burnes and Thomas Hedican as Ashland's first police officers. In short time, August Schwartz was named captain of police. The post was also referred to as city marshall, a hold over from the town government days, and as chief of police, the title used today. In the department's first years, however, the top cop was the captain.

Officers were paid nine hundred dollars per year and worked twelve-hours-on/twelve-hours-off seven days a week. These long shifts lasted until the late 1930s. The first officers received a badge, baton and belt but were not authorized to wear a handgun until 1891.

The department has had nineteen chiefs in its hundred years. In the city's early years the position was a key political plum and changed hands in accordance with the prevailing political winds. In its first eight years, Ashland had ten different chiefs.

The first chief to hold the job for many years was William T. Blair, whose twenty-four years of service is a city record. He was nicknamed "Bicycle Billy" because he rode a bike on patrol and expected his officers to do so also. Blair did authorize the purchase of Ashland's first squad car in 1931, near the end of his career. However, department policy held that the second-hand 1929 Chevrolet was to be parked at the station and used only if the distance to answer a call for help was too far to walk. The police vehicle was not used regularly until the late 1940s, when a two-way radio was installed to keep track of it.

The chief means of communication for the police in the pre-radio days was a series of red lights located throughout downtown. They could be turned on from headquarters when a call for help came in. An officer walking either the West or East End beat would, upon spotting a shining red light, call or come to the station to find out where he was needed.

At the turn-of-the-century, officers arrested lawbreakers for such violations as: sleeping in boxcars, "on complaint of wife," suspicion, being an inmate of a disorderly house, firing a gun on the street, running a house of ill-fame, fighting and drunkenness.

The life of an officer in those days was recalled in a 1941 *Daily Press* article by O.K. "Ole" Ecklo, a twenty-seven year veteran of the city police who also was elected county sheriff.

"Those were the days of wild sailors and scrapping lumber jacks," he said. "...the sailors hit for the saloons as soon as they docked and before long were picking fights. They fought until we had them locked in jail.

"There were no patrol wagons in the old times. We had to arrest our men and then march them to the cells in the old court house. Sometimes we had one in each hand and some of the fellows were big fighters.

"I wore out two bicycles. Many times I would have to hurry out to the East End or to the West End to arrest someone, and then have to leave the bike there while I led the man to jail. Then I would have to walk back for the bike. We didn't believe in riding those fellows on the handle bars..."

Other officers knocked saloon brawlers cold, then carted them to the lock-up in a wheelbarrow.

Ecklo wore the regulation tall helmet customary for police men in his day. "...they were a regular nuisance. We would get in a scuffle and ...the helmets would fly off our heads..." he said.

Key qualifications for police work then included a strong back, quickness afoot, and a willingness to knock heads. Courage was also necessary, for no wilting lily would wade into a pile of brawling loggers or dockworkers.

Police headquarters and the lock-up have been located in several places in town, with one of the very earliest being 101 East

Sergeant Ole Ecklo ready to keep the peace in 1925.

Second Street. When St. Joseph's Hospital was demolished in 1973, it was suggested that its tower be left standing and used as a police observation post, but nothing came of the scheme. Instead, police headquarters were moved to the basement of City Hall and prisoners are housed in the county jail.

The only training police officers received for many decades took place on the job. It was not until 1971 that Wisconsin required officers to be trained and certified. In 1987, an officer must receive 320 hours of intensive training to be certified.

Chief Gordon Gilbertson finds it hard to envision how the pioneer law enforcement officers managed. Today's department has eighteen sworn officers and one civilian, four police cars, modern electronic equipment, and trains continuously, yet it is difficult to provide citizens with the level of service they request.

While the picturesque days of Sergeant Ecklo are gone, some things have not changed. Officers still settle disputes and make arrests. They must occasionally be quick afoot and courage is still a qualification for the job. One tribute can be paid to the more than two-hundred men who have served as police officers in Ashland. Not one has lost his life in the line of duty.

Police Chiefs

August Swartz, 1887
John F. O'Brien, 1887
W.H. Clay, 1888
Andrew Montgomery, 1888
John F. O'Brien, 1889
J.D. Hayes, 1890
Joseph J. Kennedy, 1891-93
Gustaf Schwartz, 1893-95
Thomas Telford, 1895-97
Sumner Tanner, 1897-1903
Charles Maslowski, 1903-09
William T. Blair, 1909-33
Elmer Sanders, 1933-35
Clarence Overdahl, 1935-41
Ernest J. Hennell, 1941-59
Donald L. Tolliver, 1959-76
Raleigh L. Fox, 1976-83
Gordon G. Gilbertson, 1983-

Battling Blazes, Saving Lives

"My husband was a fireman. In 1924, he was gone all day and all night, in twenty-below-zero, working on the ore dock fire ... when he came home, his clothes were all covered with ice and he couldn't walk for a week."
Emeline Hagen

Fred and Med pulled the Ashland fire engine in the early 1900s. Andy Barkley (l to r) Jim Simms and John Cronk ride the wagon.

The famous quote, "You've come a long way baby" would best describe the Ashland Fire Department over the last one hundred years. The volunteers who started as the "Fire Laddies" in April, 1883, with one hose company, minimal equipment and training have advanced to a corps of twenty-three firefighters, highly-skilled in firefighting and specialized life-saving techniques.

Ashland was a city built almost entirely of wood. Walls, floors, even roofs and sidewalks dried to tinder in the summer sun. Sawdust piles, mill wastes and lumber stacks were also highly inflammable. Wood-fired stoves in homes, railroad locomotives hauling through town, and boilers in mills and factories all belched live sparks into the air. The heroic efforts of volunteers with buckets and wet blankets could not provide adequate fire protection. So even before Ashland was incorporated as a city, the town board organized and equipped a volunteer fire department. On June 18, 1887, Ashland's Hook and Ladder company #1 and the

Bardon Hose Company #2 were established with headquarters at the Central Hose House on the southwest corner of Fourth Avenue West and Third Street.

Fire protection headed the list of services the new city of Ashland would provide its citizens. Ordinance #1 of the City Council, passed in April of 1887, set fire limits within the business district and stipulated that buildings there be built of fireproof materials. The following year, the City took over the Hook and Ladder Company and the Bardon Hose Company and turned the Central Hose House into the Central Station. The Ellis Company #1 in the Fifth Ward, the Beaser Hose Company #3 in the Second Ward and the Vaughn Hose Company #4 in the Third Ward were also assembled. Each company consisted of a foreman, an assistant foreman and ten firemen aged eighteen to fifty. The first city budget included $1,500 to be shared by all the companies for pay and regular equipment. T.L. Scott was named Ashland's first fire chief.

By 1890, the department added two more hose companies. The Durfee Hose Company had its station at 14th Avenue West and West Second Street, while the Knight Hose Company kept its gear at the foot of Whittlesey Avenue. The first chief of this enlarged department was S.W. Tanner, who succeeded Chief Scott and who held the post until 1891. F.W. French then held the post for four years before passing it on to D.A. McCune, Ashland's last volunteer chief.

Fire protection required more than just men, horses and hoses. Until 1888, only a strong pair of lungs and a hastily-rung church bell served as fire alarms in Ashland. Then the city purchased the Gamewell Fire Alarm System whose bells are still used by the Department today.

The life of a firefighter always had its own aura of glamour and each of Ashland's companies had a long list of volunteers waiting to sign on. If a man was known to be a good family man, not prone to drunken ways, used little or no profane or vulgar language and did not spit tobacco, he was eligible for fire duty. Those who couldn't accept the risks of a firefighter's life, or who couldn't handle the drudgery and discipline were quickly weeded out and dropped from the service. In this way, the fire department maintained a roster of physically fit men of good character. However, they were still volunteers, who held regular jobs and had responsibilities to families that occasionally conflicted with their work for the fire department.

After depending on volunteers for ten years, the City Council created a paid fire corps. Twenty-one firemen, including a chief engineer, were assigned to the various hose houses. Eleven of these men would live at the hose houses and be on constant duty. Nine men would be known as special firemen and work as needed. A special fireman was appointed by the chief engineer from among those who had satisfactorily passed the

The Ashland Champion Hose-Running Team beat all competitors in 1890. No fire company at the Lake Superior Fireman's Tournament could lay a hose faster than the champ's thirty-five seconds. Vaughn Avenue was paved with planks then.

Lumberyard fires were a serious danger in Ashland's first days. Fire rages at Stern's Lumber Mill on the waterfront in this undated photo.

Barney Hagen and other firefighters battled a blaze at the Northwestern ore dock in 1924.

examination of the police and fire commission, and who worked or spent his time near to his assigned hose house. Should a special fireman live or work too far away from his hose house, he was dismissed from the department. He couldn't get to a fire in time if first he had to run across town.

The professional department brought new ordinances for better fire protection. Tampering with fire alarm boxes, or sounding a false alarm was outlawed with offenders slapped with a fine of up to $50. By 1987, this fine had been raised to $250. Fire equipment enroute to a fire was guaranteed the right-of-way over other traffic whether horse-drawn buggy or Ford flivver, and no vehicle could drive over a hose laid down for fire duty.

Louis Schaetzle was chief of Ashland's first professional fire department. By the turn of the century he was boasting that his department was never better officered, but it was in sore need of more men and better equipment. Ashland now had twelve full time firefighters, including the chief, assistant chief, three captains, four drivers and three truckmen. An additional five pipemen and four linemen were special or on-call firemen.

Equipment in service in 1901 included one chief's buggy, one double-forty gallon chemical engine, one hook-and-ladder truck, two hose wagons, one hand-hose cart, three exercising wagons and one small hook-and-ladder truck in reserve. In the course of a single year the Hook and Ladder Company made sixty-two fire runs and traveled fifty-three miles. Since they were spread out through the city, individual hose companies answered fewer calls and covered less mileage.

Because it was a lake port, Ashland required one special piece of fire fighting equipment—a fire boat. In 1901 the fireboat with its steam-powered pump was privately-owned and the city paid $300 a year to use it. This charge was part of a total fire department budget of $12,723.83. Except for the fire boat, none of this equipment was mechanized. Ashland bought its first steam fire pump in 1909 and its first motorized vehicle, a Nash hose wagon, in 1917.

Horses added to the romance of old time firefighting. Fire horses were kept in the fire house, their stalls partitioned off from the main floor by overhung doors. When an alarm rang, the doors would automatically rise. The horses were trained to leave their stalls on their own and back themselves into place beneath the harness hanging from the roof. Firemen could hitch them to the wagons very quickly and be on their way to the fire after a moment's notice.

Fire horses were special in many ways. They had to react quickly and correctly when the fire alarm sounded. They had to be brave yet manageable, ready to respond to commands while running at breakneck speeds, and able to stand patiently at the scene of a fire. Firemen came to develop strong bonds of affection for their horses and many were sorry to see the animals replaced.

Ashland was fortunate to escape the ravages of large, city-destroying fires experienced by most other pioneer communities that seemed to burn to the ground on a regular basis. Ashland's most serious fires of the horse-and-buggy days occurred on the ore docks.

In 1890, two firemen were killed and two seriously injured in a dock fire. When the widow of fireman J.J. Moore asked the council for some compensation for herself and

Northland's Dill Dormitory was destroyed by fire in 1926. Students tried to save as many of their belongings as they could.

her children, Mayor Wilmarth reported that "this city had no separate fund that could be used in such an emergency." The council then voted down a resolution to provide for the widows and children of police and firemen killed on duty.

Sentiment had changed by the time the 1891 budget was adopted. It appropriated $2,500 for a Firemen's Relief Fund, and the money was distributed to the families of those lost and injured in the 1890 fire.

In late November 1902, the Wisconsin Central Ore Dock, the world's largest, burst into a mass of flames that the fire department was unable to contain. With temperatures near zero freezing men and equipment, with immense flames and heat near the inferno, firemen had no hope of controlling the blaze. Several dockworkers lost their lives and damage was estimated at $500,000.

Horses and men were called out again in the summer of 1917 when fire broke out at the Ashland High School. Because of the height and location of the building, water pressure was low and once again the firemen's efforts were in vain. The stone walls of the high school withstood the blaze, but the interior of the building was gutted with a loss estimated at $150,000.

The 1920s brought mechanized equipment and two new fire stations. The Ellis Station was built in 1920 and the Beaser Fire House in 1921. Although remodelled over the years, these two stations continue to serve as headquarters for Ashland's firefighters. Modernization in the form of mechanization began under the leadership of Chief J.W. Sharp, who headed the department from 1910 to 1925.

Nine months after the American LaFrance pumper became the star of Ashland's fleet of fire vehicles, it was put to the test. Once again on a frigid winter night, the giant Northwestern Ore Dock #2 exploded in flames. Firefighters encountered some four hundred feet of flaming timber stretching onto the frozen Bay. So serious was the threat to neighboring docks and buildings on shore that the firemen considered dynamiting a fire break into the dock and letting part of it burn to ashes.

Instead they called for help from the Ironwood and Superior departments, who quickly raced to Ashland in their open trucks through a wind chill of minus-thirty degrees. The combined departments eventually extinguished the blaze, but not until 175 of 250 ore chutes were lost. The dollar loss was estimated at $1,500,000.

Emeline Hagen, whose husband Barney fought this blaze recalls, "he was gone all day and night, in twenty below zero . . . when he came home, his clothes were all covered with ice and he couldn't walk for a week."

35

The Scott-Taylor plant was consumed by fire in 1946.

Two years later, Ashland suffered another enormous loss due to fire. In April, 1926, sparks from a chimney atop Dill Dormitory at Northland College ignited the wooden shingles on the roof and completely destroyed the building within an hour. The fire spread through the old structure very quickly, but none of the forty women living in the dorm were harmed. Men watching the fire volunteered to save the property the women left behind and rushed into the burning building. Some of them were forced to leap from second floor balconies when the reality of the smoke and flames overcame their heroics.

One of the most spectacular blazes in Ashland's history occurred in January, 1945, when the Saron Lutheran Church caught fire. Firefighters battled the blaze, which also destroyed two nearby homes and sent threatening embers throughout the neighborhood, for seven hours. Fortunately, all 130 children attending Sunday School in the church when the fire started were evacuated unharmed. This was another winter blaze in which firemen had to fight extreme cold and ice in addition to the fire itself.

A fire to rival the Saron Lutheran disaster occurred in January, 1982, at the Cram Inn. Two people trapped inside the burning building were rescued by firemen Bob Belsky and Skip Hafstad.

The blaze started at the Cram Inn and soon spread to a vacant office building next door. Spectators clogged Second Street, hampering the firemen in their efforts to prevent flames from destroying the entire city block. In time, however, the blaze was brought under control.

For most of its history, the Ashland Fire Department has been a traditional fire-fighting organization. In 1967, it broke out of its mold and took over the ambulance service

Spectators watched the landmark Central Block go up in flames in December 1964.

previously operated as Ante's Ambulance Service. The city had been subsidizing Ante's and believed that outright city ownership would be more economical and provide better service.

The first fire department ambulance was a 1961 Ford stationwagon. It contained a cot borrowed from a local funeral home, a small first-aid kit and a resuscitator. It offered no real medical help, only transportation in time of emergency.

By 1971, six firefighters were trained as Emergency Medical Technicians or EMTS. Trained under the direction of Dr. A.A. Koeller, these men took an eighty-hour course in Red Cross First Aid and artificial respiration.

In 1987, the department has seventeen EMTS and six men trained in a First Responder course. The ambulance crew of EMTS has achieved the highest level of training and certification in its field. Eleven firemen have also taken training in the EMT Defibrillator Pilot Program to aid victims of heart emergencies.

The Ashland Firefighters are also involved in continual firefighting training. This includes the use of equipment, upgrading firefighting techniques, and the recognition and handling of hazardous materials. All are certified Wisconsin Level I Firefighters.

An important, but less than exciting chore the firemen perform is the inspection of all area businesses to detect fire hazards and code violations.

In 1987, less than one per cent of the fires in Ashland spread beyond the area where they are first encountered by the fire department. Fire damage is further reduced by the use of newer equipment and better training. Modern fire equipment is fast, powerful and extremely efficient. The Ashland Fire department carries all the practical tools of the past as well as those coming into use in recent years. Ashland has kept pace with the science and engineering of modern firefighting.

Fire Chiefs

T.L. Scott, 1887-90
S.W. Tanner, 1890-91
F.W. French, 1891
D.A. McCune, 1895-97
Louis Schaetzle, 1897-1909
J.W. Sharp, 1910-25
Curtis Markeson, 1925-35
William Saunders, 1935-40
Harry Lumberg, 1940-46
William Griffiths, 1946-63
Donald Tolliver, 1963
Walter Giese, 1963-76
Berkley Cameron, 1976-77
Gerald Giese, 1977-

1987 Ashland Fire Department. Equipment (l to r) 1980 Ford Modular Ambulance, 1978 Ward LaFrance 100 Foot Aerial Ladder, 1980 Hendrickson 1250 GPM Pumper, 1971 Ford 1000 GPM Pumper, 1954 FWD 750 GPM Pumper, 1982 Ford Tanker with 750 GPM Pump, 1982 Ford Modular Ambulance, 1977 GMC Suburban Chief's Car. Personnel (l to r) Ambulance Driver David Anderson, Ladder Driver/Alarm Operator Thomas Foris, Captain Harley Samuelson, Pumper Driver James Mattson, Pumper Driver James Morzenti, Pumper Driver Thomas Harrison, Captain Nick Rouskey, Ambulance Attendant Thomas Grahek, Chief Gerald Giese.

By Rail, Water, Road and Air

"There are many thriving commercial cities made such by railroads alone ... others ... owe their commercial importance to ... a great harbor. Ashland is assured of success ... for it has both."
Ashland Daily Press, 1893

Roads Last

Northern Pacific and Omaha Railroad trains wait at the Union Depot in 1909.

The missionaries, fur traders and earliest settlers came to Chequamegon Bay by boat. Only Indian trails penetrated the dense forest to the south, and northern Wisconsin was isolated from the rest of the world except by water. Until the railroad came to Ashland, it was easier to steam or sail to just about anywhere on Lakes Superior, Michigan or Huron than to travel to Park Falls.

When the lakes and rivers froze, travel was still possible and sometimes easier, since sleds could move heavy loads over frozen trails faster than over muddy, rutted ones. However, only a very hardy soul, like Doctor Edwin Ellis, would travel a long distance in the northern winter. He came to Ashland via dogsled from Superior to La Pointe, then snowshoed across the Bay.

As early as 1855, the state chartered a road to run from Superior to Barksdale, around the Bay and east to the Michigan line. It amounted to nothing more than a line on the map. In January of 1874, the *Press* described traveling conditions in the area as follows: "Fisher and Vaughn's two teams returned home from Duluth Tuesday with full loads of buckwheat, flour, hams and feed. They were three days on the road from Superior and traveling conditions were reported good." In warmer weather and if the road were dry, the same trip would have taken about ten days. If wet, as it usually was in spring, the road would have been impassable to all but foot traffic.

From the 1870s until the coming of the automobile, people traveled by road only if they had no choice. Rural road maintenance was left in the indifferent hands of the townships. The state was barred by a constitutional clause preventing its funding of highway work. None of the roads into Ashland—not even major routes like Highways 13 and 2—were paved until the late 1930s. Until after World War II, rail and water travel remained the fastest and most comfortable. Regular ferry schedules connected Ashland to nearby towns and to Duluth via Bayfield, while passenger trains ran the equivalent of commuter routes around the Bay.

Railroad Power

Ashland's location on one of the best protected fresh water harbors in the world was instrumental in its being chosen as the northern terminus of the Wisconsin Central Railroad. The rail link was so important that when Sam Fifield and other northern politicians overcame the opposition of southern Wisconsin legislators to the granting of land to the Central, Fifield proclaimed, "Hurrah for Governor Taylor and the Wisconsin Central Railroad. At last, justice has been done . . ."

Ashland adopted a resolution of gratitude to the governor signed by Edwin Ellis, Charles Pratt and Henry Fifield. The effect of the news on local citizens was such that the newspaper was moved to observe ". . . men who were never before guilty of wearing paper collars and boiled shirts now parade the streets with as much manly bearing as the deacon of the church."

More boiled shirts and paper collars appeared when the first train from Chicago was met by "a field of faces crazy with excitement over the event." It was marked by bonfires, a torch light parade, cannon salutes, speeches and feasting. For freight and passengers, Chicago was now only twenty-four and Milwaukee twenty-two hours away. Ashland's overland isolation was broken.

In 1882, the Omaha Railroad ran a line to Washburn and Bayfield. In a year Ashland was connected to it and the cities of the west by the Ashland Railroad Company's track to Ashland Junction. The Omaha and the Ashland built the "Shore Line" to serve the sawmills and docks on the Bay, then sold it to the Chicago and Northwestern in 1885. The Northern Pacific had already linked Ashland to Superior in 1884, and one year later the Milwaukee, Lake Shore and Western built Ashland's first ore dock and a rail line connecting it to Hurley. The Northwestern, which would become the dominant railroad of

Wooden rail cars carried ore onto the Ashland docks. When the floor of the car opened, ore fell into chutes below, then into waiting boats.

Ore boats at the Milwaukee Lakeshore & Western docks in 1888. This was Ashland's first ore dock. Ore carriers required as many as four tall masts and steam engines to move their heavy loads.

the Iron Range, soon acquired this line. About this time the shore line or "scoot" extension to Washburn and Bayfield was completed. The fifth and last railroad into Ashland was the Duluth, South Shore and Atlantic, which arrived in 1893.

Even before the last spike was driven, Ashland's rail-born prosperity seem assured. "There are many thriving commercial cities made such by railroads alone. There are others that owe their commercial importance to the advantages of a great harbor. Ashland is assured of success in either case for it has both," boasted the Daily Press in 1893.

The four railroad lines serving the city in 1892 hauled over eight billion pounds of freight, with about 4.5 billion pounds of ore alone. "When the ore business is under full headway," claimed the Daily Press, "there are at least 365 arrivals and departures of trains per day." If those numbers are accurate, one train arrived at or left Ashland every four minutes. (The reporter is probably referring to the number of individual cars and not entire trains.)

In 1895, Ashland County put up $120,000 to build the Peerless Railroad to connect the city to Minneapolis via Moquah. About twenty-five miles of track were laid, but the connection with the line south was never completed. The Peerless ran until nearby timber was cut, then rusted into the earth.

Rail depots were clustered in the center of the city between Ellis and Seventh Avenues. The last station to remain in service was the Northwestern on Seventh. Ashland's last passenger train left this depot in 1968.

Railroads remained at the heart of Ashland's economy as long as the city depended on timber and ore for its livelihood. When those industries died, so did a bit of Ashland.

Deep Water Port

The city was the hub of a network of rail and water transportation lines, the place where track met lake and cargo was shifted from one to the other. The importance of this connection was made plain by James J. Hill, the rail baron who built the Great Northern. "Certainly you feel the deepest interest in your harbor and the depth of water in your harbor and the Soo canal, but your greatest harbor, the one that must not only bring everything that comes and goes by water, is the terminal facilities."

George R. Stuntz and Frederick Prentice built the first commercial dock in Ashland in 1854. A few years later the shore was crowded with sawmills and docks. The bay front was the center of activity both day and night, with trains and ships handling ore, coal, timber and manufactured goods throughout the shipping season. Logs filled the water in wait for their run through the saw mill. The smell of wood and coal fueling steam boilers, the hiss of locomotive engines, the squeal of brakes, the roar of hematite in the chute on its way into the hold of an ore carrier, the clank and clangor of heavy industry in the machine age filled the air of a prosperous, hard-working city.

The early ore boats were made of wood, with the largest having a capacity of 2,600 tons. Steel ships could carry up to five times as much ore and could be loaded in only two hours instead of an entire day. In 1943, a year of heavy wartime production, between five and six millions tons of ore were shipped from Ashland's docks. In the 1950s ore shipments declined to about fifteen million tons for the entire decade.

In the years prior to World War I, the Great Lakes states had become the industrial heartland of America. The steel, auto, and many allied industries were dependent on fast, inexpensive water transportation on Lakes Superior, Michigan, Huron and Erie. World War I created a vast new international market for the goods of the Lake states and pointed out the need for improved access from the Lakes to the Atlantic Ocean.

The St. Lawrence Seaway Project was born and both Wisconsin and Ashland played a leading role in its development. The state named a Deep Waterways Commission with a two-fold task. First, it was to lobby the Canadian and United States governments to widen and deepen the channel of the St. Lawrence and St. Mary's Rivers so large ocean-going vessels could navigate on the Lakes. It was also to study and supervise the improvement of deep water harbors in Wisconsin.

Ashland, of course, was one of these harbors, but the city's connection with the Seaway project was more intimate. Ashland attorney C.A. Lamoreux headed the Commission from its inception in 1919 until 1932. When the Seaway was finally opened in 1959, Ashland could take bittersweet pride in having a part in it. Iron mining in the Penokees was drawing to a close and, just when the means to ship huge loads of hematite overseas became available, there was nothing more to ship. In time, the decline of the American steel and auto industries made the Seaway even less important.

Pleasure and Passengers

From the first days of settlement, the last melting of ice on the Bay was an event worth celebrating. It signified not only the arrival of the commercial vessels, but also the start of the pleasure boating season. Throughout the warm months, excursion boats carried passengers on the Bay, to the Apostle Islands, and north to Washburn and Bayfield.

The Steamer *Emerald*, licensed for 500 passengers, was one of the largest passenger boats on the Bay. The *Plowboy, Fashion* and *Lucille* were also popular. Booth's Line ran daily trips to Duluth from the dock at the foot of Ellis Avenue on *Hunter* and *Dixon*.

By 1904, the *Chequamegon* and *Mary Scott* were operating out of the Commercial Dock, and the United States and Dominion Transportation company was running the *Moore* and *S.B. Barker* between Ashland, Duluth, Houghton and Port Arthur.

Passenger ships were intended to do more than carry people around Lake Superior. They were seen as means for bringing

A wooden coal hauler from Cleveland berthed at the Columbus & Hocking Coal and Iron Company dock.

The "Reserve" at Wisconsin Central ore dock during World War I. In 1918 boats like this carried more tonnage out of Ashland than passed through the Panama Canal.

41

The *Emerald* carried up to five hundred excursionists to the Apostle Islands at the turn of the century. She sank near Barksdale where the hulk is still visible.

immigrants to Wisconsin and the west. James J. Hill, whose railroad ran from Duluth to the Pacific Ocean, saw Great Lakes steamers as his means to compete with eastern rail lines for immigrant traffic. " ...we are building ...steamers," he said in 1893, "which will carry passengers from Ashland to Buffalo in forty hours ...We will be disappointed if they do not make the run to the Soo in seven hours. I see no reason why the traveler landing in New York with $100 in his pocket should not come west upon the fastest line of steamers in the world."

The Lake Michigan and Lake Superior Transportation Company provided weekly transportation between Chicago and Duluth ports and in between too. The *Manitou, City of Duluth, City of Traverse, Peerless,* and *Jay Gould* were said to be "the finest vessels ever seen on the lakes presenting many novel and agreeable features for the comfort, convenience, and safety of the traveling public."

Trolleys and Buses

Ashland's population settled along the Bay stretching from Lake Park to beyond Sanborn Avenue. The great distance between one end of town and the other created demand for some means of public transportation. In 1887, the Ashland Street Railway Company began carrying passengers in horse-drawn cars. Five years later, the company merged with the failing Ashland Lighting Company to form the Ashland Light, Power and Street Railway Company and retired its horses.

The first president of the company was Doctor George Harrison, but in 1908 Arthur E. Appleyard acquired control of the stock. In 1922, all properties were merged into the Lake Superior District Power Company.

Generally, the cars ran from Prentice Park to what is now Bretting's and what was then Parishville. The main route was a loop from

Lake Park via Second Street, up Twenty-Second Avenue East to Sixth Street, down Fourteenth Avenue East to Second Street and then to Sanborn Avenue and to the cemeteries—almost six miles. A track on Seventh Avenue West ran from Second Street to the Northwestern Depot. A short spur on the end of the line at Sanborn Avenue led to the sand pit and was used for hauling sand and gravel. A power house on the corner of Prentice Avenue and St. Clair Street supplied power for the whole line.

By 1901, the company had three open and seven closed street cars, and riding the open cars in summer was a popular pastime. In the 1920s, the cars were painted bright yellow with red trim, but the color scheme was changed to orange and white for the 1930s. Car Number Fourteen had a special mahogany color scheme and the snowplow was painted a serious red. The cars ran from 6:10 AM to 11:50 PM—with three on weekdays and four on Sundays and holidays.

The Great Depression forced cutbacks on both track and service, while the popularity of autos soon silenced the trolley bells. The last street car ran in September, 1933.

Bus service started immediately and followed the street car route. In time buses also ran south of the railroad tracks, but the whole system died in 1977. Four years later, under federal, state and local government sponsorship, the Bay Area Rural Transit was organized and runs buses to Bayfield, Odanah, Red Cliff, Washburn and Mellen.

Other bus companies serving the area

Ashland Street Railway Car No. 2 ran on Second Street until the electric cars arrived in 1893. Peckhams Chinese Restaurant was located at 819 West Second Street.

Lake Park at the end of the trolley line was a good place for picnics. Old trolley at left provided shelter from the rain.

Previous Page
In the late 1970s, this 1,000 foot-long ore boat sat out a strike in Ashland. Ed Erickson of Bayfield cut the boat free from the dock with a chainsaw and the Coast Guard cleared a path through the lake ice to open water.

Dr. William Rinehart, his wife and her sister motored through the country in one of Ashland's first cars circa 1900.

include Greyhound, Wisconsin-Michigan Trailways and Four Star Line. In addition, the Lake Shore Bus Company provides charter service for schools, churches and groups.

Drays and Automobiles

The first automobile owned in Ashland was an Oldsmobile belonging to Doctor J.A. Marchessault. It caused quite a stir when it sputtered down Second Street in May, 1903. Doctors were usually the first in their community to own cars, since they still made house calls then. Quick transportation was a necessity.

Other cars soon followed the Olds. Doctors Harrison, Rinehart and Dodd all bought one and so did Joe Woodhead. Small boys found hitching rides on the back of his car so much fun that Dr. Rinehart installed a battery with a live wire on the rear end to keep them off. Marchessault and his Olds gave Ashland two more historical landmarks. The first recorded tow in Ashland took place when the Olds broke down and L.A. Giese used his horse and wagon to pull it home. Marchessault himself was accused of Ashland's first traffic law offense, but a jury acquitted him.

The auto spelled the end of Ashland's livery and dray services. W.J. Armstrong and J.H. Murray ran stables and rented horses, carriages, wagons and sleighs. Only the wealthy kept their own horses and carriages in their own barns. For most of Ashland's population, foot power was much more in use than horse power.

City Airport

The site of the original Ashland airport was purchased by the city in 1928. It was on Ellis Avenue Road, two miles south of the city. This airport served the city during the early days of commercial aviation. Two-seater bi-planes, Ford Tri-Motors, Douglas DC-3s, barnstormers and pioneers flew into and out of the old airport.

In 1958, the airport moved to its present site on Sanborn Avenue and was certified for service by North Central Airlines. President John F. Kennedy landed at the airport in September of 1963, two months before his assassination. Shortly after, the field was renamed the John F. Kennedy Memorial Airport.

Several commercial airlines have had

regularly scheduled flights to and from Ashland, but in 1987, only charter and private aircraft use it.

In 1986, an average of 6.8 aircraft per day landed at the J.F. Kennedy Memorial Airport. In that year 2,508 pilots signed the log. An estimated additional fifteen percent land but fail to register.

The first airplane in Ashland landed on the Bay about 1910. It's an early Curtiss model.

Edith Dodd Culver, 1893-

Edith Dodd was the second of the four children of Doctor and Mrs. John Dodd. She grew up in Ashland when "it was the land of opportunity for the young in heart." Since her father established his hospital in the family home, Edith grew up as one of "The Hospital Children."

She was educated in Ashland schools, then at Milwaukee-Downer, Smith, and the University of Wisconsin. She married H. Paul Culver in 1916. They had three children, Paul, Edith and John.

Edith's husband, a member of the Early Birds of Aviation, was one of four army pilots chosen to fly the first regularly scheduled air mail flights that began in 1918. She wrote many articles about her experiences as a pioneer aviator's wife. Her first book, *The Day Air Mail Began*, received an award from the Wisconsin Writer's Council.

Her second book, *610 Ellis and the Hospital Children*, published in 1978, told of childhood days as the daughter of one of Ashland's most prominent physicians. Her most recent book, *Tailspins*, published in 1986, tells of the early development of aviation and the part she and her husband played in it.

Mrs. Culver currently makes her home in Santa Fe, New Mexico, but regularly visits her home town.

A Bird's-Eye View of Ashland, 1886

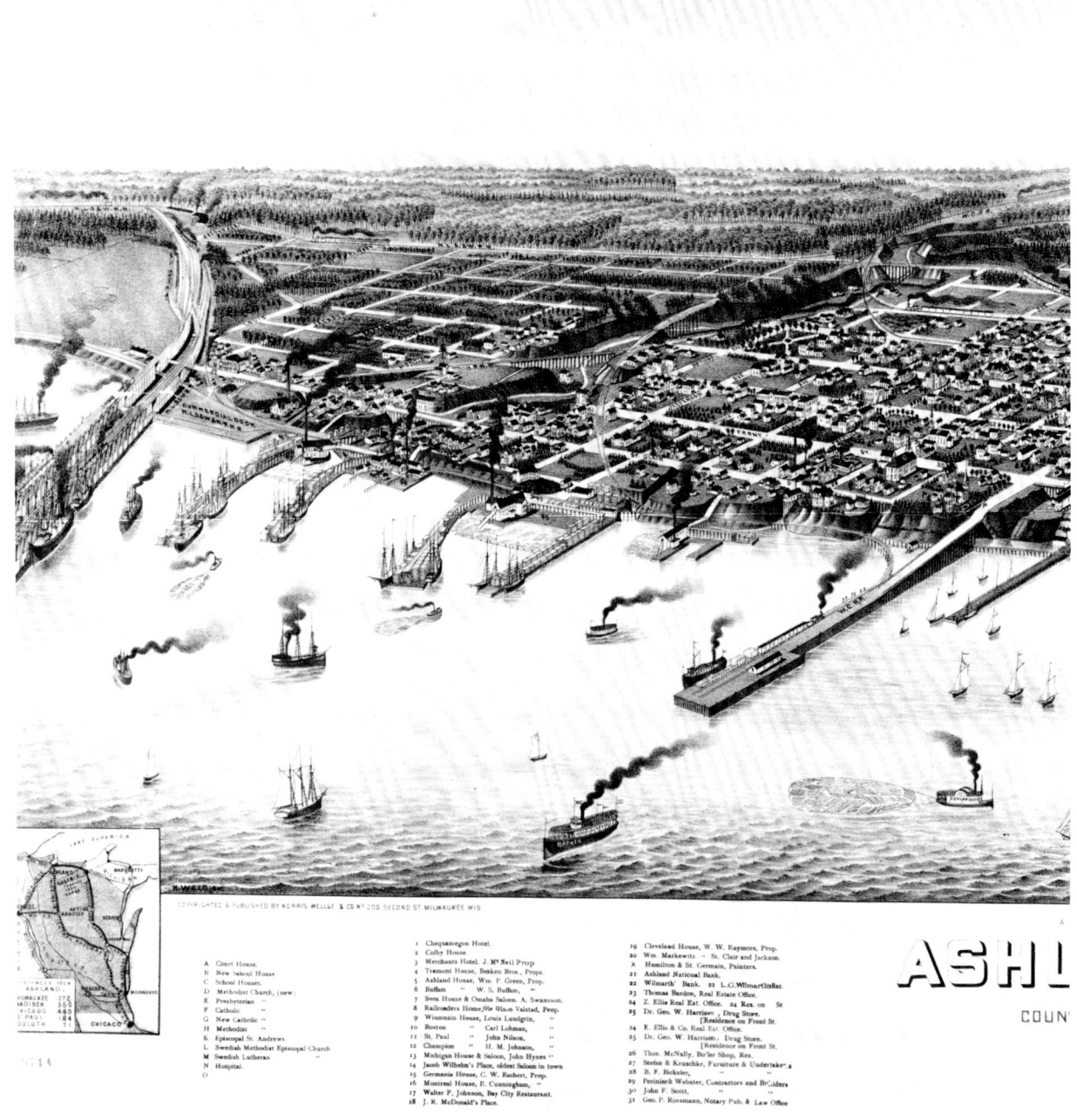

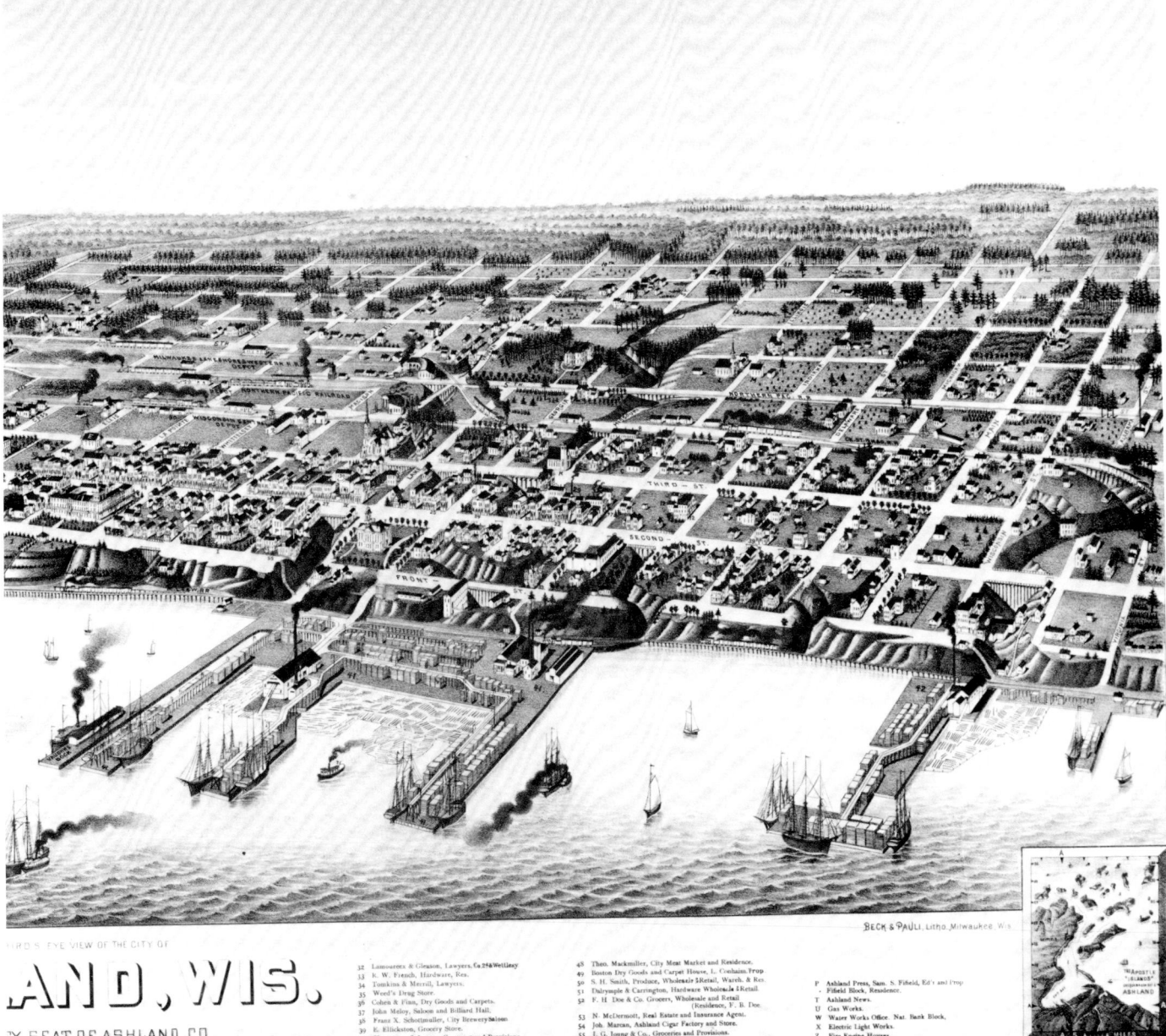

Optimists and Opportunists

"Ashland is emphatically not a speculative town. Ashland is a business town. The growth is simply the result of utilizing accumulative advances."
Ashland Daily Press, *1893*

Lumberjacks stacked logs into huge piles so a photographer could take a "folly shot" to impress viewers with the abundance of timber in the Ashland area. This stack contained 263 logs and nearly 19,000 board feet.

The fur trade was the forebear and the longest-lasting of all businesses in Ashland. Radisson, Groseilliers, and the Chippewa they traded with were the area's first businessmen, and the traffic in pelts they began lasted for two centuries before any white man thought of settling here. Furs were traded for trinkets, tools, weapons and whiskey—a natural resource exchanged for the trappings of civilization. As Ashland's economy developed, this kind of exchange was typical. The natural wealth of lumber, stone, ore, agriculture, and the pristine pleasures of clean water, air and beautiful scenery were traded for manufactured goods and services.

The fur trade also initiated what became another permanent trait of Ashland's economic life. The Bay and the city on it became a necessary link—the narrows of an hourglass—connecting the flow of goods and people to and from the Wisconsin hinterland and the international world of Great Lakes trade. Furs in the 1600s, lumber in the 1800s, iron ore until a few decades ago, Ashland was a middle link between the land to the south and the water to the north.

Martin Roehm and his family were Ashland's first Yankee farmers and this enabled them to stay at the Bay in the 1860s when virtually everyone else left. They raised cattle that grazed on wild pastures in the Marengo River Valley and faced the farmer's perennial problem of marketing their surplus production in a unique way. To sell their stock, the Roehms drove them downriver from Marengo to Odanah, then along the lake to the tip of Chequamegon Point, where Martin swam the cattle across the Bay to the market at La Pointe.

Ashland itself became a booming market for cattle and many other goods in 1872 when the Wisconsin Central began railroad construction south from town. Over two hundred buildings sprang up on the edge of the woods in the spring and summer of that year and approximately twelve hundred railroad men created a demand local merchants were happy to fill.

This first boom lasted until the end of the year when work on the road halted. Ashland's business people then experienced their first recession, but the city did not die. Optimism remained high and several entrepreneurs risked their fortunes in the new town.

Thomas Bardon came from Superior and started a real estate and insurance office that is the fore-runner of today's Lamal Agency. E.F. Prince organized a delivery route to Duluth by boat in summer and by sled in winter in connection with the Lake Superior Express. Emil Garnich and his partner Irvin Leihy opened the hardware store that became E. Garnich & Sons Company.

Of these three original Ashland businesses, only the Lamal Agency is still in existence. In 1884, Peter Lamal joined Bardon and gave his name to the business. Lawrence Lamal became associated with the agency in 1933 and operated it until 1978. He then sold it to Carolyn and Ed Malmberg, members of another old Ashland business family.

A band of trumpeters helped celebrate the opening of the Garnich Building.

Logs and Lumber

Ashland's lumber industry also began in 1872 when W.R. Sutherland built the Ashland Lumber Company on the lakeshore. Copper mining on Isle Royale created a demand for milled timbers and planks, and Sutherland was

Thomas Bardon, 1848-1923

A Kentucky native, Thomas Bardon started his working life as a railroad engineer who helped push the Northern Pacific west from Superior. He opened Ashland's first real estate office in 1872, and soon became the city's largest landowner and taxpayer. He was one of the most successful businessmen on the shore of Lake Superior, with extensive timber holdings in Canada and valuable iron ore holdings in the Gogebic Range. He also owned Ashland's first pulp mill, incorporated its first bank, taught in the first city school and held interests in the street railway, electric and gas plants. He was elected mayor four times.

THOMAS BARDON,

FIRE INSURANCE DEPARTMENT.

Following Companies Represented:

Pennsylvania, Penn.,
North British and Mercantile,
National, Hartford,
Concordia, Milwaukee,
Phœnix, London, England,
Liverpool, London and Globe,
Niagara, New York,
Ætna, Hartford, Conn.,
Sun Fire Office, England,
Denver Insurance Co., Denver, Col.,
Lloyd's Plate Glass Insurance Co., of New York City,
Commerce Insurance Co., Southern California,

Home, New York,
Underwriters, New York,
Insurance Co. of North America,
Germania, New York,
Connecticut, Hartford,
Springfield Fire and Marine,
Hartford, of Hartford,
Heckla, Madison, Wis.,
Phenix, Brooklyn, N. Y.,
Hamburg, Bremen,
Caledonia Insurance Co., Glasgow, Scotland,
St. Paul Fire and Marine,
Western, Toronto,

ALL LOSSES PAID AT THIS OFFICE.

618 SECOND STREET WEST,   ASHLAND, WIS

Captain Doherty ran a sawmill located on the Bay between Ninth and Twelfth Avenue East in 1888.

Woodworkers turned out arched moldings for church windows and other decorative pieces at the Scott-Taylor mill.

in the right place at the right time. Three years later the Union Mill Company built the Durfee mill and in 1878 the Muellwe & Ritchie Mill, later known as the Mowatt Mill, went up just west of the present Soo Line dock. The last of these early mills was the Superior Lumber Company, or Keystone mill, erected on the Reiss Coal dock site in 1882.

Ashland quickly became a sawmill town with the shoreline from Prentice Park to what is now Bretting's covered with logs, slabs, sawdust piles and milled boards. In 1893, ten mills cut an estimated three hundred billion board feet of lumber. About ten thousand lumberjacks spent four hard winter months cutting trees in the hinterlands and earning about one dollar each a day or about 1.4 million dollars a season. Although many loggers were farmhands away from home in southern Wisconsin and who returned there in spring, many other loggers moved into Ashland and worked in the mills from spring to fall or until the logs gave out. Nearly all of this lumber as well as boards from mills away from the lake was sent out of town by boat, and Ashland was an even larger lumber shipper than miller.

Scott-Taylor

With all this lumber in Ashland, it was only natural that a planing mill should appear. John F. Scott, who came to Ashland in 1883, and Frederick F. Hubbell, who came in 1886, and James H. Taylor, an excellent mill man who joined on in 1887, formed The Scott, Hubbell and Taylor Company. They manufactured finished sashes, doors, blinds, moldings and other wood products.

Hubbell dropped out of the company in 1895, but Scott-Taylor developed into a diversified mill and woodworking plant. Standard woodwork was milled but so were specialty pieces for churches, schools, libraries and commercial buildings. Scott-Taylor prospered until the changes in architectural tastes and industrial technology reduced demand for intricately milled moldings and precisely-machined wooden containers. The plant closed in 1974. Its presence is still felt in Ashland, however. Many of the planer blades used on Scott-Taylor moldings were sold to Larson Picture Framing where they could continue to shape wood into beautiful patterns.

James River Paper

It in the nature of business to deplete a resource, find a substitute, then develop an industry to utilize it. With all the fine timber cut and the hardwoods rapidly disappearing by the turn of the century, Ashland capitalists turned to lower grade logs to start a paper industry.

In 1902, the Ashland Pulp and Paper Company, the first on Lake Superior, was founded. The plant produced tissue and other light weight papers until the 1920s when it became part of the Menasha Printing and Carton Company. In the 1930s, the "Tux" and "Compact" napkins were developed and the plant then concentrated on the production of napkin papers.

The Menasha Company merged with the Marathon Corporation, and in 1956, Marathon sold the Ashland plant to the American Can Company. James River purchased the operation in 1982.

Larry Grymala operates a Number One Rewinder at the James River plant.

The James River plant of 1987 occupies 128,000 square feet. It has two paper machines, twenty-three napkin folders and one sleeve machine. It employs 217 people with an annual payroll of $6.6 million. James River turns out twenty thousand tons of tissue paper per year and ships 1.4 million cases of napkins annually.

Development Schemes

For people in business, the most significant event of Ashland's first decade of development occurred on June 2, 1877, when the first Wisconsin Central train from Chicago and Milwaukee pulled into town. Three hundred cheering Ashlanders met the train whose presence meant so much to the city's development. The link connecting the port city to the interior was now complete. Most Ashland boosters saw the city's future tied to the lumber industry, or to ore mining. A few looked beyond the time when these two resources would be depleted and hoped to see northern Wisconsin develop into a prosperous farming region with Ashland as its hub.

One of the first institutions organized to promote Ashland's commercial potential was the Chamber of Commerce. It had seventy-five members at its start in 1883 with Sam Fifield as president, W.R. Durfee as vice-president and Sam Vaughn as treasurer.

Six years later, a group of local boosters persuaded the city council to issue one hundred $1000 bonds "for the advancement of commerce and manufacturers." Citizens approved the issue by a vote of 640-7. The next year Sam Fifield requested that the council hire James E. York for three months at $1,500 to tout Ashland as a manufacturing site for eastern investors.

Bond money was used to help the Northern Grains Company set up its flour mill in the city, and given to D.A. Kennedy to start a sawmill. It was also used to pay the expenses of Doctor George Harrison who joined Thomas Bardon on a trip to London to attract English capital to Ashland. They later asked the council to pay the expenses of three Englishmen who wished to investigate investment possibilities in Ashland.

Six months later, Mayor W.W. O'Keefe asked the council to rescind the bonds since money appropriated wasn't used to attract new business but was "simply transferred into the hands of city property owners in payment for a piece of their property." In addition Bardon and Harrison, who had returned from Europe, had yet to report to the council. "I cannot understand," said O'Keefe, unless it be ...understood by us as a failure of their mission, or it may be that they are busy entertaining the three men we sent the $300 to pay their passage over."

The bond issue was cancelled and only $14,750 was spent. Such promotional schemes were common for new settlements on the make. Whether they were right or wrong, depended on their success. If another new industry had appeared in Ashland because of

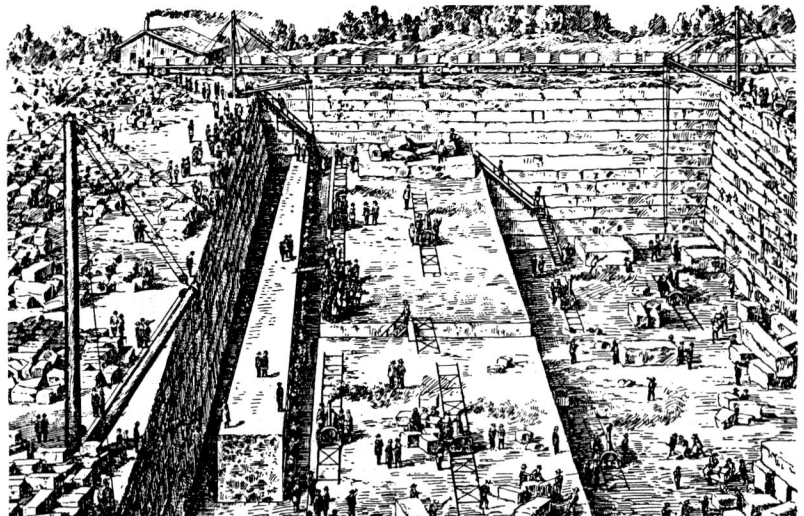

A VIEW REPRESENTING A SECTION OF THE PRENTICE BROWN STONE QUARRY AT HOUGHTON, WISCONSIN, SHOWING THE GREAT MONOLITH BEING BROKEN FROM ITS BED THE 18TH OF NOVEMBER, 1892. LENGTH ONE HUNDRED AND FIFTEEN FEET, TEN FEET AT BASE, FOUR FEET AT TOP, AND IS THE LONGEST MONOLITH EVERY QUARRIED BY OVER NINE FEET, BEING FORTY-SIX FEET LONGER THAN CLEOPATRA'S NEEDLE, ERECTED BY VANDERBILT IN CENTRAL PARK, NEW YORK CITY.

Main Office, Ashland, Wisconsin.

The Ashland *Daily Press* captioned this sketch: "A view representing a section of the Prentice brown stone quarry at Houghton, Wisconsin, showing the great monolith being broken from its bed the 18th of November, 1892. Length one hundred and fifteen feet, ten feet at base, four feet at top, and is the longest monolith ever quarried by over nine feet, being forty-six feet longer than Cleopatra's Needle, erected by Vanderbilt in Central Park, New York City."

the $300 spent on travel expenses for Englishmen, then the bond issue would have been a brilliant stroke.

Brownstone Monolith

Another brilliant stroke was attempted by Ashland's quarrymen, who shipped the first brownstone out of the Bay in 1870. It was called "Ashland stone" and thousands of tons of it were shipped down the lakes to build Milwaukee's courthouse and erect other handsome, durable public and private buildings in Chicago, Brooklyn, Buffalo and Manhattan.

Ashland brownstone possessed the desirable qualities of softness when first cut out of the earth and durability after it had seasoned. It was easily worked, but solid and strong. Up to eight quarries were in operation in the 1880s with Frederick Prentice's digs at Houghton Point the largest. In 1892, a total of 2,313,000 cubic feet of brownstone was quarried.

Prentice hoped to vividly display the strength and beauty of Ashland stone and promote his home town at the Chicago World's Fair of 1893. He had his workers quarry the world's largest stone monolith, a colossus ten feet square at the base and 110 feet long. When raised at the Fair, the monolith would, like the Eiffel Tower in Paris and the Statue of Liberty in New York, stand as a symbol of the power and progress of the people who engineered it.

Shipping such a huge item down the Lakes to Chicago was a formidable but not insurmountable problem. Financing the project was harder. The recession of 1893 crippled Prentice's operations and the huge block was stranded in the quarry. In time it was cut into smaller blocks used in many building projects. Its fate presaged that of the brownstone industry. Though the supply of stone was virtually inexhaustible, demand was not. The development of iron and steel skeletons for multi-story buildings eliminated the need for heavy stone walls and brownstone was replaced by other materials.

Iron Range Connection

Early surveyors and settlers knew copper and iron ore was present in the Ashland area, but no one really tried to exploit the lode until storekeeper Nat Moore discovered a chunk of clear hematic ore under the roots of a fallen tree. A boom similar to the California or Alaska gold rush resounded in Ashland. Population soared to an estimated 18,000 as newcomers poured into town to take part in the building of what was called the second Pittsburgh. Popular logic held that an abundant supply of iron ore and hardwoods for charcoal would prompt construction of blast furnaces and iron mills in Ashland, which, as both a railhead and a lake port, could ship everything it could make. Prosperity based on another natural resource and an industrial plant to boot had to follow.

A stock exchange opened to trade mining stocks in Ashland. George F. Merrill, who accepted the logic of the iron boom, built a house and paid for the plumbing and heating with $1,000 worth of stock options sold on the exchange. He put his own money into several thousand shares of stock and was so confident that he refused to sell it at two dollars a share. After the iron bubble burst in 1887 he was happy to sell the stock for four cents a share.

Iron mining did develop into a solid business for Ashland and nearby communities, but not on the quick-rich basis many hoped it would. The mines were located about forty miles from Ashland and the city became an important port for the transport, not of finished iron products as many hoped it would, but of raw ore instead. The second Pittsburgh was indeed built, and just about this time; not in Ashland, but in Gary, Indiana.

Vast quantities of iron ore were shipped by rail from mines on the Wisconsin-Michigan border east of city. At one time four ore docks were in operation and trainload after

trainload rumbled through town to unload.

Only one iron mill, The Ashland Iron and Steel Company, processed ore in Ashland. It was the largest charcoal-iron blast furnace in the world, and the City of Ashland donated a total of fourteen blocks with extensive frontage on the Bay to get the company started in 1886.

The Hinkle furnace the company used was nearly twice as large as any previously-built blaster of its type. On a daily basis it produced 150 tons of castings, roughly enough to cover about one half of a football field. At its peak in 1891, the furnace produced 37,192 tons of iron. It survived until 1921 and closed because of the development of Bessemer steel-making process.

The blast furnace re-opened for about a year in 1924-25 as part of the Charcoal Iron Company of America. The final closing was due to depletion of the hardwood forest which supplied it with charcoal. The Japanese who had been importing the acetate of lime by-product of the plant developed a substitute they could buy closer to home, thereby proving that Ashland had a stake in world trade from its first days of industrial development.

Granite Quarrying

In the 1930s, the American Black Granite Company took over the blast furnace buildings and grounds for a finishing plant for black granite quarried near Mellen. Arthur E. Appleyard managed the operation that became one of the largest employers in Depression-era Ashland. The original company lasted until the late 1930s when plastic facings for building stone proved too hard for even granite to overcome.

Not all black granite quarrying ended, however. The original grave decorations for the John F. Kennedy grave in Arlington National Cemetery are made of stone quarried at Mellen and finished in Ashland. Kennedy himself selected black granite for his grave stone when he visited Ashland in September, 1963, two months before he died.

Lime Kiln

Mining of another sort supplied raw material for the Ashland Lime, Salt and Cement Company, organized by W.O. Lamb in 1887. This operation took limestone shipped all the way from Kelly Island in Lake Erie and baked it in a special kiln that transformed it into the

Builders of the Ashland Iron and Steel Company Blast Furnace hoped it would make the city America's second Pittsburgh.

These Kilns used sawmill waste as fuel to cook limestone into cement and other products. Ashlander Tony Leciejewski leveled them with dynamite in 1931.

white powder used for plaster, mortar, and other lime-based products with salt as a by-product. The kiln took six hours to turn stone to powder and its fire, fueled by sawmill wastes, never went out.

Ashland's location on the lake, its excellent railroad connections and its abundant supply of cheap fuel kept the limestone kiln in town. In 1893, Ashland Lime, Salt and Cement, was shipping between seventy-five and one hundred cars of salt and cement per month.

C.G. Bretting

The North Star Iron works moved to Ashland from Minneapolis in 1888 to be closer to iron and cheap water transportation. The name was changed to the Parish Manufacturing Company, which made mining and sawmill machinery, Corliss Engines and a complete line of boilers and power transmitting machinery. In 1890, Christopher George Bretting purchased the Parish Iron Works and formed the C.G. Bretting Manufacturing Company which still occupies its original site on Lake Superior in east Ashland.

From 1890 to the 1920s, the company produced machinery and equipment for the sawmill industry. During the first of those four decades, Ashland had the world's largest concentration of sawmills, and Bretting supplied the machines they needed to cut and shape wood. Christopher Bretting enjoyed the boom years but did not live to see the decline of the lumber industry. He died at the St. Louis World's Fair in 1904.

His wife Jane and their oldest son Ralph continued to run the company and shifted to the manufacture of mining equipment. In 1929, Christopher Bretting's youngest son Lyman returned to Ashland with an Engineering degree from M.I.T. and took over management of the company.

By the 1950s, the decline of the mining industry prompted Bretting to change its line again. Tad Bretting joined his father Lyman in 1958, and by the early 1960s Bretting was concentrating its efforts on the design and manufacture of folding equipment for use in paper tissue and napkin plants. In the 1970s, Bretting entered the export market, and by 1987 about twenty-five per cent of its machinery was exported overseas to England, West Germany, The Netherlands, Italy, Switzerland, Finland, Australia, Mexico and Malaysia. Three-quarters of Bretting's output is purchased by the American and Canadian divisions of paper companies like Fort Howard, Scott Paper, Kimberly-Clark,

Workers posed with their tools aloft at the North Star Ironworks circa 1900. They are identified as Johnson, Benson, Green, Elstrom, Larson, Urbom, Parson and Blixt.

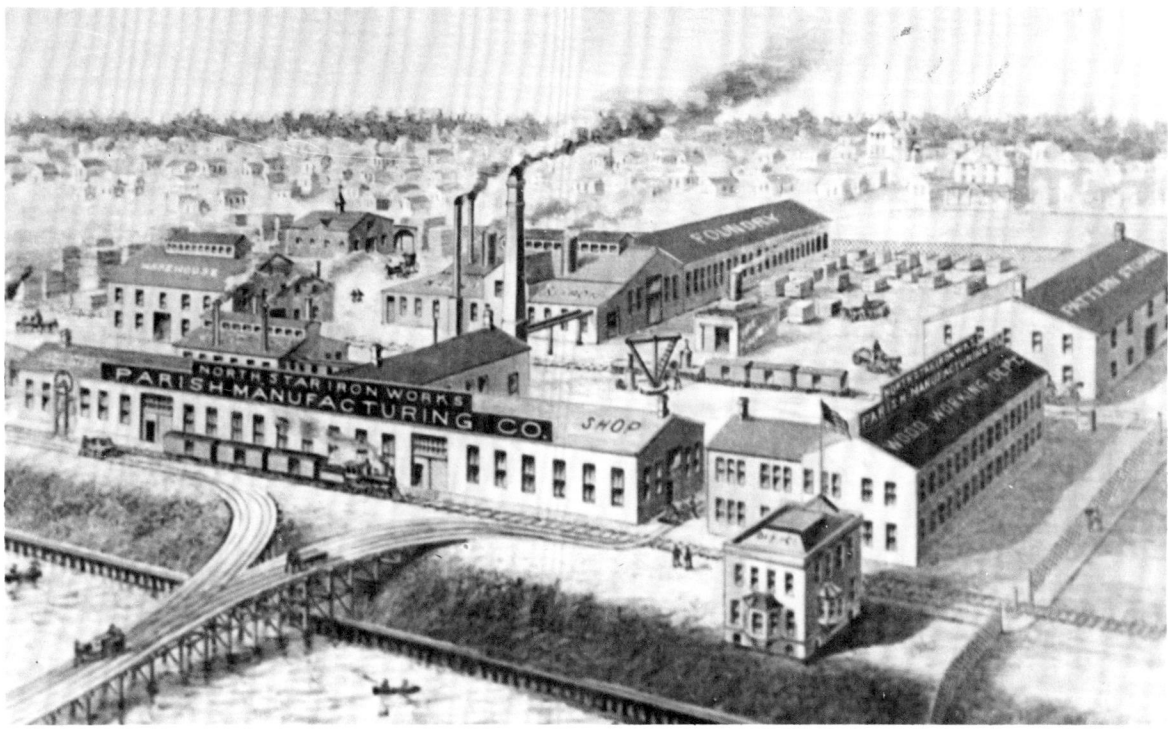

C.G. Bretting began as the Parish Manufacturing Company Foundry and evolved to meet the needs of the lumber, mining and paper industries.

Georgia-Pacific, James River and Wisconsin Tissue Mills.

The Bretting line has expanded from napkin folders to include interfolded and "C" fold paper towel machines, facial tissue interfolders and non-woven folders and interfolders. It is a prime supplier of automatic, state-of the art-folding machinery. The company has grown from twelve employees in the early 1960s to 225 employees with an annual payroll or more than five million dollars. Not only does the company attract scores of visitors from overseas to Ashland, but six technical service engineers go on frequent trips to service Bretting machines around the world.

Malmberg's

Bretting is not the only Ashland business to survive nearly a century of operation. In the spring of 1889, Sebe Malmberg and his elder sister left their native Sweden for Ashland. Malmberg was in his early twenties and had completed an apprenticeship in watch and clock making. He decided to open a repair shop in Ashland because of the large Scandinavian population in the area.

His first shop was in the ravine area of Second Street between Vaughn Avenue and Sixth Avenue West, but he soon moved to the central business district across from the Knight Hotel on East Second. He later moved to 112 Second Street West and remained there until his death in 1929.

Malmberg and his wife Gina were childless, and Gina prevailed on Sebe's brother Axel and Axel's son Roy to emigrate from Sweden and take over the business. They arrived in 1930 and kept Malmberg's in the family. In 1978, after nearly fifty years in the business, Roy Malmberg retired and left management of the family shop, now incorporated, to his son Curtis.

The business is still owned and operated by the Malmbergs. Officers and shareholders are all family members. Curtis Malmberg is president; Richard, vice-president; Edwin, secretary; and Susan Malmberg Riddell, treasurer. In 1989, the Malmbergs will celebrate a century of continuous family operation of their store in Ashland.

Columbia Furniture

Another immigrant, Russian-born Sam Sherbacov, founded a second long-lasting family business in Ashland. In 1891, Sherbacov opened the Columbia Furniture Store at 215 Second Street East but soon moved to the Wilmarth Block on Second Street East.

By 1905, the *Daily Press* was announcing that the Columbia Furniture Company had all the furnishings necessary to make a home beautiful and complete. Furniture, stoves, carpets, linoleum, glassware, crockery and cutlery were all available. Many pairs of newlyweds started housekeeping with

E.J. Born opened his jewelry store at 317½ West Second Street in 1890. The predecessor of today's Ashland Jeweler, Born later moved to 402 Second Street West.

Robert Oien opened his store in 1954 and has remained on West Second Street ever since.

furnishings from Columbia.

Alec Sherbacov, Sam's son, joined the business in 1919 and managed the store through the rough years of the Depression. At the end of World War II, Alec's nephew William Boutwell joined the operation and is currently serving as president.

The New England Store

The New England Store was the largest dry goods establishment of 1890s Ashland. In 1893, it occupied three floors in the old Knight Block and was considered to be Ashland's most handsome store. It boasted separate departments for underwear and linen, carpets and rugs, ladies dress goods, gloves and hosiery, and ribbons.

By 1905, George A. Sparling was the proprietor, and the store was heavily stocked with dry goods, carpets, ready-to-wear ladies and children's clothes, notions, draperies, rugs and lace curtains. Fifteen clerks staffed the counters and registered sales on electric cash machines.

Although not as large as it once was, the New England Store still exists. Donna Wheeler purchased it fourteen years ago from Margaret Erickson. Some of the original showcases and cash registers are still in use at the 216 Fourth

Avenue West location. When Wheeler bought the store, she considered changing the name, but decided not to since Ashland has "always" had a New England Store.

Emil Garnich & Sons

Emil Garnich and Sons was another century-old Ashland business. Garnich began selling hardware to lumbermen, miners and railroaders in 1872. Twenty-one years later he built a brick building at 410 Second Street West but had to move to larger quarters in 1895. After a fire in 1914, Garnich built a large wholesale establishment on Seventh Avenue West.

Although the company celebrated a century of life in 1972, it survived for only three more years. When fire destroyed its building in 1975, E. Garnich and Sons Hardware Company closed its doors for the last time.

Tomlinson Construction

The oldest general contracting firm in Ashland is Frank Tomlinson Company, Inc., founded in 1888. Tomlinson was a masonry contractor with Archie Donald and Company, but left to form a partnership with a carpenter named Dan Egan.

In 1920, they built the Northern National Bank on the corner of Second Street and Fourth Avenue West. They also built the Ashland National Bank on Second and Ellis. The distinctive stonework of both buildings is typical of the Tomlinson style.

In the midst of the Depression in 1933, Tomlinson started his own contracting business by building a new home for Dr. Clyde Smiles. His two sons, William and Ed, worked with their father until Frank retired in 1953. William and his son Paul took over the business and incorporated it in 1959. Paul Tomlinson became president in 1970 and will pass the title and the family business to his son Steve, the fourth generation of Tomlinsons in the construction business. The company will be one hundred years old in 1988.

Power and Light

The Ashland Electric Light Company began generating electricity in 1886, but demand for power in the days of steam engines was scant. Restricted to supplying power only for lighting, the Ashland utility went bankrupt. Then Dr. George Harrison provided demand for electric power by replacing the horses of the Ashland Street Railway Company with electric trolleys. In 1896, Harrison merged the two companies and they struggled down the line into solvency together.

In 1908, Boston financier Arthur E. Appleyard purchased the operation and ran a combined light, power, gas and trolley utility. He also bought a hydroelectric plant on the White River, and in 1915, started construction of a new steam plant at the site of the present Bay Front Generating Plant.

By 1922, the Big Falls Water Power Company, located in Ladysmith, had changed its name to Lake Superior District Power Company and purchased the Ashland utility. Except for a period of retrenchment in the 1930s, the Power Company has grown with the times. In 1948, a new building, boiler, and 20,000 kilowatt turbine generator was

The New England Store ready for Christmas about 1910. (l to r) Jeanie Ritchie, Helen Giezewski, Mr. Douglas (the floorwalker), Floss Waterbury, Hazel Masters, Jerry Sullivan, Helen Radik, Harold Brown, Mary Scharding, Paulie Hines, (rear) Luke Olson, Olive Finn.

Steve, the fourth Tomlinson to run the century-old family construction business.

The Lake Superior District Power Plant in 1948.

The Lake Superior District Power Company conducted a Laundry School in the 1920s to encourage women to buy and use electrical appliances.

installed at Bay Front, and the tall stacks and huge coal pile at the plant became familiar waterfront scenes.

In 1986, a new fuel system design to utilize wood and reduce the need for coal went on line. Wood from local sources will replace an estimated 17,000 tons of coal each year. Burning wood will also reduce sulfur dioxide and fly ash emissions, thereby improving air quality along the Bay.

Other experiments in using wood to make electricity include the burning of whole trees without trimming limbs, debarking, shredding or chipping as well as burning old railroad ties in an environmentally safe manner.

Northern States Power is continuing the Ashland business tradition of using natural resources to maintain quality of life.

Telephones

In 1882, only six years after it was invented, a telephone was installed by the Wisconsin Telephone Company in the Ashland American Express Office. Telephone use grew slowly at first, then picked up after 1900.

Ashland was served by two telephone systems in the early 1900s, and two sets of lines ran down the streets. The Ashland

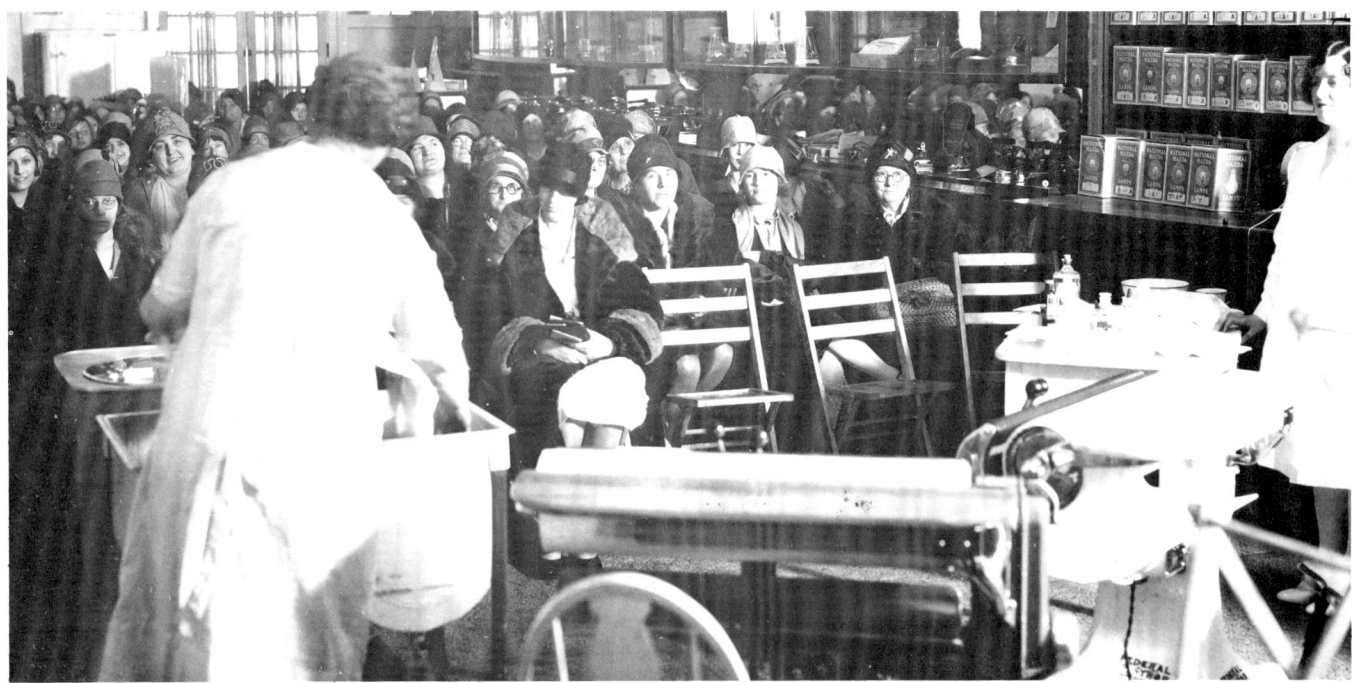

Home Telephone Company started with six hundred subscribers in 1902 and doubled to twelve hundred in 1905. It was locally managed by W.F. Shea, W.R. Durfee and C.A. Lamoreux and charged a one dollar per month residential rate with a two dollar commercial fee. The other company was the Wisconsin Telephone Company managed by Charles J. Good. Competition ended in 1919, when the Home Company became part of the larger Wisconsin Telephone grid.

Cutover Colonization

In 1891, vast tracts of logged-over railroad land south of Ashland were thrown open for settlement. The land was free, and, although of questionable quality for farming, attractive to immigrants from Europe and the United States. The railroads, local and state political leaders, and the University of Wisconsin urged settlers to try and scratch a living out of this Cutover ground that had grown mainly pine trees and sphagnum moss for thousands of years.

In Ashland, the law firm of State Senator A.W. Sanborn, Frank Lamoreux, Allen T. Pray and James W. Goode, sponsored a Cutover colonization scheme. They succeeded in attracting over three hundred Czech and Slovak immigrant families to the vicinity of Ino, Moquah and Benoit.

Others believed that, instead of clearing the stumps and rocks for row crops, the Cutover could be turned into a large pasture. In 1904, Frank Catlin and J.S. Miller started raising sheep on the enterprise known today as the Catlin Farm. Shortly after, the Chequamegon Stock Ranch and the Eileen Stock Farm began operations, and the Dixon brothers put two thousand sheep out to pasture amidst the stumps near Marengo.

Part of the program to encourage migration to the Cutover was a university experimental farm in Ashland. Dr. E.J. Delwiche conducted the first experiments at the Harrison farm on Ellis Avenue and helped another medical man, Dr. Adellon Andrus, to set up the first modern dairy farm in Ashland County.

Delwiche and other university people worked on the problems of growing grain, hay, orchard and vegetable crops. By 1913, as other natural resources were running out, the possibilities of agricultural development prompted Ashland and Bayfield counties to make a joint donation of 180 acres of land for university use at Ashland Junction. This

The exchange at one of Ashland's two turn-of-the-century telephone companies. Many businesses were connected to both lines so all their customers could call.

L. Larsen and Co. Grocers. Louis Larsen, Jens Wilman, H. Peter and A. Hansen ran the store at 322 9th Avenue West.

Albert W. Sanborn, 1853-1937

A.W. Sanborn was a Vermont native who had established a successful legal and political career in Portage County prior to his arrival in Ashland in 1895. He practiced law in partnership with several attorneys before establishing the firm of Cate, Sanborn, Lamoreux and Park in 1897.

A prominent Republican, Sanborn delivered the nomination speech for President Benjamin Harrison at the party convention in 1888. He also served as State Senator for the Ashland area from 1904 until 1912.

For his work in helping Slovak farmers colonize the Moquah region of Bayfield County, he was affectionately known as "Daddy Sanborn." He was also recognized for his efforts by the University of Wisconsin. The little Slovak community eventually prospered and expanded along the line of the Northern Pacific Railroad to Dauby, Benoit and Ino.

When Moquah settlers needed financial help, "Daddy Sanborn" borrowed it from a bank and loaned it to them at the same rate of interest as he had borrowed it. He helped buy horses and first rate Guernsey cattle and supported schools that taught English and American citizenship.

Sanborn left a legacy to working people all over the country when he wrote and ushered through the legislature Wisconsin's pioneering Workmen's Compensation Law. Like other Ashland leaders, Sanborn also served on the board of Northland College.

---

experimental station, the first established outside of Madison, has since helped northern farmers master the skills necessary to raise crops and livestock in a decidedly inhospitable environment.

Since the rural area around it never developed into a wealthy agricultural region, Ashland never built much of an farm-service sector in its economy. The cash that a large number of prosperous farmers might have put into the local economy never appeared, neither did the grain and livestock that might have been shipped out of Ashland's port, nor the people who might have moved to the city and found jobs in the agricultural sector. Ashland's development depended on the natural wealth of the region around the city. Because of its small success, farming could not play a very large role in Ashland's growth.

Frank S. Dhooge was an exception to the rule of Cutover farm failure, but he was a far cry from the typical Cutover settler. Dhooge was a prominent Ashland merchant who also operated a 250-acre farm near the city. In 1905, his fifty pure bred Shorthorns enabled the Dhooge Creamery to produce three hundred gallons of ice cream a day as well as several hundred pounds of Grade A butter. He also raised and sold milk, cheese, vegetables and fruit plus 360 hogs for the Ashland market. The Dhooge operation literally put food on Ashland's dinner tables and dominated the local agricultural market.

Despite the success of the farm station, farming was not widely successful in the Cutover. Settlers who had come to the land full of hope at the turn of the century were bankrupt and broken by the 1920s. Foreclosures, tax sales and abandoned homesteads were common sights in Ashland, Bayfield, Sawyer and Iron counties in the decade prior to the infamously hard times of the 1930s. In 1932, seventy-five farmers gathered at the court house in Ashland but failed to halt a sheriff's sale of their land.

Significantly, in 1891 an elevator able to store 150,000 bushels of grain had been built in Ashland. It grossed over one million dollars in its first year of operation, but little of the grain it ground was locally-grown. Nearly every barrel of flour was made from wheat shipped to Ashland by boat. Not much would change over the years, as agriculture would remain only a marginal enterprise in northern Wisconsin.

Frank S. Dhooge ran Ashland's largest general store in the 1890 s. Dhooge's sold everything from cream to meats to sweets.

Simon Anderson's Meat Market at 1211 West Third Street. Sawdust on the floor, pickles in the barrel and cold meats on the counter were standard features. Customers could sit on a stool and sample the wares.

Legal Profession

The Ashland County Bar Association and the Bar Association of the Fifteenth Judicial Circuit Court were formed about the same time in 1856. J.J. Miles, John H. Knight, William M. Tomkins, George F. Merrill, E.H. Hayes, J.Q. Hayes and Ed. F. Gleason practiced in Ashland prior to incorporation.

In 1887, George W. Cate and John F. Dufer formed the predecessor of the firm of Clark and Clark. 1987 is its centennial year. Many prestigious Ashland attorneys were part of this firm, including State Senator A.W. Sanborn, Frank Lamoreux, Allen T. Pray, James W. Goode, Theron P. Pray and Dale R. Clark. Scott W. Clark joined his father Dale in 1980 and gave the firm its present name.

While a member of the firm, Senator Sanborn helped lead the state legislature to enact important industrial legislation: workmen's compensation, women and child welfare rules, the income tax, and the creation of the Industrial Commission that was the predecessor of the Wisconsin Department of Industry, Labor and Human Relations.

Other law firms in 1987 include Wartman, Wartman and Dallenbach; Jacobs, McDonald and Silc; Anich and Peterson; Mark L. Perrine; and David Siegler. Robert Eaton is the District Attorney.

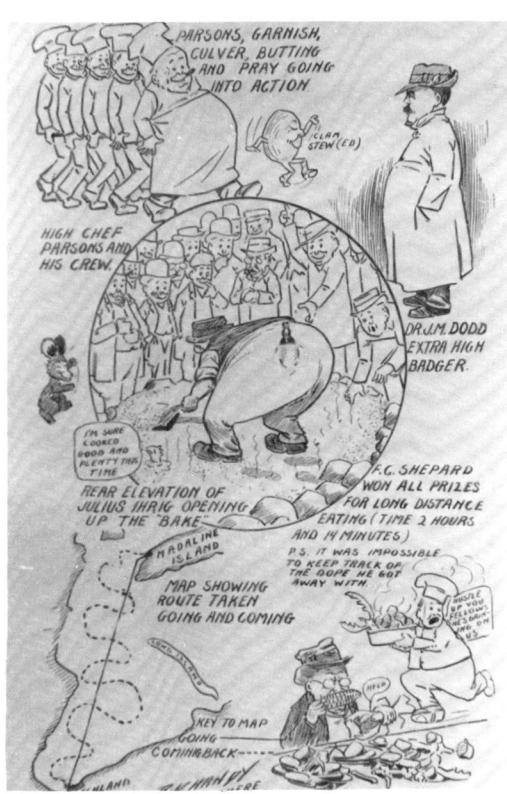

Ashland business leaders entertained each other at clambakes like this one sponsored by the Badger Club in 1916. The menu featured steamed Little Neck clams, baked bluefish, steamed lived lobster and north Wisconsin milk-fed chicken.

Clarence A. Lamoreux, 1860-1945

Clarence Lamoreux moved to Cumberland, Wisconsin, from his native Portage County in 1881. While there he practiced law, ran a newspaper, managed the post office and directed a band. He was superintendent of schools for Barron County.

He came to Ashland in 1884. Five years later he founded the firm of Lamoreux and Gleason with E.F. Gleason. He was a member of the Knights of Pythias, Elks, and the Presbyterian Church choir. He also served as president of the Ashland County Bar Association for ten years, a role that earned him the title of *Mr. Law*. In 1899, he won a Republican seat in the Wisconsin Senate and was involved in politics his entire life.

He also served for many years on the Wisconsin Deep Water Ports Commission and worked for improvements on the Great Lakes Waterway that resulted in construction of the St. Lawrence Seaway.

In 1905, the *Press* quoted his expression of every Ashland booster's view of the city. He said, "Ashland is bound to advance with its unlimited quantities of timber ...the finest harbor on the great chain of lakes, the finest grass country, all of which will contribute to its rapid growth and upbuilding ..."

Angvick's sold home furnishings and provided funeral services from this Second Street location.

Du Pont Dynamite

The clearing of the stumplands and mining provided a nearby market for another Ashland industrial product. The dynamite plant of E.I. Du Pont was established in 1905 just around the tip of the Bay in Barksdale. Two years later the Ashland *Daily Press* could report that the plant turned out 74,000 pounds of dynamite in one day, a new world's record.

Du Pont came to the Ashland area for the same reasons other plants located here. A natural resource in the form of the potash necessary for the manufacture of high explosives was abundant, and Ashland's rail and water transportation links were excellent. The Ashland area was also large enough to supply a good labor force, but small enough to minimize the threat to life and limb should a serious accident occur.

The start of World War I in 1914 made dynamite a good investment, and Du Pont enlarged the Barksdale works. In a year the monthly payroll was about $35,000, and many Ashlanders made the daily commute around the tip of the Bay on bicycles.

By 1929, Barksdale was one of the largest dynamite plants in the country, able to turn out eighty million pounds of TNT a year. 250 buildings were contained in the two thousand acre compound. During World War II, Barksdale became the largest producer of TNT in the United States. Several serious explosions occurred over the years, blowing out many of the windows on Second Street. A number of lives were lost.

The plant closed in 1974.

Munsingwear

Ashland's workers turned their efforts to less destructive pursuits in 1948, when the Munsingwear Plant opened. A year earlier Clarence Tolg, a Munsingwear vice-president, studied the city's suitability for the factory by perching himself atop an orange crate on Second Street and taking a random head count. When asked what he was doing, Tolg said he was trying to determine if Ashland could support a new industry.

The Ashland Chamber of Commerce took a more conventional approach and sent a seven-member committee to Munsingwear headquarters in Minneapolis. The trip was a success and Munsingwear opened its first plant in the building that now houses Larson Picture

Frame. Within its first year of operation the plant grew fast enough to employ 195 people.

In 1969, Munsingwear moved to its present location on Seventeenth Avenue and by 1986 employed 274 people making men's clothing.

Larson Picture Frame

Another post-World War II business venture to find success in Ashland is Larson Picture Frame, which moved to the city in 1959. Expansion came quickly in the 1960s as Larson found a ready market for its original molded wood designs. The business became a leader in manufacturing ready-made picture frames and marketing them on display racks in craft and gallery shops.

Roger Larson, who started the framing business as a hobby, sold it to Craig Ponsio and Lee Anderson in 1981. Growth continued, with the Ashland plant handling both manufacturing and distribution. Since 1982, additional distribution centers have been added in Denver, Dallas, Chicago, Atlanta and Los Angeles. Larson Picture Frame is a national operation.

All manufacturing of moldings and frames is done in Ashland with locally grown and milled wood. The plant has been modified twice in the 1980s and enlarged once. As the company continues to grow additional expansion of the Ashland plant is likely to take place.

Ashland Forge

The city's manufacturing base expanded in 1974 when Ashland Forge began working steel. Eight drop hammers, two coining presses, four grinding and polishing machines, eight burnishing barrels, a tool and die plus a

Roger Larson began his Framing Company in a garage in the 1960s.

Hardee's is Ashland's largest fast-food restaurant. A 145-seat facility was built in 1986 to replace an older, smaller Hardee's next door.

scissors plant make up the operation.

Shortly after opening Ashland Forge had twenty-three employees. The recession of the early 1980s reduced the work force to two, Ken Kramer and Martin Marita. The recent addition of the scissors works and the economic recovery have restored the number of employees to fifteen, with future growth expected. During the thirteen years Ashland Forge has been in business, it has produced over thirteen million forgings for Duro Metal Products of Chicago and other customers, with ninety per cent of the forgings going to Duro Metal.

Reversing the flight of business from the Midwest to the Sun Belt, Howard Yefsky of Ashland Forge purchased American Scissors of Spartanburg, South Carolina and moved the operation to Ashland in 1986. The production goal for the scissors plant is 2500 pairs a day to meet a federal contract.

Banking

Ashland's industrial and commercial development revolved around its banks and savings institutions, all of which were located in the central business district on West Second Street. Ashland National, First National, The Northern National and Security Savings Banks were all open for business by 1890.

Banking ran its normal course in Ashland until the Great Depression. Slowdowns in the steel industry threw miners and sailors out of work. Large-scale lumbering was already over. A severe drought compounded the problems of hard-pressed farmers.

In January of 1933, depositors afraid of losing their savings forced the Northern National and Ashland National to close. Both banks were placed in receivership, but ended up paying a good percentage of money owed depositors. Ashland spent most of 1933 without a bank, with unemployment at a record high, and with the city paying its workers in scrip, because tax payments were in arrears. By the end of 1933, the Northern State and Union National Banks opened under the supervision of the state banking commission and with deposits guaranteed by the federal government.

The beginning of Ashland's centennial year finds the city growing. A Civic Center and a new Hotel Chequamegon opened in 1986. The old brownstone Soo Line Depot is destined for preservation and remodeling instead of the demolition suffered by many other Ashland landmarks.

The future looks bright. Ashland continues to be a retail center for most of northern Wisconsin. Hunt's grocery is building a large new store on the east side. Tourism continues to grow and bring new dollars to the area. A new marina just opening in the Centennial summer will bring more visitors to town.

In the past one hundred years Ashland has seen many changes. The boom years of the 1880s and 1890s were followed by the Depression of the 1920s and 1930s. Another fifty years have passed and signs seem to indicate a new period of prosperity is on Ashland's horizon.

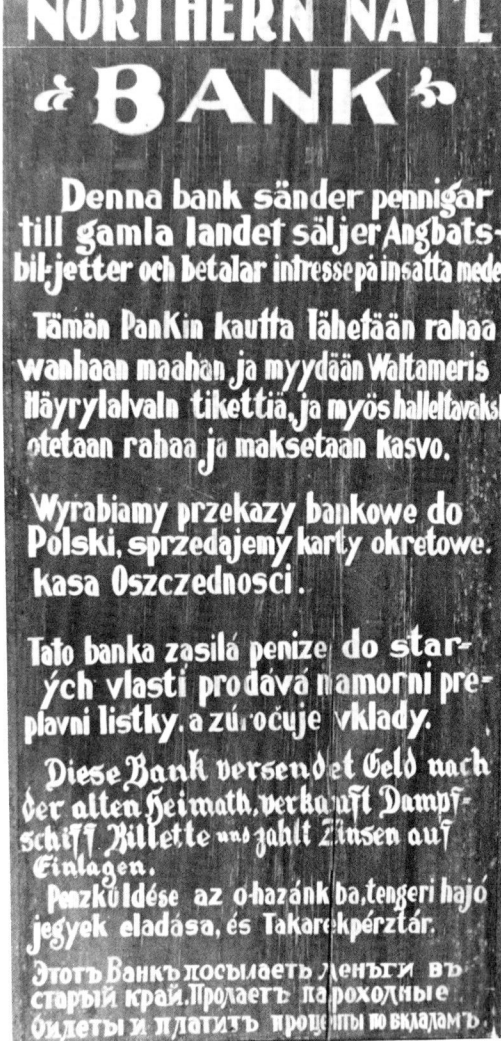

This sign hung outside the Northern National Bank in the 1800s. It says, "This bank sends money to the old country, sells steamship tickets and pays interest on deposits" in Swedish, Finnish, Polish, Czech, German, Hungarian, and Russian.

The Pulp Hoist

Large tug at right pulled log raft into position in front of pulp hoist pier. Small tug at left center is bringing log boon around raft to close opening to lake and roll logs into the pen.

Pulp hoist workers sorted logs and steered them with pikes towards the crane to be loaded in railcars for shipment. Logs were hauled across Lake Superior from Minnesota or Canada in huge tows that were a one-of-a-kind operation. Ashlander John Walter spent his working life with the pulp hoist and is the unofficial historian of the operation.

Communications

"What? A daily paper in this town? You've ruined me...you'll send me to the poorhouse."
Sam Fifield, as told by Joe M. Chapple

The Ashland *Press* had offices on the second floor of the Fifield Block at 115 Vaughn. The American Express Company occupied the first floor.

In the summer of 1872, a lumber scow carrying an unusual cargo appeared at the Ashland dock. Perched atop the stack of boards filling the scow were cases of lead type, bundles of paper, wooden forms, and a heavy iron flat-bed printing press. Sam and Hank Fifield were bringing the printing plant for Ashland's first newspaper from Bayfield. Since no road ran up the hill from the dock to the new building the Fifields had built for the paper, the two brothers recruited a team of volunteers to lug their gear up the bank. The press itself was too heavy to be so manhandled, so the Fifields and their new neighbors loaded it onto an ox-sled or "go-devil" and the patient beasts pulled it into town.

The first issue of the Ashland *Weekly Press* had been printed a week earlier in Asaph Whittlesey's barn near Bayfield, but the Fifields were in a hurry to get the Ashland newspaper plant where it belonged. Since the plaster on the walls of their new building hadn't quite dried, they set up the press and other equipment beneath a tall tree just outside. In short time, they had the type set, the cylinder inked, the paper in its bin. While the bright June sun shone in the leaves overhead, there appeared the first issue of the *Press* printed in Ashland.

Although not the only newspaper in Ashland's history, the *Press*, from its very first days, was the most successful and influential. In short time it became a leading voice calling for the development of Ashland and northern Wisconsin. It also became the vehicle whereby the members of a remarkable family placed their imprint on their place and times.

As John C. Chapple tells the story, his elder brother Joe Mitchell Chapple, "had blown into Ashland from a country printing office in Dakota" and gone to work for Sam Fifield. By 1888, Fifield's printing press was no longer in the yard, had, in fact, been replaced by a modern steam powered machine that was "a pretty nifty plant." Fifield

Sam S. Fifield, 1839-1915

Sam S. Fifield was born in Maine in 1839. By the time he was twenty-one, he was a printer's apprentice at the Taylor's Falls, Minnesota *Reporter*. In 1862, he moved across the St. Croix River and purchased the *Polk County Press*. Taken up with Republican fervor during the Civil War, Fifield turned the *Press* into the leading supporter of the Republican Party in northern Wisconsin. Seeing the opportunity offered by the Wisconsin Central's arrival at Chequamegon Bay in 1872, Fifield moved north. He and his brother Henry brought the name of the Polk County newspaper to Ashland when they founded the *Weekly Press*. Like many other pioneers, Fifield had his fingers in many pies. He managed the old Chequamegon Hotel and a resort on Sand Island. He also founded the Ashland National Bank and the city's first Masonic Lodge.

Fifield was also astute enough to hire Joe M. Chapple and not fire him after Chapple turned the *Weekly Press* into a daily while Fifield was out of town. Instead Fifield sold the paper to the first of the Chapple clan to make his mark in Ashland and turned to politics.

He served as chairman of the town board prior to city incorporation, state assemblyman, senator, and lieutenant governor of Wisconsin, ending his career as Ashland postmaster.

was losing interest in the paper and, shortly after it became a daily, he sold it to Joe, the first of many Chapples to edit and manage it.

Like other newspapers of its day, the *Press* was expected to promote Ashland to the rest of the world. In Joe Chapple's first years as editor, Ashland's boom was at full speed and his work was made easy. The *1893 Annual Edition*, the prime source for reporting the history of its times, was also a very impressive printing job. At a time when pictures appeared only rarely in newspapers, the *Press* had pictures of practically every business and professional man in town, of nearly every church, school, business and house, including many interiors. So impressive was this edition that 10,000 extra copies of it were shipped around the country by rail to promote the city.

Shortly after he produced the *1893 Annual*, Joe Chapple left Ashland for Boston where he published *The National Magazine* as part of the Chapple Publishing Co. Over the years many Ashland *Press* people moved to and from Boston to work for both Chapple firms. Joe passed management of the *Press* to his brother Bennett, who soon left to found a paper in Phoenix, Arizona. The Ashland operation was left in the hands of another brother, John C. Chapple, who remained at the paper until 1910. The Chapples then sold the paper to School Superintendent J.T. Hooper who in turn sold it to an ex-Milwaukeean named Greene.

John C. Chapple, 1875-1946

Born in LaPorte City, Iowa, Chapple came to Bayfield at the age of thirteen. The son of newspaperman William Chapple, young John had worked with his three brothers at their father's paper in LaPorte.

In 1890, Chapple went to work at the Ashland *Daily Press*, which his brother Joe had recently purchased from Sam Fifield. Except for one six-year period, Chapple would spend the next fifty-six years of his life in association with the *Press*. He held every position from "printer's devil" to editor-in-chief and gained renown as *The Squibber* who used only a few words to convey a large load of wisdom.

He also served as a member of the city council for four years and chairman of the county board for two years. Starting in 1909, he won five successive terms to the Wisconsin Assembly. Chapple was also Ashland postmaster for thirteen years and was famous for leading community singing sessions. He was a Northland College graduate, a Thirty-Second Degree Mason and a member of Rotary, Knights of Pythias, Odd Fellows, Elks and Eagles.

He is best remembered as north Wisconsin's Will Rogers—the Ashland *Squibber* whose philosophy was, "We do not know all the answers, but we can be kind."

In 1915, the unsung member of the Chapple clan, John C.'s wife Myrta, entered the picture. She too had worked on the *Daily Press* from the 1890s and, when Greene wanted to sell it, she bought it. Husband John C. returned and edited the paper until he died in 1946, and son John B. soon took up the reporter's post he has held to this day.

John C. was the famous and much-beloved "Squibber" whose motto for his paper said, "We don't know all the answers, but we can be kind." He shared editorial duties over the years with Guy Burnham, avid collector and compiler of Chequamegon lore.

Myrta Chapple took an active role in managing and editing the paper until the early 1950s. When she died in 1973 she completed one of the longest newspaper careers of any woman in the nation.

In 1956, the *Press* was sold to the Superior *Telegram* and has remained a part of that company ever since. The current general manager is Byron Johnson, and Virginia Burtness is the news editor.

The *Press* is not the only newspaper to appear in Ashland. The *News* was founded by John S. Knight and was the first daily newspaper in Ashland. Edited by Burt Williams, it survived in tough competition with the *Press* until 1915, when it was purchased by the Chapples. Williams also published a weekly society paper called *The Chequamegon*.

The Ashland *Chronicle* lived a short life in 1880 when Doctor W.M. Tompkins extended his practice into publishing. The *Times* of J.A. Monger also appeared briefly. The *Chequamegon Critic*, part newspaper and part magazine, was published by James Duket.

The *Frihet* and the *Posten* were Swedish language weeklies and the *Herald* a German paper that survived until their readership felt comfortable with English.

J.F. Miles published a labor paper called the *Appeal* and Roy Beebe put out the *Lake Superior Farmer* in the 1890s. Later papers were the *Call* and the *Journal*.

Radio

Word of Ashland first floated over the radio waves in January, 1925, when a radio station billing itself "The Voice of the Wilderness" put on an "Ashland Night." The Ashland Chamber of Commerce, Doctor Rowley, Professor Steinmetz and Postmaster Chapple and C.W. Pefferkorn were serenaded over the air. A handful of listeners in Ashland heard the serenade, and at least two hundred radio fans in other parts of the country wrote friends in town to say that they had heard the salute.

The next month, Chamber of Commerce President Fred Brown appointed a committee to decide if Ashland should have its own station. In March, Northland College installed a radio so its students could hear President Calvin Coolidge's inaugural address. The signal was clear until other Ashlanders turned on their sets and drowned Coolidge's words in static.

By the end of the month Ashland station WTNB, "Where the North Begins," was broadcasting from City Hall. Phone calls from listeners confirmed that the signal was reaching as far as Mellen, Bayfield, and Superior. A Saturday night musical program received nearly one hundred requests, and soon Ashland radio had is own theme song. Written and published by band director Theodore Stenimetz, the lyrics ran as follows:

> When you land in Ashland, the North begins;
> With smiles and the glad hand, you're
>   welcomed in;
> You'll find the people kind and free,
> They're always happy as can be;
> Boy, Ashland is the town for me,
>   where the North begins.

WTNB remained on the air through the Depression but was replaced as the Ashland station by WATW in 1940.

Another popular local radio station is WBWA which was founded on October 5, 1981, and is located in Washburn. Although its primary audience is Washburn, Ashland and Bayfield, it also serves Minnesota's and Wisconsin's northern shores on Lake Superior and western Upper Michigan.

Television

The first television sets appeared in Ashland in the late 1940s, and the new medium brought the same changes to the city as it did throughout the nation.

Ashland was too small to have its own television station but large enough to have its own cable-TV firm. The first co-axial cable franchise was granted to Bay Television, Inc. in July, 1965. They ran the first cables into Ashland homes in the 1960s. This franchise changed hands several times and was last sold to Marcus Communications in 1982. By 1987, 2,705 of Marcus's 132,000 subscribers in Wisconsin were in Ashland. Because of cable's public access channel, it can be said that the city has its own station.

John B. Chapple

"I don't know where else I'd want to go," John B. Chapple, 87, said of his full-time job as a reporter for the *Daily Press* in Ashland.

Chapple doesn't let his age stop him either—there's too much to do. "I love it," he said of his years as a reporter. "Everyday is a new day in the newspaper business." Does he get tired? "I haven't been mentally tired yet. When I get physically tired, I take a nap."

Chapple was born into the newspaper world on November 20, 1899, in Ashland, the son of John C. and Myrta Bowman Chapple, originally from LaPorte City, Iowa.

John B. Chapple attended school in Ashland and graduated from Ashland High School in 1917. He attended the University of Wisconsin-Madison for one year and joined the United States Army during World War I in 1918. In the army, he taught college students enrolled in the Reserve Officers Training Corps at the University of Kansas.

Following the war, Chapple worked at various journalism jobs, including stints with the Milwaukee *Sentinel* and Milwaukee *Journal*. In 1919, he went back to college, this time to Yale University and graduated in 1924 with a degree in philosophy. While a student, he met his future wife, Irene McDonnell. They celebrate their sixty-fifth wedding anniversary this year.

So, seeing the flaws in the American economy, he went to Soviet Moscow in 1927. His ten days in Moscow were eye-openers. He didn't find "heaven on earth," but found a system where the individual was sacrificed for the good of the "world revolution."

"I came back to my newspaper work in Ashland and kept my mouth shut," Chapple stated. Back home, he gradually developed his theme of the "American Way of Life." He became very involved in politics and defeated incumbent United States Senator John Blaine for the Republican Senate nomination in 1932. Only thirty-three years old, Chapple ran for the Senate as a conservative Republican in the year of a liberal Democratic landslide. Franklin D. Roosevelt's presidential coattails were long enough to carry Democrat F. Ryan Duffy to the Senate and defeat Chapple. He ran again in the Republican senatorial primary of 1936, but was defeated by Robert F. La Follette, Jr.

He returned to the *Daily Press*, remained there and has become the unofficial historian for Ashland. He is the city's booster and encyclopedia. If someone needs to know some fact—see Chapple.

The history of the Chapple family and John B. in particular is closely linked with the history of Ashland. As the people remember the city on its Centennial, John B. Chapple—poet, song-writer, historian, father, husband and reporter—will also be remembered.

John B. Chapple ready for work in 1987.

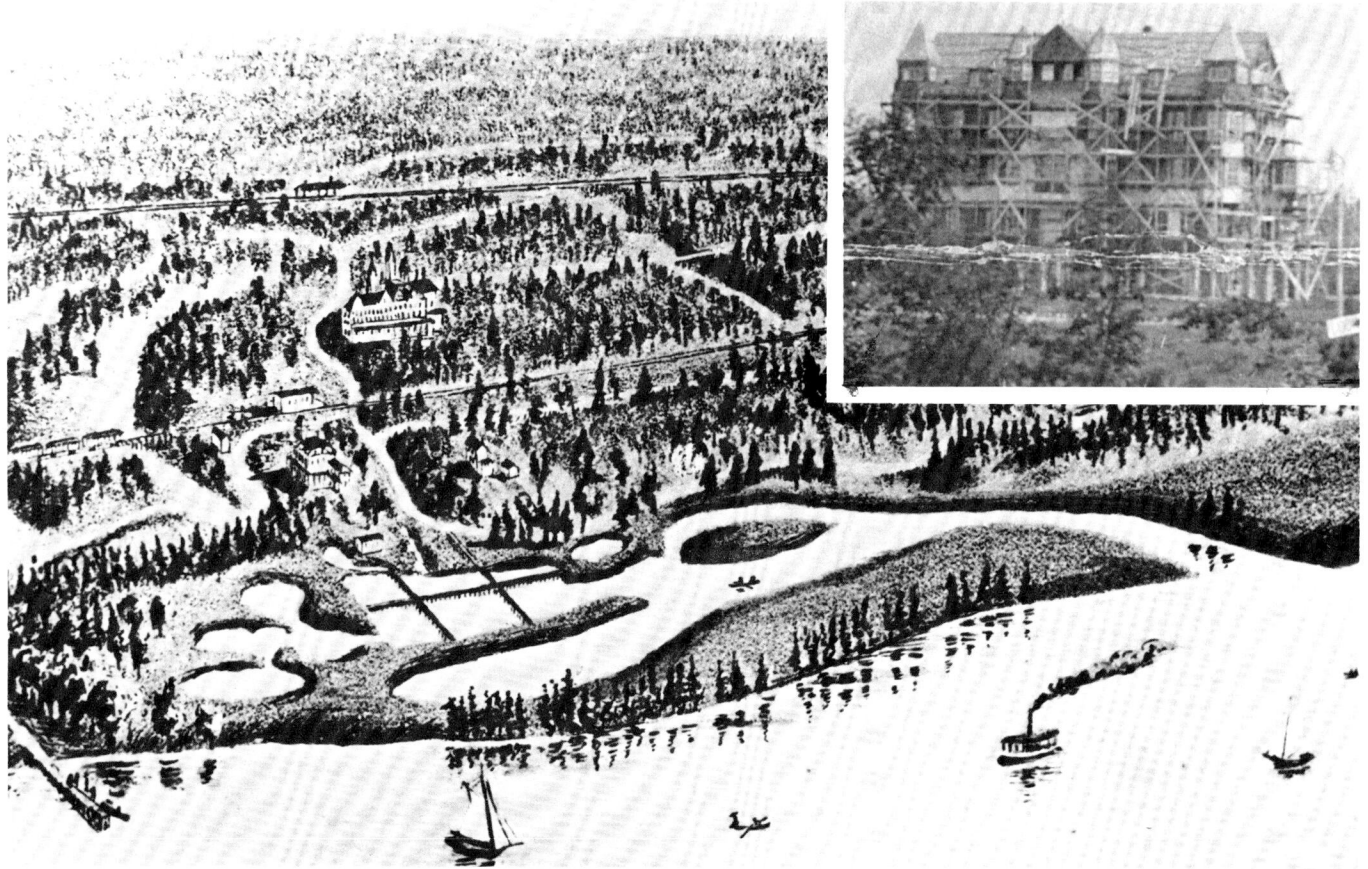

The Medical Center of the North

"Well, I had hay fever so bad living in the southern part of the state. Everybody said, 'Go north, go north', so we came north...Now I don't seem to have it anymore."
Ethel..., a Court Manor Nursing Home Resident in 1981

Prentice Park was once intended to be the grounds of a elaborate spa for patients seeking healthful northern water and fresh air. The centerpiece of the park was the Booth tubercular sanitarium. (Inset) No expense was spared for the proposed fifty patients, including a complete system of baths. The building burned down one month before opening in 1893.

Residents and visitors at Chequamegon Bay are fortunate to have the excellent medical facility located at 1615 Maple Lane. The 115-bed Memorial Medical Center, opened in 1972, is the culmination of a community effort to raise financial support and meet administrative, legal and governmental requirements. The 1968 meeting of representatives of Ashland's two existing hospitals, Trinity and Ashland Community, was attended by Reverend R. Dean Johnson, John Engholm, Don Smith, Clarence Van Remortel, Richard Wartman and William Schuler.

The present hospital boasts of one of the finest nursing and ancillary staffs and a thirty-seven member physician staff representing thirteen medical and surgical specialties. The hospital offers computerized axial tomography (CAT Scan) and other modern technology not usually found in a hospital of its size.

Memorial Medical Center provides care for patients from as far as one hundred miles east, seventy miles south and thirty miles west as well as offering additional care at six satellite clinics. As the largest employer in Ashland and three adjoining counties, and with a twelve million dollar budget, Memorial Medical Center has a powerful economic impact on all of northern Wisconsin.

The Memorial Medical Treatment Center, formerly Trinity Hospital, provides comprehensive treatment for individuals and families with chemical or alcohol dependency problems. The unit was established in 1974.

The first hospital administrator, Clarence Jouppi, was succeeded in 1974 by current administrator Lowell Miller. Current hospital board members are Steve Ave, Les Beecher, Yvonne Gilbert, Donald Johnson, Don Marcouiller, Lowell Miller, Robert Stanley, Robert Paulik, Robert Philby, John Reardon

(President), Howard Sandin, Donald Smith, Robert Stilin, Fred Tidstrom and Richard Wartman.

One must go back to Doctor Edwin Ellis to start tracing Ashland's medical history. When he arrived at the Bay with his family in 1856 surveyors were just laying out the village of Bay Port.

Four months later, Doctor Myron Tompkins arrived and built the fourth house in the settlement. Apparently, the cool northern climate brought him to Ashland, since in Illinois he had been plagued by "ague and rheumatism." The move must have suited him, for his ailments were relieved and he is thus credited with being the first to promote the area's healthful climate. In 1893, the *Daily Press* stated, "Ashland is a famous resort for hay fever sufferers and for those suffering from asthma and lung complaints." This announcement coincided with the opening of the elegant resort hotel, The Chequamegon.

The healthful qualities of cool northern air and fresh lake breezes were widely assumed in the 1900s. Industrialization had brought unprecedented progress, but not without a price. American cities were crowded, foul-smelling and smoke-filled. The atmosphere in summer was particularly unpleasant. Those who could afford to get away, did get away and the health care establishment in Ashland owes much of its beginning to the understandable desire of sick people to seek a healthy climate.

At the same time, Ashland itself was the hub of a developing industrial region. Logging, mining, foundry work, railroading and shipping were dangerous occupations and Ashland's growth as a medical center was tied to the growth of these industries and the toll they took on their workers.

In addition, Ashland grew very quickly. The arrival of ten thousand people to a raw settlement in only a few years placed great demands on both private and public health services. For example, typhoid fever broke out in 1893, first in the logging camps, then the city. Water lines contaminated with sewerage spread the disease and confronted Ashland with its first major public health problem. Construction of a modern water filtration plant—a service not many communities had—began. Lake Superior water was made safe, but not until many people suffered and died.

Doctor George W. Harrison opened his practice in Ashland in 1881. A political leader who served as Ashland's second mayor and a businessman who helped found the Ashland Lighting and Street Railway Company, Harrison was one of many Ashland medical men whose interests lay well beyond the bounds of their profession.

Doctor Edwin Ellis was both founding father and community builder. His legacy is acknowledged by a plaque on Ellis Avenue which proclaims him "The Father of Ashland." In a 1905 *Daily Press* article, Doctor John M. Dodd, another community-minded physician, remarked of Ellis, "Besides taking part in almost every enterprise having to do with the growth of the city, he found time to keep pace with the rapid strides of medicinal and

Dr. William Rinehart in surgery with his brother George anesthetizing a patient with an ether cone. George was on call from his job as an auto mechanic.

Nurses at Dodd's Hospital circa 1900. Trainees were to be at least twenty years old and "strong, and healthy, obedient, kind, cheerful and not given to gossip."

The original wooden St. Joseph's Hospital is to the right in this photo. The brick 1890s structure served patients until its demolition in 1974.

In 1917, Ashland General Hospital was established to provide the community with a non-sectarian facility. Doctor Dodd commented on the evolution of Ashland's hospitals in 1916 when he said, "From an institution conducted by religious orders, supported by voluntary contributions and devoted to the charitable relief of the sick it has grown in many communities, into a business enterprise, supported by its earnings and conducted on business principles."

Ashland General remained non-sectarian until 1946 when it became Trinity Lutheran. In 1972, Trinity closed and the old Wilmarth mansion that housed it became the site of the Memorial Medical Treatment Center.

St. Joseph's Hospital opened its nursing school in 1912 and graduated 449 nurses before closing in 1946. Ashland General opened with a school for nurses and it trained 111 women before closing in 1938.

Nursing was not considered an appropriate calling for women in the 1880s. Home was the proper place for health care and women who needed it or supplied it were restricted to their own houses. Men, like loggers, miners and railroaders who worked away from home, needed hospitals because they couldn't return home to be nursed by family. The first women who ventured into a hospital ward full of ailing lumberjacks weren't accepted as fully respectable by many. However, the quality of the care they supplied soon made women an indispensable part of the health care picture. In 1901, Doctor Rinehart started Ashland's first nursing school for women.

St. Joseph's was not Ashland's first hospital. The earliest health care facilities were converted boarding houses or the physician's own home. Patients often cared for each other or depended on the doctor's family.

Doctor William Rinehart started his Ashland Hospital and Doctor C.F. Merkle the Lake View Hospital to care for sick and injured lumberjacks. They sent salesmen to lumber camps to peddle tickets that varied in price from $3.50 to $10.00. Each ticket bought a logger a prescribed period of hospitalization. Most loggers, aware of the dangers of their occupation and the unwillingness of their employers to provide medical assistance, bought the tickets. Doctor Rinehart worked for the American Hospital Aid Association, which had established a chain of what were called "ticket" hospitals in the north woods. Rinehart found the system so profitable, that he kept it even after the Association dissolved.

Ashland had a number of basically one-

other sciences, and his name will always be associated with the great and good in Ashland's history."

Ellis donated many properties for community and business purposes. His sale of shoreline land to the Wisconsin Central for right-of-way spurred Ashland's great 1880s boom.

In the midst of that boom, in 1884, the Sisters of the Catholic Church, Poor Handmaids of Jesus Christ, came to Ashland to establish a hospital. They started in a small frame house across the street from the Catholic church and cared for seventy-six patients in their first year. Additions to the small building, called St. Joseph's Hospital, were made in 1885, 1888 and 1892. A new hospital was built in 1905 and enlarged to 120 beds in 1912.

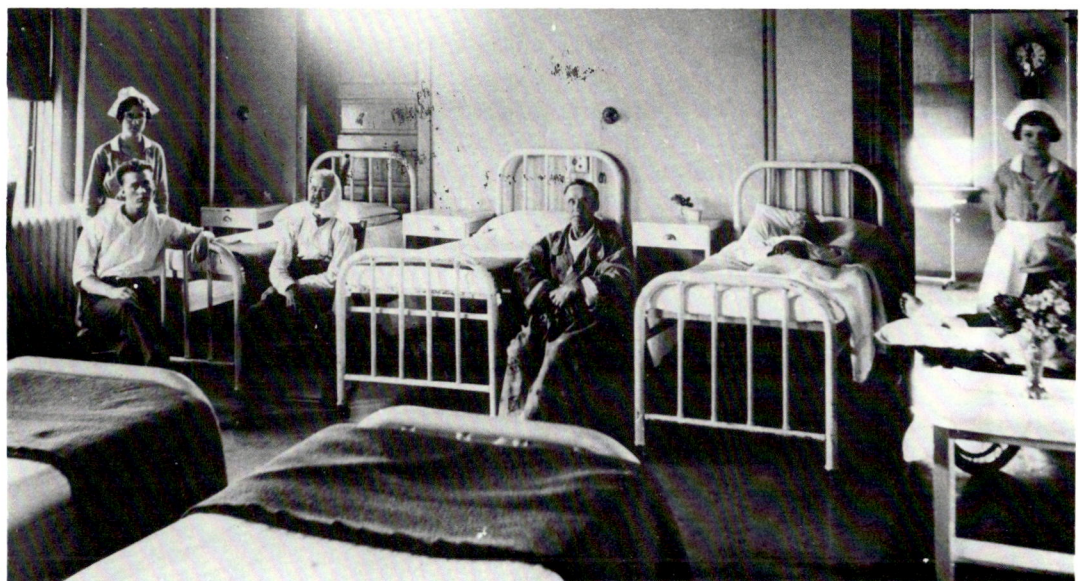

A ward at Ashland General Hospital. Opened in 1917 in the old Lewis Wilmarth mansion, the hospital remained in service until 1972.

doctor hospitals, including A.J. Hosmer's Michigan-Wisconsin Hospital and the Swedish-American Hospital next door. In time these small operations closed and St. Joseph's was Ashland's only hospital.

In 1912, St. Joseph's Hospital School of Nursing opened with seven students under the supervision of Sister M. Landelina. Classes were taught by hospital physicians, nurses and technicians. St. Joseph's Nursing School and, later, Ashland General's, offered career possibilities to young woman from the entire Ashland region.

St. Joseph's Nursing School remained open until 1946. For sixteen of its thirty-four years, it was under the direction of Sister Mary Victoria. 449 nurses graduated to careers that took them all over the country to serve the sick in the spirit of their *alma mater*.

Doctor Rinehart was a progressive-minded man. In 1887, shortly after the development of x-ray technology in Germany, he set up and used one of the first x-ray machines in Wisconsin. He and Doctor Fred Jenner Hodges published papers on their work in *The Western Clinical Recorder*, a journal that was one of Wisconsin's first professional medical publications.

For Ashland, Rinehart's most significant accomplishment was to bring Doctor John Dodd to the city in 1891. Rinehart and Dodd ran a 75-bed hospital for four years, until Dodd set up his own facility. This hospital became the scene of his daughter Edith's reminiscences which she published in her books *610 Ellis* and *The Hospital Children*. Dodd himself was a highly successful surgeon and civic leader. He served as president of the Northland College Board of Directors for many years and as mayor for four terms.

Dodd's hospital was famous for its nursing and emergency care, two vital services in a city where industrial accidents were everyday occurrences. But not all emergencies at Ashland's hospital were the result of workshop accidents. The first days after Buffalo Bill's Wild West Show came to town, many children hurt themselves trying to duplicate the show tricks, keeping doctors and nurses busy.

In the 1920s and 30s Dodd was the most prominent medical man in Ashland. He was chief surgeon at Ashland General. Doctor William Tucker became chief surgeon at St. Joseph's in 1920. He came to Ashland from the Mayo Clinic and immediately began a busy practice here.

Tucker operated Monday through Saturday, from early morning until afternoon, with major and minor cases of all types. General, orthopedic, urologic, obstetric and gynecological surgery were included on his list of specialties. He developed a widely-known reputation, and patients travelled up to 150 miles for his care. He worked in Ashland for over fifty years until his retirement in the mid-1970s.

Doctor Joseph Jauquet is a forty-year veteran of medical practice in Ashland who still serves on the staff at Memorial Medical Center. He came to Ashland upon the invitation of Doctor Tucker and maintained Ashland's tradition of excellent medical care.

When Jauquet arrived in 1947, most physicians had their offices on the second floor of the old Knight Hotel. It was the professional center for the city's doctors and

Previous Page

The 1946 graduating class of St. Joseph's Hospital School of Nursing. (bottom l to r) Frances Turner, Lorraine Gillen, Betty Sterk, Toni Mallach, Eileen Cronemiller, Marge Okonek. (2nd row) Sister M. Fabiola, Ruth Jolicouer, Marie Katherine, Helen Nigard, Marlys Cudmore. (3rd) Alice Berg, Jeanette Pimple, Blanche Brandt. (top) Phillis Lewandowski, Liesse Garvin, Irma Amelung.

John M. Dodd, 1866-1950

John M. Dodd came to Ashland in 1889 following his graduation from Starling Medical College in Ohio. An orphan who lost his parents when he was two years old, Dodd worked his way through college as a carpenter. Upon receiving his medical degree he went to work for the American Hospital Association, a chain of medical facilities offering a sort of health insurance plan to loggers in Wisconsin. As Dodd described the system, "Tickets were sold to the men in camps, for from five to ten dollars a year, which entitled them to medical and surgical service and care in a hospital." Dodd started a so-called "ticket" hospital in Rhinelander, then moved to Ashland to work with Doctor William Rinehart, who ran his own ticket facility here.

In 1894, he opened Dodd's Hospital where he specialized in surgery and nurses' training. In 1904, he became chief surgeon at St. Joseph's Hospital and remained there until he helped found Ashland General in 1916.

Dodd was of the second generation of Ashland leaders, younger than the pioneers who founded the place. He was nevertheless cut of the same cloth as the older men. A civic leader, he served as mayor in 1910-11 and opposed the adoption of the commission form of government. During World I he led a victorious campaign to persuade Ashlanders to ban the sale of alcoholic beverages six months prior to the advent of national Prohibition. He served as mayor again from 1933 to 1939.

Dodd was president of the Northland College Board of Trustees from it inception until 1944. He also led the Ashland Advancement Association, a group committed to bringing new industry to the city and the Outdoor Art League, which planted shade trees, shrubs and flowers in the denuded pioneer town.

Dodd summed his life of community service with words that could apply to other distinguished Ashlanders as well. He said, "One who settles in a growing frontier community and becomes part of it cannot help being drawn into its activities. The medical man comes into close contact with individual and community problems ... and in every community the doctor will be found to have had an active part in the upbuilding of village, town, city and surrounding country ..."

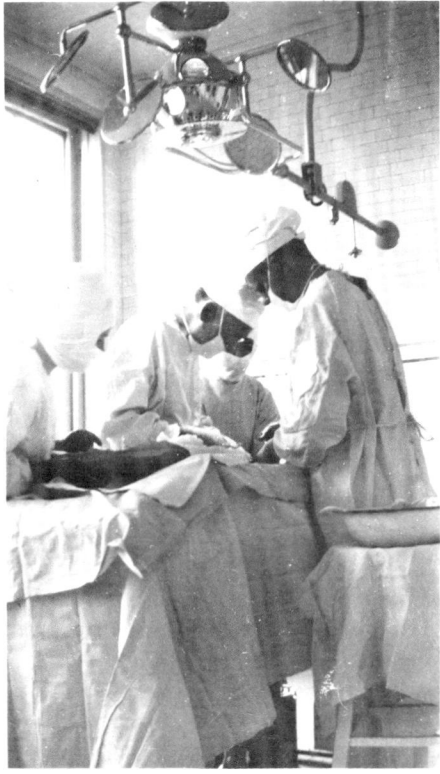

Nurse M. Cudmore, Dr. William Tucker, nurse E. Amelung and Dr. A. Lamal performing a vein ligation.

dentists. In 1987, Ashland's thirty-seven doctors keep office space in the Medical Center adjacent to the hospital and in the Chequamegon and Ashland Clinics downtown.

Medical practice in Ashland has come a long way since Edwin Ellis snowshoed across the Bay in 1855, but one fact hasn't changed since those pioneering days. Ashland has been the medical center of northern Wisconsin for all of its history. While other industries have boomed and burst, medicine has made steady progress. That progress helps explain how the city survived its first century. In many ways, the most successful patient of Ashland's health care profession is Ashland itself.

Dentistry

A century ago a typical northwoods dentist traveled from lumber camp to mining town pulling teeth and peddling dentures. Ashland's dentists—Doctors Lee, Forester, Borecky, Ellison and Penn—had offices in the Knight Hotel and later moved to Doctor Dodd's Medical Service building when he tried to organize a group practice.

Local dentists made one of their greatest contributions to dental health when Doctors Martin Thorsen and A.G. Sell succeeded in persuading the city council to fluoridate the water supply. Along with Milwaukee, Ashland was the first city to so treat its water.

Ashland dentists have always been leaders in the profession and community. Doctor Carl Hambach, Sr., served the profession as trustee and president of the State Dental Association. Doctor Fred Tidstrom was recognized as citizen of the year for his service to the Boy Scouts, school board and Memorial Medical Center. Doctor John Reardon is current president of the hospital board. Doctor A.G. Sell was trustee and, with the state aeronautics board, was instrumental in construction of the Ashland-Bayfield county airport.

Dentists practicing in Ashland in 1987 are H.O. Branzell, Glen Grage, Carl Hambach, Jr., L.K. Patterson, Edwin Ellison, A.G. Sell, John Penn, Martin Thorsen, Eugene Newhouse, Doug Larson, William Leakey, John Reardon and Fred Tidstrom.

Doctor Jim Pletz was the first orthodontic specialist at Memorial Medical Center. He was followed by Doctors Frank Worms and Tom Lovlien. Doctor Kyle Tidstrom is currently training to be an oral and maxillo-facial surgeon at Mayo Clinic.

Modern hospital dentistry has become an elective treatment modality at Memorial Medical Center and the dental staff meets monthly for continuing education and quality assurance review.

Memorial Medical Center opened its doors on October 9, 1972, following the merger of Ashland Community Hospital and Trinity Lutheran Hospital. There are 105 medical-surgical beds, 10 in mental health and 36 at Memorial Medical Treatment Center. MMC offers may hospital services and educational programs to residents of Ashland and neighboring communities.

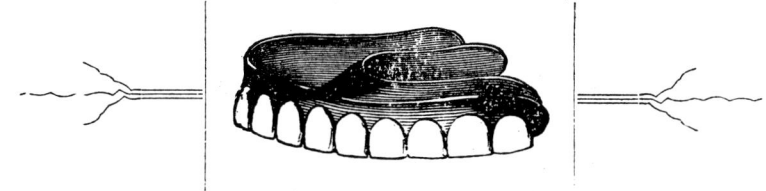

DR. N. BOOTH,
DENTIST,

Painless, Safe and Harmless Method for the Extracting of the Teeth.

LARGEST AND BEST DENTAL OFFICE IN THE STATE.

ROOM 4 VAUGHN LIBRARY BUILDING,

Ashland,   -   -   Wisconsin.

A Center of Learning

"Ashland takes special pride in its schools, public and private. Its public school system is second to no other city in the state."
Ashland Daily Press, 1893

The first class to graduate from the new Ellis Avenue High School in February 1905. Pictured here are Flossy Bradley, Clara Sinrud, F. Kepler, Winnie Garnich, Anna Holston, Blanch Seek, Faye Lamoreux, K. Kelly, Alma Angvick.

The history of education in Ashland is one of diversity. Public, private and church schools have served the educational needs of children longer than the city has been in existence. Over the years, preschool, elementary, secondary, vocational and college-level educational institutions have helped prepare both children and adults for life.

Ashland county levied its first school tax in 1860. Local population was so small that the $3.97 collected was deemed large enough. In 1872, the Town Board organized School District #1 and appropriated $3,000 to build a school in both Ashland and the neighboring village of Bay City. The Bay City school was later used as the County Teacher's College and the Ashland facility became known as the Ninth Avenue School. A Mrs. Kittredge was the teacher at Ninth Avenue, and Thomas Bardon instructed students at Bay City. After he went on to become President of Ashland's National Bank, Bardon kept a picture of his first students called "The Boys of '72" on the wall of his office.

Growth in the Ashland district was steady throughout the 1870s and early 1880s. It exploded after 1887. Superintendent J.M Turner saw school enrollments rise from 1,189 in 1887 to 1,864 in 1889 to 2,805 in 1891. Any school system at any time would be severely strained by such growth and Ashland hustled to keep up. By 1893, the district had completed and staffed a high school, two grammar schools, eleven intermediate and primary schools, plus a night school. Thirty teachers, roughly one for every ninety-five students, worked in eight different buildings. School enrollments had increased so fast that, even in a city crowded with lumber, sawmills and carpenters, there were fifty more pupils than desks.

In addition to the public schools, St. Agnes Catholic had 140 pupils enrolled when it opened and the German Lutheran and Saron Lutheran churches also operated schools. Two German immigrant women named Schultz opened a private kindergarten that survived for about a year, and a Professor Parsons conducted free night classes in business arithmetic, bookkeeping and writing that were "an excellent opportunity for clerks and others . . . unable to attend day sessions." As if all this activity wasn't enough, Ashland subscribed $30,000 to a fund organized by Doctor Edwin Ellis, outbid other cities, and saw the new North Wisconsin Academy rise on the southern outskirts of town.

Ashland's commitment to education was serious. Superintendent Junius T. Hooper, who managed the system from 1899 to 1905, was one of the most talented administrators of his day. In order to encourage reluctant parents to send their youngsters to Ashland's first public kindergarten in 1902, he brought three faculty members from the University of Chicago to speak at a public meeting at the Presbyterian Church. Hooper believed in what would now be considered a rigorous classical regimen for students and he made Ashland the first school system in Wisconsin to teach algebra and Latin to eighth-graders. He also began the first classes for handicapped children in the state. A builder as well as an educator, he won over reluctant taxpayers and built a new, ornately-designed high school in 1904. Enrollment that year was 2,859 but Hooper had succeeded in increasing the faculty to seventy-one teachers working at ten schools. He had established such a glowing reputation that when he left Ashland he was named Director of the Wisconsin School for the Blind in Janesville.

Hooper and other early superintendents were fortunate to receive strong backing from Ashland's civic leaders. Thomas Bardon, Edwin Ellis, Lewis Wilmarth, Emeline Vaughn, Christopher Bretting, George Merrill and other prominent people took the lead in publicly supporting the schools. Wilmarth was so flattered a school was named after him that, "It was his yearly custom during apple blossom time to carry huge bundles of apple blossoms to the faculty of the school and when the teacher would open the door of his

Beaser School students at a 1908 picnic. Teachers were Daisy McLaughlin and Alma Angvick. In the class were... Christopherson, Jennie Anderson Papadakis, Ester Anderson Feldt, Alma Seestrom, Mary Pernier, Mildred Fineauer, Elvera Halvorson, Hjalmer Sandstrom, Clarence Newman, Clarence Talaska, ...Ronning, Hugo Ledin, Harold Thines.

Lewis C. Wilmarth, 1833-1907

As a young man Lewis Wilmarth was a firebrand Abolitionist who rode with John Brown in the Kansas anti-slavery battle. Just before Brown's fateful raid on Lawrence, Kansas, Wilmarth left the band and turned his energies to the real estate business. He bought and sold 160 acres in downtown Topeka, Kansas, then moved to Ashland where he became a leading banker and realtor.

He was the designer, builder and owner of five of the largest business blocks in Ashland and owner of extensive acreage outside the city. A Rhode Island native who had attended the finest schools in the eastern United States, Wilmarth had the largest collection of books in Ashland. He was a generous supporter of education, and one city school is justifiably named after him.

Confident of the quality of the buildings he designed and built, Wilmarth refused to insure them for fire. He never lost a dime on fire damage. He was also interested in politics, serving as mayor, councilman and county supervisor.

Flora Jane McDonald taught at Ashland High for many years. Her 1940 Social Problems class wrote a history of the Ashland school system.

or her room he would be greeted by the fragrant sight of apple blossoms."

In the 1890s, the Board of Education sponsored an ambitious building program that funded the Wilmarth, Beaser and Ellis Schools. Built of imposing brick and stone, nearly a century old, these three structures have been remodeled only once and are still in use. They are a brick-and-mortar legacy of a generation willing and able to lay permanent foundations for a sound educational system.

All of Ashland's schools were neighborhood centers, the location of sports events, plays, and pageants. They remain so to this day. Most former students remember the curriculum as hard and discipline strict. "I went to the Ninth Avenue School," Florence Brenseke recalls, "We had some excellent teachers who were very, very strict . . . Miss McKevitt and Delia Childs. My fourth grade teacher once said on a Friday, 'Don't come to school on Monday unless you know all the tables to twelve.' I almost had a nervous breakdown, but I learned them, and I've never forgotten them."

Ashland's population and its school enrollments peaked just prior to World War I. No new buildings were necessary until the early 1930s. The Dodd gym was constructed in 1936, and named by vote of the citizens after the mayor who was also a medical doctor and popular civic leader. The gym became the site of the triumphs and tragedies of Ashland athletic teams, a hall for dances and plays, and a concert house where local and visiting musicians played.

If there is one field of study Ashland schools have consistently excelled in, it is music. Music was part of the daily curriculum for all grades and Ashland's bands gained regional and national renown. Music played a large role in the curriculum at Northland College and the influence of teachers and students there spread through the city.

In 1924, the City Council appropriated $3,000 and hired Director Theodore Steinmetz to organize a city band. This group soon acquired 263 members and became the first of Ashland's World's Biggest Boys' Bands. In the 1930s, Ted Mesang was director and the high school band regularly performed in regional and national music festivals. The lives of the students themselves and of all Ashlanders were enriched by the city and the school system's dedication to musical education.

In 1950, the Wisconsin Department of Public Instruction ordered small rural districts to consolidate into larger districts with a high

The sixth grade class at the Middle School circa 1980. Mary Anne Paitl is the teacher.

school and kindergarten. Soon after, the Towns of La Pointe, Gingles, White River and Marengo joined the Ashland City School District. They were later joined by parts of the Towns of Eileen and Kelly in Bayfield County. By the end of the decade the Town of Sanborn and Odanah were also part of the district.

The Ashland District is unique in that it is the only district in Wisconsin divided by twenty miles of Lake Superior water. Because the distance they must travel is so great high school students from La Pointe once boarded in Ashland but now attend Bayfield High School.

In 1967, De Padua High School closed and its students transferred to Ashland High. The transition was made easier by the District's hiring of two of the Catholic sisters to teach in the public schools, another Ashland and Wisconsin first.

In that same year, the Joint City School District was dissolved and the Unified School District created. This removed the schools from the budgetary control of the City Council and set up an independent school board with its own power to levy taxes, set policy and supervise administration.

Just as it had forced the system to enlarge its grade schools in the 1950s, the post-World War II baby boom generation pushed Ashland to build a new high school in 1973. The building is modern and flexible and can house up to 2,000 students. By 1983, a new middle school was built and junior high students moved out of the old high school building.

Education has always been of vital concern to the citizens of Ashland and they have continue to support a fine educational system for more than one hundred years.

Wisconsin Indianhead Technical Institute

Vocational service for the city of Ashland began about 1920, as a result of earlier state legislation and in answer to the needs of the citizens. Classes were held in the main building of the high school and on only two evenings a week. The curriculum included shop, mathematics, drawing, typing, stenography, sewing, English, reading and citizenship. H.O. Eiken was part-time director and the enrollment numbered eighty-four.

By 1940, classes in painting and decorating and barbering were added to the curriculum and enrollment expanded to six day students in apprentice programs and 188 evening

Vocational education in Ashland has existed for more than sixty years. The present Beaser Avenue location of the Wisconsin Indianhead Technical Institute was dedicated in 1970 and has expanded twice.

students. Rinaldo Bonacci was director and he worked long and hard to improve and expand vocational education. The old Post Office building (1987's City Hall) was turned over to the Vocational School board for establishment of the school. Two years later the Defense Training Program dominated the curriculum just as World War II dominated the entire city.

Citizens voted in favor of a post-war referendum to build a new vocational school but Mayor Harry Van Guilder refused to authorize a bond issue and no further action was taken.

The vocational school always cooperated with local industries to help train manual workers and by 1966, thirty-five students were involved in on-the-job training in addition to class work. A total of two hundred students were enrolled then.

All programs at WITI are certified by the state and receive full accreditation from the North Central Association of Colleges and Secondary Schools.

In addition to on-campus programs, the Field Service provides classes in all communities in the District. Thousands of adults are served in afternoon or evening classes from the Ashland Campus.

Wisconsin has a proud heritage in the area of Vocational, Technical and Adult Education. The WITI-Ashland Campus is an integral part of this heritage in northern Wisconsin. Education Districts as they now operate were organized in 1970. In that year Ashland WITI left the City Hall Building that had housed it for fifty years and moved to its new facility on Beaser Avenue.

Enrollment and programs expanded in the 1970s, requiring two additions to the building, including a Tourism Facility completed in 1980.

Ashland Teachers College

The Ashland County Training School was established in 1914. It was part of a state system inaugurated to quickly train teachers to staff schools in remote northern communities. Originally in Mellen and later Butternut, the school moved permanently to Ashland in 1920. Located in the old city hall, the school was re-named Ashland County Normal. J.M. Lorscheter was the first principal in Ashland. He was succeeded by A.J. McDermott, who presided until the school closed.

The Normal School awarded graduates a two-year license permitting them to teach in elementary schools with the provision that they complete further educational requirements for their bachelor degree within a six-year period. It launched many deserving young people into teaching careers they might not otherwise have had and was a leading educational force in northern Wisconsin. The messages of learning, culture and knowledge of the wider world that Normal School graduates brought to isolated northern communities were invaluable.

In 1953, the Normal School became known as the Ashland County Teachers College, but was still housed in the city hall building. As time passed, the need for teachers in rural areas grew less urgent and regular four-year colleges and universities were able to meet it. In 1971, Ashland County Teachers College graduated its final forty-two students. In its fifty-six years of life the School sent out a total of 1,439 teachers.

Northland College

As Ashland celebrates its centennial in 1987, Northland College begins to prepare for its own centennial now just five years away. Founded first as the North Wisconsin Academy, the College has been a central educational and cultural institution here in northern Wisconsin. Since that organizing meeting on August 6, 1892, when the founders stated that "the institution should be open to all students of both sexes and all races," Northland has been a major force in educating the young of this area, in enriching regional cultural life, in enhancing environmental decisions, and adding to the quality of life.

The first students entered the North Wisconsin Academy in the fall of 1892. The Reverend Edward Payson Wheeler became the first president of the institution. Wheeler Hall, named for him, is a replica of an historic building on the Beloit College campus.

The original aim of the Academy was to offer secondary education to students of the region for whom no high schools were available. High schools then operated in Ashland and Superior, but youngsters in Prentice, Park Falls, Mellen, Hayward and other communities had no place to continue their education beyond primary level.

With the expansion of high school throughout the north, the trustees determined in 1906 that post-secondary education should become the major theme of the institution.

Accordingly, North Wisconsin Academy was renamed Northland College in 1906. Secondary instruction continued under the title of the Northland Academy.

From its inception, clergy and lay people of the Congregational Church played a central role, along with Ashland civic leaders, in founding and nurturing the new institution. Believing that true religion was bolstered, not threatened, by the pursuit of truth and vigorous educational bodies, the Congregational Church sought everywhere to praise God by opening schools. Northland remains in that broad tradition that affirms the Judaeo-Christian heritage which called forth this seat of learning and teaching.

So the small school, hugging the northern rim of Wisconsin, started its post-secondary life as a liberal arts college and a teacher training institution with special emphasis in music education. Later milestones along the way included the long presidency of Dan Brownell (1913-1942), the struggle for survival during the Depression and World War II, accreditation by the North Central Association in 1957, and the more recent introduction of the distinctive liberal arts environmental curriculum.

Now in this transition year when Northland is seeking a new president, it is serving more than six hundred students. It has achieved a national reputation in environmental education. It has pioneered in the development of its Native American studies

Rev. Melmon J. Fenenga was principal of North Wisconsin Academy and first president of Northland College.

Malcolm McLean has served as president of Northland College with dedication and effectiveness since 1971. He has firmed and deepened the roots of this institution which he has referred to as "the gnarled tree above the timberline."

Sigurd Olson, 1899-1982

Sigurd Olson was born in Chicago, but his life and heart belonged to the northern wilderness. He graduated from Ashland High School in 1916 and made his first major canoe expedition to the Quetico-Superior wilderness in 1922.

He was the bard of the *voyageurs* and an unrivaled teacher of environmental ethics who helped found the modern conservation movement. In his books he bespoke his love for the wild streams, shaded forests and crystal lakes of the unspoiled country where he felt truly at home.

He was honored with many degrees, citations and awards from around the world. He spoke a language of nurture and caring for the land and waters that was universally understood. He lived right and was fortunate to die as he had lived. At the age of eighty-three he set off into the woods on snowshoes and never returned alive. Before he left his cabin near Ely, Minnesota, he typed his own epitaph. "A new adventure is coming up," he wrote, "and I know it will be a good one."

---

program. Creation of the Sigurd Olson Environmental Institute in 1972 pushed Northland forward in regional service.

The budget for all this amounts to $6,312,325 this year, of which salaries and fringe benefits add up to about $2,500,000. The College occupies approximately seventy acres of land in the southern portion of Ashland and operates out of thirteen major buildings.

Northland particularly seeks to serve the areas for which it is named through education, of course, but in many other ways—through seminars and workshops, through counseling of college-bound students, through scholarships for north Wisconsin students, through a full arts and lecture series, through the Sigurd Olson Institute's Island School program, through community use of athletic facilities, through involvement of its faculty and staff in the life of Ashland.

Being a good neighbor is a major goal of Northland College which, just slightly younger than the city in which it is located, salutes Ashland on its centennial and promises another one hundred years of cooperation.

The Vaughn Library building. Rent from stores, apartments and professional offices supported the operation of the library, an unusual but successful relationship that lasted until the Great Depression.

The Vaughn Library

Libraries have always played an integral part in Ashland's history. The first Library Association was formed in 1872. The preamble to its constitution states its objective as, "mutual intercourse and improvement through the collection of a library, the establishing of a reading room, or by any other means that may be found advantageous." For three years the Association held weekly meetings with varied programs that included debates, music, essays, and lectures.

The Association hoped to serve more people by allocating one hundred dollars to purchase books that were kept in the town clerk's office. The collection grew thanks to the generous donations of Association members. In 1876, encouraged by the response of citizens to the library in the clerk's office, the town started its own library in the same premises. It remained in operation until the Vaughn Library opened in 1888. The town library was now "completely overshadowed by the superior advantage of the new library." It soon closed and gave its collection to the high school.

The 1893 Annual Edition of the *Daily Press*, remarked that "in the twilight of the Nineteenth Century nothing is more prized and more highly indicative of a progressive and aggressive city than a free public library." Samuel Stewart Vaughn certainly agreed. He had spent extensive time and energy planning such an institution. Vaughn himself was not from a wealthy background and envisioned a free library where citizens from all economic levels would have ample opportunity to educate themselves in comfortable and hospitable surroundings. He died before he could see his dream materialize. It was his wife Emeline who competently and energetically carried out the project.

The crucial date in Ashland's library history is November 16, 1888—dedication day for the Vaughn Library. Emeline Vaughn built a three story building on Vaughn and Second Street to house the library. Rental income from the F.J. Pool Company on the first floor and offices on the third supported the library located on the second. In this respect Ashland's mercantile library differed from nearly all other independent libraries being built around the country at the time.

At the dedication Vaughn spoke with pride of her husband and his dreams for the Ashland library. "I have faithfully tried to carry out my husband's plans and place before the public a library which should be of a high moral standard and of permanent benefit to the city." She explained her concern for moral standards in her restrictions for the library. "No infidel or atheistic works are allowed here, or can ever be placed on these shelves." In regard to fiction Vaughn spoke of the growing number of novels that did not meet her standards of morality. She said she "will not assume the responsibility of placing before the young people of this city books that drain away all practical sympathy and leave no force of love and helpfulness for actual life." Despite these restrictions, Vaughn's contributions to the book and periodical collections were most generous.

She concluded her dedication speech by saying, "It is in every sense a free library, non-sectarian and with only those restrictions necessary for the comfort of patrons and safety of books. It comes to you free of debt, as a gift from Samuel Stewart Vaughn.

The Vaughn Library was impressive—well-lighted and homey. The collection included five thousand volumes and one hundred periodicals " . . . leading dailies, standard monthlies, religious, German-American, Scandinavian-American papers . . . the leading scientific and mechanical journals. The Bible in different languages is also found on the tables, which gives the room a high moral tone."

In addition to the periodicals, reference works, children's literature and fiction, there were impressive collections in the sciences, history and public documents. The *Daily Press*

George Rinehart, Thomas Bardon, M. Hunt and Dr. J.A. Marchessault in the well-lit and stocked reading room of the Vaughn Library circa 1900.

assured its readers that, "Every book is carefully examined before being entered ...No one need have any fear ...they will get anything trashy, for the books are the very cream of literature, long experience having taught the ones selecting which to choose."

The library has continued to flourish through the years, its collection growing from the original five thousand to the present thirty-four thousand volumes.

In 1937, the library moved to the ground floor of the building in order to make room for the Works Progress Administration offices the city was forced to supply. With its rental income lost, the Vaughn nearly closed. However, the city government was persuaded to appropriate $6,620 and the library remained open.

The city appropriation stayed the same for eighteen years. It wasn't until 1955 that Ashland could supply $14,145 to hire a full-time librarian. In 1982, the library underwent major renovation and restoration that preserved historical significance yet maintained modern practicality.

In addition to the Vaughn, other libraries played an important role in Ashland. The YMCA contained a library of five hundred volumes in the late nineteenth century.

The public school system maintained a library ever since the town library turned over its collection of five hundred books in the late 1880s. Today Ashland has libraries at the high, middle and elementary schools containing forty-three thousand volumes.

Another important library is the Dexter Library of Northland College. It has functioned ever since the college began in 1892. It moved to its present location in December 1970 and has holdings in excess of eighty thousand volumes.

Ashland is also home of the Northern Waters Library Service. Originating in 1959, the NWLS originally served four counties, but since 1972 its range has extended to the eight counties in the northwestern part of the state. This library's collection numbers about thirty-four thousand volumes and its outreach programs serve individuals in rural areas.

Emeline Patrick Vaughn, 1841-1901

Emeline Vaughn married her husband Sam in 1864 and came with him to Ashland a few years later. She assumed a role of leadership in social and church affairs. After her husband's death in 1886, she built the Vaughn Library in his memory.

In her dedication address she said, "When failing strength compelled him to give work to others to complete, he folded his hands and went to his rest with the assurance that it should go on ...I have faithfully tried to carry out my husband's plans and place before the public a library ...It comes to you free from debt, as a gift from Samuel Stuart Vaughn ..."

Vaughn was astute enough to provide for the library with rental money from a store and offices in the building. Thanks to this arrangement Ashland's library paid for itself until the Depression of the 1930s.

She was also a three-time president of the Monday Club, president of the Vaughn Choral Club and an active supporter of the Presbyterian Church as well as taking part in the Vaughn Literary Society and the State Federation of Women's Clubs.

Samuel Stuart Vaughn, 1830-1886

Sam Vaughn was one of the first Yankees to settle at Lake Superior. He was nineteen when he left Ohio for Eagle River, Michigan, and twenty-two when he first came to La Pointe in 1852. In 1856, he pre-empted a claim to 160 acres in Ashland and also opened the first store in Bayfield. While there he also built the first stone building and sawmill as well as running his general store.

Vaughn was convinced that northern Wisconsin needed a railroad and worked to bring one to the region. In 1871, he laid out Vaughn's Subdivision of Ashland just in time to profit handsomely from the city's first boom. He moved to Ashland, opened a store and sold supplies to the railroad as it built its way south to Mellen. When he died in 1886, Vaughn left an estate valued at $300,000-$500,000.

The Ashland Chronicle

1659 — Radisson and Groseilliers arrive at Chequamegon Bay.

1665 — Claude Allouez builds mission of Saint Esprit.

1854 — Chippewas cede land in Wisconsin to United States.
— Asaph Whittlesey and George Kilborn start first settlement at Ashland.

1855 — First mail addressed to Whittlesey arrives.

1856 — First plat of "Ashland" registered.

1860 — County Population: 450.
— U.S. Post Office recognizes "Ashland" as the official name of the Bay settlement.
— Ashland County formed.
— Ashland County collects $3.97 school tax.

1863 — Ashland deserted by all but the Roehm family.

1869 — Settlers return.

1870 — County Population: 211.
— First Ashland brownstone quarried and shipped.

1871 — Ashland County issues $200,000 in bonds for aid to the Wisconsin Central.
— Colby House Hotel opens.

1872 — W.R. Sutherland builds Ashland's first sawmill.
— Sam and Hank Fifield print first issue of Ashland *Weekly Press*.
— Town board organizes School District #1 and appropriates $3,000 for schools at Ashland and Bay City.

1873 — First telegram sent from Ashland.
— Wisconsin Central builds 1,500-foot Commercial Dock.

1874 — Hudson Bay Company closes its post.

1875 — Central School built on Second Street.

1877 — Wisconsin Central completes rail connection of Ashland to Chicago.
— Chequamegon Hotel opens.

1878 — Ashlanders visit Bayfield by boat on January 1.

1880 — Town of Ashland Population: 951.

1881 — St. Agnes School opens.
— Wisconsin Central starts to use refrigerator cars from Ashland to Milwaukee.

1883 — St. Paul, Minneapolis and Omaha Railroad arrives.
— City threatened by huge forest fire.

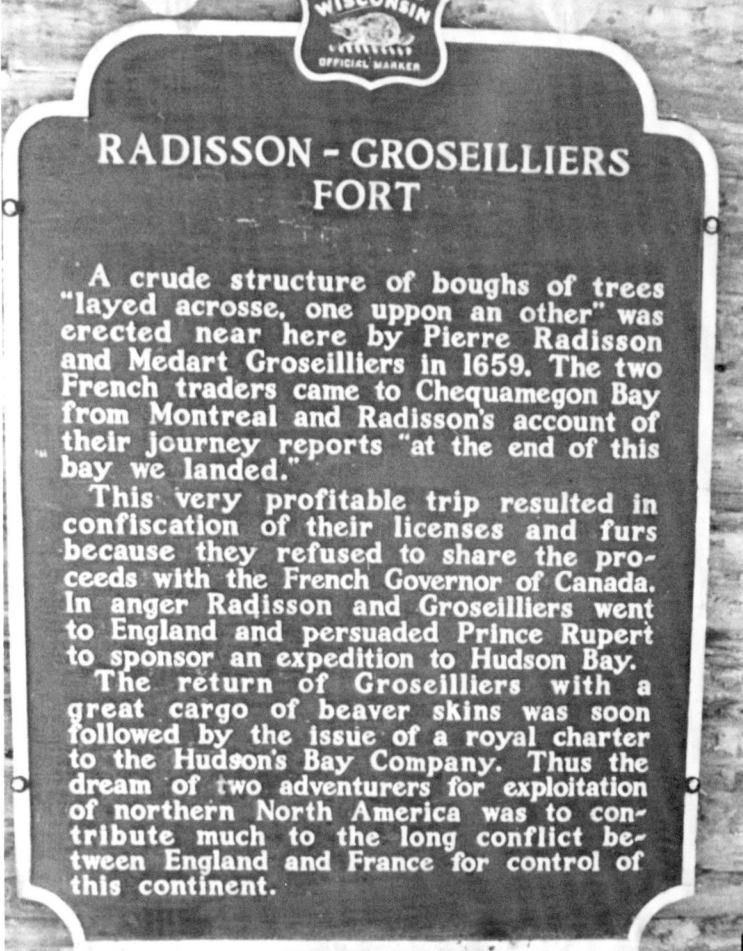

1884 — Thomas Bardon incorporates The Ashland National Bank.
— St. Joseph's Hospital opens.
— Railroad tracks extend along the Bay front.
— Northern Pacific Railroad arrives.

1885 — First fire hydrants installed.
— Nat Moore finds hematite beneath fallen tree. Iron boom begins.
— Milwaukee, Lake Shore & Western arrives from Hurley.

1886 — Sam Fifield starts First National Bank.
— Ashland schools graded and six teachers employed.

1887 — State legislature incorporates City of Ashland.
— 1,189 students in public schools; 140 at St. Agnes.
— Volunteer Hook & Ladder Co. #1 organized.
— Frederick Fischer opens The Northern National Bank.
— Ashland horse-drawn street railway starts to run.

Historical marker at Maslowski Beach.

Picnickers at Madeline Island. From the first days of settlement Ashlanders enjoyed picnic excursions to the Apostle Islands.

The view from the gazebo of the Old Chequamegon Hotel was used to promote tourism to Ashland in the 1880's.

1888 — Ashland *Weekly Press* becomes a daily and is purchased by Joseph M. Chapple.
— First class graduates from high school.
— James York builds blast furnace.

1889 — Voters approve $100,000 development bond issue.
— Wisconsin Central (Soo Line) depot constructed.
— Bare-knuckles champ John L. Sullivan fights in Ashland.

1890 — City Population: 9,956.
— John Knight builds the Knight Hotel.
— Christopher Bretting forms C.G. Bretting Manufacturing Co.
— J.S. Ellis forms Security Savings Bank.
— German-Lutheran school opens.
— Ore dock fire kills two firemen.

1891 — Boston company buys the local water utility.
— 2,805 pupils in public schools.

1892 — St. Agnes Catholic Church built.
— Gordon's Business College holds first classes.
— Monday Club starts to meet.
— Northern Wisconsin Academy opens after Ashland contributes $30,000.
— World's largest stone monolith quarried.

1893 — Electric street railway starts to run.
— First Presbyterian Church built.
— 10,000 copies of Annual Edition of *Daily Press* distributed around the country by rail.
— YMCA starts.

1894 — Present Ashland City Hall built as U.S. Post Office.
— Typhoid rages through lumber camps and city.

1895 — Ashland County begins to build Peerless Railroad to Minneapolis. Track approaches Ino, then stops without ever carrying a passenger. Cost to the County: $120,000.

1896 — Buffalo Bill Cody brings Chippewa and Sioux chiefs together to sign a "peace treaty" during his Wild West Show.
— Two men die in Shores Lumber Co. fire.

1897 — Four railroads in Ashland: Chicago & Northwestern, Northern Pacific, The Omaha, Wisconsin Central.

1898 — Ashland volunteers march off for the Spanish-American War.
— Wilmarth School built.

1899 — Six students enrolled at North Wisconsin Academy.

1900 — City Population: 13,074.
— Beaser School in session.

1901 — Dr. William Rinehart starts Ashland's first nursing school.

1902 — Three die in Northwestern ore dock fire: Gus Drolson, Les Fins, and firefighter William Lindbloom.
— Robert M. La Follette campaigns in Ashland.
— Ashland Home Telephone Company starts with 600 subscribers.
— Collision on Ashland Street Railway line; three cars damaged and several persons injured.
— Mass meeting for women's suffrage held at Methodist Church. Main speakers are Superintendent Hooper and Northland's Professor Fenenga.

Ore from mines like these near Ironwood, Michigan, made Ashland a vital link in the industrialization of the Midwest.

When Buffalo Bill Cody brought his Show to Ashland in 1896 he staged a peace pow wow between the Sioux in his show and some local Chippewa. The gathering was intended to end decades of conflict between the tribes.

Buglers of the Second Regiment, Wisconsin National Guard, at the time of the Spanish-American War. Claude Talaska and Mr. Benedict are in top row, center.

1903 — Dr. J.A. Marchessault drives the first auto into town, a one cylinder Oldsmobile. He is soon joined by Joe Woodhead, Dr. Harrison, Dr. Rinehart, Dr. Dodd and their cars.

1904 — Du Pont gunpowder plant at Barksdale opens.
— Ashland High School opens.
— Rural Free Delivery begins out of Ashland Post Office.

1905 — City Population: 14,519.
— Iron ore drilling begins in Ashland County.
— Swedish and German Singing Societies active in city.
— Ashland schools receive a gold medal at the Louisiana Purchase Exposition in St. Louis.

1906 — Elks open clubhouse on Third Avenue.
— White River power dam built.
— 800 new citizens naturalized in Circuit Court.

1907 — Aksel Holter promotes national ski tournament at White River.
— The Princess, Bijou and Lyric movie houses open.

1908 — Slovak and Croation immigration to Moquah, Ino, and Benoit begins.

1909 — Ashland Power Company purchases White River Hydro-plant.

1910 — City Population: 11,594.

1911 — Voters choose commission form of city government.
— Frank Oscar Anderson, A.M. Raarup and C.E. Bloom organize the Andersonville Cooperative Cheese factory on Sanborn Avenue—the first farm cooperative in northern Wisconsin.

1912 — Fire Department becomes official recorder of temperatures for the city.
— St. Joseph's School of Nursing accepts first students.
— Commission system of government adopted.

1913 — University of Wisconsin Experimental Station set up at Ashland Junction.

1914 — World War I starts in Europe.
— Bridge and causeway work begun on Fish Creek Marsh.
— Fire destroys the Garnich Block on Second Street.
— Royal Theater opens.

1915 — New county courthouse completed.
— Ashland football team plays Milwaukee for state championship.

1916 — Ashland National Guard and Ashland Machine Gun Company sent on border patrol during Mexican Revolution.
— Ashland General Hospital opens.
— Sigurd Olson graduates from Ashland High School.

1917 — Ashland High School damaged by fire.
— Ashland General Hospital established.
— United States enters World War I.
— 1,400 county men enter military service.
— John Philip Sousa Band plays in Ashland.

1918 — World War I ends.
— Twenty-eight Ashland men die in service.
— Tonnage shipped out of Ashland exceeds that of Panama Canal.
— Spanish flu takes seventy-eight lives in the county.
— Ashland votes to go "dry."

1919 — National Prohibition begins.
— Home Telephone and Wisconsin Telephone companies merge.
— American Legion plants elm trees on "Memorial Highway 13."

1920 — City Population: 11,334.
— Beaser Avenue is first paved street in Ashland.

1921 — Ashland Vocational School begins classes.
— City Dock collapses during Memorial Day Ceremonies.

1922 — Second Street is paved with bricks from Stuntz to Ninth Avenue West.
— February blizzard shuts down city.

1923 — Ashland Fire Department gives up horses for trucks.
— C.F. Latimer donates Manual Training Building to high school.
— Tug Butterfield tows pulp barges from Port Arthur to the Commercial Dock now leased to Consolidated Paper Co.

1924 — Northwestern ore dock destroyed by fire.
— 15 MPH speed limit on Ashland arterial roads.
— First air mail stamps arrive at Ashland Post Office.
— Tornado strikes outskirts of city, kills six.
— First free chest clinic scans patients for tuberculosis.
— North Wisconsin Rod & Gun Club organizes.
— Frank Hughes shoots trap for the U.S. Olympic Team.
— Old Settlers Club organizes.

1925 — WTNB, "Where The North Begins," radio airs its first show.
— Two Norwegian ships, first ships of foreign registry, deliver nitrate of soda to Du Pont dock.

William Jennings Bryan (center), who ran for President three times, visited Ashland. He posed with Ashlanders at 400 East Front Street.

The "liberated" Ashland High School Girls Basketball team. Known as "the Invincible," they are: Vivian Nelson, Violet Anderson, Catherine Whittier, Adeline "Happy" Gordon, Laura Thibedeau (star forward), Dorothy Hitter, Isabelle Paton and Marie Coan.

1926 — Dill Dormitory fire at Northland.
— Ted Mesang becomes city bandmaster.

1927 — Memorial Hall dedicated at Northland.
— Guy Burnham, author of the definitive history of the Chequamegon region, *The Lake Superior Country in History and Story* writes first column for the *Daily Press* on June 28.

1928 — De Padua High School opens with 58 students.
— Rotary Park sports programs begin.
— City buys airport site.
— President Calvin Coolidge visits Ashland.
— Steam-powered pulpwood hoist starts loading logs.

1929 — Ashland celebrates its Diamond Jubilee.
— Six airplanes, including a Ford Tri-Motor twelve seater help open Ashland's first airport.
— Stock market crash starts Great Depression.
— Carl Sandburg visits Ashland.

1930 — City Population: 10,622.
— Helen Baker Jenner starts The Ashland Foundation with a gift of $25,000.

1931 — City gives free temporary lodging to 2,999 women and children.

1932 — Bayfield folks visit Ashland by boat on January 1.
— John B. Chapple defeats Republican Senator John Blaine in the primary but loses general election to F. Ryan Duffy.

1933 — Ashland banks close.
— City issues scrip money to pay city workers.
— Ashland becomes northern Wisconsin headquarters for the Civilian Conservation Corps.
— Prohibition ends.
— Highway 2 becomes first concrete road in the county.
— Last trolley car makes its run.
— 1,226 people in National Recovery Act Demonstration Parade.

1934 — Scarlet fever forces temporary closing of Ninth Avenue School.
— 1,353 people hired for public works projects in the county.
— Ashland Brewery reopens.

1935 — Original Harlem Globetrotters play at Ashland.
— City builds a new municipal dock and garage.
— J.C. Penney store opens.
— De Padua High basketball teams plays in finals for National Catholic championship.

1936 — Highways paved to Odanah and Washburn.
— Northwestern Ore Dock #1 dismantled.
— Presidential election vote: Roosevelt 523, Landon 8.
— John B. Chapple challenges Robert La Follette, Jr., in Republican Senatorial primary.
— Slot machines banned.

1937 — Bay movie theatre opens.
— American Black Granite Company ships $48,000 order to Florida.
— Ashland Brewing Co. closes.

1938 — Voters say no to sewerage plant proposal.
— First air mail shipment of 1,000 letters flies off.
— Admiral Leahy honored at American Legion Convention.

1939 — New Post Office begun.
— New Highway 13 bridge over White River completed.
— World War II begins in Europe.

1940 — City Population: 11,101.
— WATW radio goes on the air.
— Seventy-one new homes built in Ashland.
— F.W. Woolworth builds a new store.
— First peacetime draft takes seventeen Ashland men.

1941 — United States enters World War II. Guards placed at Ashland Junction, ore docks, Fish Creek Bridge.
— Vocational school (WITI) opens in old Post Office.

1942 — U.S. Signal Corps School opens.
— National Guard Company formed.
— Rationing begins.
— Blackout rules enforced, Christmas lighting restricted.
— Military guards ore docks and Ashland Junction.

1943 — Gordon's Business College closes.
— WPA passes from existence.

1944 — Coach Roy Melvin changes name of high school teams from *Purgolders* to *Oredockers*.

1945 — World War II ends.
— Fire at Saron Lutheran Church.
— City Council denies petitions to close taverns on Sundays.
— Pullman car service ends.

1946 — Scott-Taylor Company fire.
— Ashland General becomes Trinity Lutheran Hospital.
— Varsity basketball team ranks fourth in state.
— Varsity football team is champ of Michigan-Wisconsin Conference.

1947 — Voters pass referendum to built a new vocational school.
— Referendum to adopt city-manager government succeeds.
— Splicedwood factory moves to Ashland.

1948 — Munsingwear moves to Ashland.
— Charley Winnegar pays tribute to Admiral Leahy at Homecoming Celebration.
— Voters approve switch to city-manager government.
— Joseph Warren selected as first city manager.

1949 — Wisconsin legislature passes school district consolidation law.
— City beaches posted for polluted water.

Built in 1915, the Ashland Lighthouse is a rare example of the use of reinforced concrete for lighthouses. 58 feet tall, it is the only significant structure of its kind on the Great Lakes.

A promotional button for the Ashland Brewery. It made beer until Prohibition, switched to soda, then went back to beer.

In January 1946 the staff of the *Daily Press* entertained a reporter and photographer from *Life Magazine* who were visiting Ashland.

1950 — City Population: 10,640.
— Ashland fluoridates its water system.
— Rural school districts begin consolidation with Ashland.
— City Council adopts petitions to change names of roads: "Lover's Lane" is now "Maple Lane;" "Garbage Ground" and "Jones Road" become "Woodbury Lane."

1951 — High School band plays at Chicagoland Music Festival.
— City Council passes motion to hire a policewoman but no one is hired.

1952 — Prime Minister of Sweden visits Ashland and is hosted by Tage Erlander and John Anderson.

1953 — Korean War ends. Nine Ashland County men died in service.
— County Normal School becomes County Teachers College.
— High School Band, directed by Francis White, wins first place in the U.S. for its recording of *Stars and Stripes Forever*.
— Kiwanis Club places large white pine log on display in Memorial Park.

1954 — Ashland celebrates its centennial of settlement.
— High School band plays at American Legion Convention in Oshkosh.
— High School dedicates Dr. Edwin Ellis plaque.
— President Turbeville of Northland College and Cora Angvick begin movement to establish a historical museum in the Vaughn Library Building.
— City Council passes motion to sell only pasteurized milk in Ashland.

1955 — Lakeshore School closes.
— Varsity football goes undefeated.
— City Council debates removal of Ellis Avenue center boulevards.

1956 — *Daily Press* sold to *Superior Telegram*.
— Civil Defense organization created.

1957 — Northwestern ore dock closes.
— Voters chose to return to mayor-council government.
— City Council enacts first zoning ordinance.

1958 — New St. Agnes grade school opens.
— Chamber of Commerce erects *Wishing Well* at Maslowski Park.

1959 — Ashland Sewer and Water Utilities combined.

In 1948, Charley Winnegar and Admiral William Leahy posed with the staff of the *Daily Press* while visiting for the Homecoming Celebration.

A high point of the 1954 Centennial of Settlement was a beard contest. Brothers of the Brush vied for the title of best and bushiest.

1960 — City Population: 10,132.
— John F. Kennedy begins his Presidential campaign in Ashland.
— Voters pass referendum on dog leash law.

1961 — Soo Line takes over old Wisconsin Central Railroad.
— Ashland participates in Circle Tour around Lake Superior to promote tourism.
— City accepts bid of 14.8 cents per gallon for fuel oil.

1962 — City purchases first comprehensive liability insurance coverage and adopts first littering ordinance.
— Columbia Furniture warehouse burns.

1963 — President John F. Kennedy visits Ashland to dedicate Apostles Islands National Lakeshore and to pick out a black granite tombstone.

1964 — Large "American" crane expands pulp hoist operation.

1965 — Soo Line ore dock shuts down.
— Chequamegon Symphony Orchestra founded.

1966 — Upon petition of the Chamber of Commerce, city council adopts the petunia as Ashland's official flower.

1967 — First Ashland soldier dies in Vietnam.
— Fire Department takes over ambulance service.
— De Padua High School closes.
— Unified school district formed. City district dissolves.

1968 — United Way Fund Drive underway.

1969 — City Council approves license for Whispering Pines Trailer Court.
— City supports construction of Project Sanguine/Elf.

Sitting Bull guarded the entrance to Bob Parson's Cigar Store at 409 Second Street West for over fifty years. Parsons was a mecca for politicians and citizens discussing problems of the city, nation and world.

93

President John F. Kennedy, Governor John W. Reynolds (l), and Senator Gaylord Nelson visited Ashland for the dedication of the Apostle Islands National Lakeshore in 1963. Flagbearer in dark uniform is Andy Thone.

Following Page

Mrs. Sam Fifield's Sunday School Class. (l to r, top) Daisy Bailey Ritchie, Anna Mattson, Maggie Young, Agnes Ritchie, Elizabeth Biksler Palchim, Amie Baker, Louise Jacobson. (2nd row) Miny Young, Dora Hanson Ruggles, Miss Kinney, Elsie Semple. (bottom) Mittie Smith, Cora DuMeg Ballard, Rose French Johnson, Ida Pearce French, Mollie Jacka.

1970 — City Population: 9,615.
— Ashland's last passenger train leaves Northwestern Depot.
— WITI moves to new Beaser Avenue Campus.

1971 — Ashland County Teachers College closes.

1972 — Memorial Medical Center opens.
— Last cordwood log raft towed across Lake Superior.
— Ashland Pulp Hoist closes.

1973 — New High School opens for classes.
— Energy crisis restricts Christmas lighting.

1974 — Scott-Taylor closes.
— Du Pont-Barksdale plant closes.
— St. Joseph's Hospital and Knight Hotel razed.

1975 — Gibson Store opens.
— City receives $300,000 grant to renovate City Hall.

1976 — Ashland High School Band plays at Wisconsin State Fair.
— Second Street re-surfacing project begin.

1977 — City bus service ends.
— Renovated City Hall dedicated.

1978 — Oredockers win district football title.

1979 — Small Cities Grant improves parks and housing.
— City council votes 6-5 in favor of Mayor Stephen R. Zohimsky's resignation. He refuses.
— Voters reject proposal to build a new marina.

1980 — City Population: 9,115.
— First annual *Nutcracker* performed.

1981 — Bay Area Rural Transit starts to run.
— Sigurd Olson Environmental Institute dedicated.

1982 — Sigurd Olson dies.

1983 — Middle School moves out of old high school building.
— Varsity girls softball team wins district championship.
— Soo Line gives Pulp Hoist Dock to Northland College.

1984 — Oredockers take Division 2 state football title.
— Varsity girls basketball team is second in state.
— City buys Pulp Hoist Dock for $147,000.

1985 — Grand Re-Opening of Pamida Store.
— City receives $1,154,000 in grants for new marina.

1986 — Varsity baseball teams wins district championship.
— Civic Center opens.
— Pulp Hoist Dock becomes The Ashland Marina.
— Long Island officially added to National Lakeshore.

1987 — Ashland celebrates its Centennial as a city.

Of Faiths Diverse

"Without churches a city is lost to itself and the world."
Ashland Daily Press, *1893*

United Methodist

The Methodists established the first church in Ashland in 1872, when Reverend and Mrs. W.G. Bancroft answered a call from Mr. Bennett of Bayfield and came to Chequamegon Bay by boat from Milwaukee. The first service was held in the store of R.W. French, with the counter as pulpit and nail kegs as pews. Spirit was strong, however, and the fourteen-member congregation pledged about a thousand dollars for a new church building.

The depression of the 1870s forced the Methodists to sell their building and the congregation all but dissolved. Nevertheless, a small church was built on Seventh Avenue West.

As the economy improved in the 1880s, more Methodists moved to Ashland. Reverend F.M. Haight arrived in 1888 and in a year church membership reached 150. A new church was built on the corner of Sixth Avenue West and Third Street.

First Methodist Church

95

The church enjoyed a period of tranquility and growth until the 1930s, when the Great Depression caused hardship to everyone. By the end of the decade membership reached 160. In 1947, a new organ was purchased and a new chancel built. A new parsonage was acquired that same year.

In January 1955, over two hundred people gathered at First Methodist, on one of the coldest nights of the year to observe the open house at the newly-remodeled church. The work included two new entrances and the laying of footings for the new exterior of Norman brick.

In the 1970s, the parish was reorganized and pastor Fred Thomas took up residence in Washburn. In 1987, the United Methodist church continues to serve Ashland as it has for the last 115 years. The current pastor is Reverend Steven Foster.

Nidaros Norwegian-Danish Lutheran Church

Good Shepherd Lutheran

Movement to establish a Norwegian Lutheran congregation in Ashland began in 1876 when Pastor Musens, from Scandinavia, Wisconsin, held a worship and communion service at the old Ninth Avenue School.

Eight years passed before an organizational meeting was held and the name Nidaros Norwegian Evangelical Lutheran Congregation was chosen. Nidaros is the old name of the Norwegian city of Trondheim, from which many Ashland Norwegians had emigrated.

Worship was held alternately in the schoolhouse, in the Swedish church building on Ellis Avenue, and in a hall located on Eighth Avenue and Third Street which belonged to the First Episcopal Church.

Pastor Amundsen served the congregation on a monthly circuit and was paid a fee of $10 plus food and lodging. A collection taken at the meeting after the pastor was hired amounted to $6.50, considered a goodly sum from only thirteen members.

In 1887, three lots on the northeast corner of Ninth Avenue West and Third Street were purchased for the sum of $3,000 at eight per cent interest. A constitution was adopted, a Sunday School, Ladies Aid and Young Girls Mission Society organized.

Many young Norwegian immigrants came to Ashland at this time to work in the lumber camps, mills, and railyards. Church membership grew and in 1889, N. Stensland was appointed to draw plans for a church building. Carpenters and laborers volunteered their labor to complete the main body and bell tower of the church that year. The church was dedicated in 1892 with a seating capacity of three hundred.

A branch church was organized in the east end of Ashland for the convenience of members who lived in Bay City. This congregation was called the Oslo Church.

Women were given the right to vote at the annual meeting in 1899 and a parsonage was constructed in 1901.

The first hymn books used at Nidaros were Lundstad's Psalmbog and most members used the small word editions they had brought from Norway. The large reed organ used in the church required pumping with foot pedals or a hand lever at the back of the instrument. Usually two boys were hired to man the lever at five cents a service.

The Reverend M. Halvorsen was called as pastor in 1907. He was the first Nidaros pastor to own a car. He also introduced an extra monthly Sunday evening evangelistic service in English. The seventy-eight member Oslo congregation disbanded in 1920. Their building was sold and the funds used to purchase an altar with a picture of Jesus and Peter which is now in the narthex of Good Shepherd Church.

Sunday services at Nidaros were conducted in English, with the last half in Norwegian for older members. By 1934, Norwegian was spoken only during the first Sunday of the month and one Sunday evening service each month. The by-laws were translated into English in 1941. The name of the congregation was changed to Nidaros Evangelical Lutheran Church in 1942, after the congregation joined the Lutheran Free Church.

The annual beef and lutefisk supper was cancelled in 1942 because of coffee and sugar rationing. The church also frequently experienced a shortage of funds, especially to pay the fuel bills, and the Ladies Aid and Ladies Guild always came to the rescue.

A fire caused by lightning in July, 1949, destroyed the tower and cracked the bell, but the building was saved by members of the congregation who manned hoses and kept the fire contained until the fire department arrived. The by-laws were changed in 1951, and the section prohibiting saloonkeepers and others engaged in un-Christian business from becoming members was deleted.

During Pastor Helland's ministry in 1960, plans were made to build a new church which was completed in 1965. The new church was dedicated as Good Shepherd Lutheran church in December of that year.

A year of celebration and thanks to God marked the first one hundred years of existence for Nidaros-Good Shepherd and culminated in a huge Homecoming weekend in July, 1984. The logo adopted for the Centennial Celebration, "Forward Through Faith," continues to be the goal of the Good Shepherd Lutheran church congregation as it moves into its second century of worship and service to God.

Presbyterian Church

United Presbyterian-Congregational

The United Presbyterian-Congregational Church is the result of a federation in 1943 of the First Presbyterian and the First Congregational.

The roots of the Presbyterian church go back to July, 1880, when nineteen charter members formed the initial congregation. The first church building was located at Third and Ellis and still stands today. The present brownstone and brick structure was built in 1897 and a pipe organ installed in 1900.

First Congregational was formed in August, 1887, and this year marks its centennial. In 1889 a new church was built on Fourth Avenue and Eighth Street. With the merging of the two congregations, the church building was sold to the Assembly of God congregation.

The present membership of the Presbyterian-Congregational Church is approximately 430. The church is noted for the beauty of its building and sanctuary and its stained-glass windows. It has an admirable history of ministry and service in Ashland, with both ministers and members as community leaders.

Doctor Carlton Koons organized the first Boy Scout Troop in Wisconsin. Doctor Martin Kausler initiated radio broadcasts of church services and witnessed the building of an educational wing on the church. His wife, Eloise, organized a large youth choir called the Choralettes. The church has been privileged to host the annual Christmas Community Concert, sponsored by the Wednesday Music club, since its inception in 1929.

The United Presbyterian-Congregational Church continues as a center of Christian fellowship and ministry for many Ashlanders. This year the church will commemorate the centennial celebration of the founding of the Congregational Church. A major renovation and refurbishing of the sanctuary and a new, ramped entrance to the church dining room have recently been completed. The present pastor is Doctor Darrel M. Robertson.

Salem Baptist

On July 8, 1883, eleven Swedish immigrants met to discuss the possibility of having a Baptist Church in the Ashland area. Seven years later in December, 1890, forty-five charter members met and organized the Swedish Salem Baptist Church. A lot was purchased on Second Avenue East and Seventh Street for $900. Reverend Gust Lundquist was chosen as first pastor.

Salem Baptist was Ashland's first foreign-speaking congregation and the city's fifth Protestant church. Like other ethnic churches, it was founded to serve the religious needs of immigrants who wished to worship God in their native language.

Salem remained a Swedish-language church until 1946. The children of the founders spoke English and so did many other non-Swedish members of the congregation. Services were conducted in English and the "Swedish" prefix was dropped from the name.

Growth and change came to Salem, and in 1951 an educational building for a larger Sunday school was built. The present church on Beaser and Sixteenth Street was completed in 1983 at a cost of $598,408. The sum was substantially financed by the congregation. The two-level building has 15,500 square feet and is divided into sanctuary, offices, classrooms, library, fellowship area and recreation hall. The sanctuary seats approximately 375 people.

Members and friends of Salem contributed approximately 15,000 hours of volunteer labor to construct the new facility.

Reverend Ronald E. Valente was installed as Pastor on June 15, 1986. The present membership is 262 people of wide and diverse backgrounds who attend Salem from a large surrounding area encompassing the community from Mellen to Bayfield.

Swedish Salem Baptist Church

Emmanuel Baptist

On September 8, 1985, the Apostle Islands Baptist Church and the former Northland Baptist church of 701 Ellis Avenue merged and took the name of Emmanuel Baptist.

Northland Baptist was founded in 1977 with Reverend Jay Varner as first pastor. Reverend Timothy Branton came as pastor in March of 1980 and held the pulpit for five years. Reverend Daryl Taylor followed Branton and is the current pastor.

The Apostle Islands Baptist church was organized in May of 1983 with Reverend Bradley Berglund as pastor. In January of 1985, the congregation purchased the old Salem Baptist church building at 623 Second Avenue East.

This venerable old building now serves as meeting place for the combined membership and also houses the Apostle Islands Christian School, a ministry of the church.

St. Andrew Episcopal

Before Ashland developed into a city, occasional services were held by various missionaries of the Episcopal Church who came from considerable distances to look after those of the same household of faith. The first regular services under a Lay Reader began in 1879 in homes of the congregation.

By 1880, there were twelve families and forty souls in the congregation. They held their first service on St. Andrew's day that year. The Bishop of Fond du Lac came to celebrate Mass and to confirm.

The following year St. Andrew's was organized as a mission and admitted to the Diocese of Fond du Lac. Of that same twelve families and forty souls, ten were now communicant members. In 1883, Father Howard St. George, then resident priest at Christ Church in Bayfield, took charge of St. Andrew's. By 1886, under Reverend Joseph Moran, St. Andrew's accumulated the wherewithal to build a church building on the southeast corner of Eighth Avenue West and Third Street. First services were held there on St. Andrew's Day, 1886. In 1892, St. Andrew's became a parish.

In 1900, construction of the present building began. The design is considered a classic example of pure "Victorian Gothic" and was built in modified cruciform. Its unique beauty derives from its interior facing of smooth brick, and its "hammer-beam" roof. The project was underwritten by Judge J.W. Cochran, cost $24,000 and was completed in 1904. The original wooden structure was sold to the Swedish Evangelical Mission and sometime later was struck by lightning and destroyed by fire. The High Altar and the Reredos in the present building are from the original church, having been moved when the present church was completed.

An interesting feature of the Reredos is its likeness to a great bedstead which, with its overhanging canopy, actually represents the theological concept of the Church as the Bride of Christ. The Rood-beam, which separates the Choir from the Nave and carries the Great

Episcopal Church

Rood, or Crucifix, was added in 1941 and was the gift of Mr. and Mrs Walter Hodgkins in memory of their mothers. The figures of the Rood Group were carved in Oberammergau, Bavaria. The Stations of the Cross came from Italy and are carved in lemon wood. They were the gift of the late Frank Tomlinson, founder of the Ashland firm which bears his name, and a mason who helped build the church. The Side Altar was added sometime in the 1950s, the gift of John Kendrigan in memory of his wife, Allie. The Tabernacle above the High Altar was added in 1967 by Mrs. Mary Grigsby in memory of her husband, Doctor Roll Grigsby. The candlesticks on the High Altar were given by Mr. and Mrs. Robert Fluskey.

The Baptismal Font at the back of the church is a particularly beautiful place. It was given by Mr. and Mrs. Allen T. Pray in memory of a son who died at an early age. Another item of interest is the Eagle Lectern on the Gospel side of the Chancel. Its origin is obscure, but it is a classic example of the woodcarver's art, and is one of the particular treasures of St. Andrew's.

St. Andrew's celebrated its centennial in 1981. At that time Father Douglas E. Culver was Pastor. He served the congregation for seventeen years. Father Samuelson Rogers is serving as the interim priest at the present time.

Swedish Mission

First Covenant Church

The First Covenant Church had its official beginning in 1892, when a small group of young Swedish immigrants who had been exposed to the Mission Friends in Sweden began to meet. They were served and encouraged by itinerant ministers, including C.A. Soderman, J.J. Peterson and N.O. Olson.

Five young men were the nucleus of the this early church. They were C.J. Lindahl, J.M. Johnson, Louis Newquist, Anton Oberg, and N.G. Nelson. They established a Swedish Mission Church with a Sunday School and young people's program The first four Sunday school teachers were requested to find their own pupils, who they instructed in their native Swedish. To assist in this teaching, a "Swed school" was held in the summer months. As use of English spread, Swedish was used only in special evening services.

Services were first held in the vacated Swedish Baptist Church at Third Street and Tenth Avenue West. The next meeting place was the former First Presbyterian Church at Third and Ellis. A new church building was erected at Second Avenue West and Eighth Street in 1893, under the direction of Olaf Johnson. This building was moved to the present site at Sixth Street and MacArthur Avenue in 1902, under the ministry of Pastor Carl Olson.

In 1894, the church became affiliated with the Swedish Evangelical Mission Covenant Church of America, known today as the Evangelical Covenant Church.

The Reverend Soderman served as pastor until 1894 and was followed by several pastors who stayed for short periods of time. In 1895, with a membership of twenty-one the church called a permanent pastor, Reverend Isaac Skoog, who served until 1897.

Over the years, the church building has been improved and enlarged. In 1923, a basement was added and, later, the church tower was removed, a new entrance added, and the sanctuary extensively renovated.

By the time the church celebrated its Fiftieth Anniversary, 252 members had been received and over two hundred youths confirmed.

During the ministry of Reverend Frederic Medary, 1958-62, the church became known by its present name. The word *Covenant* comes from the Swedish word *Forbund*, which carried the idea of coming together as a group. It closely relates to the early nickname, *Mission Friends*. Historically, the movement began in the Lutheran State Church in Sweden, as groups gathered in their homes for Bible study. The watch words of the early movement were: "Do you know Jesus?" and "Where is it written?" The denomination was founded in 1885 when a group of Christian pioneers met in Chicago and covenanted to support a common missionary work in America and abroad.

The church is a member of the Northwest Conference of the Evangelical Covenant Church. It has close fellowship ties with churches in the Lake Superior District of this Conference. The church shares in the camping ministry of Covenant Park Bible Camp near Mahtowa, Minnesota.

The church has an active Covenant Women's Group and a Brotherhood group. A Sunday School program for all ages is held during the school year.

Esther Swanson, a life long resident, is currently the longest-lived active church member. She joined the church in December of 1922 at the age of fifteen.

The church celebrated its seventh-fifth

anniversary in 1967, while Reverend Walter Snell was pastor. In August 1982, the church celebrated its ninetieth anniversary, while Reverend Carl B. Johnson was pastor. Reverend Johnson retired in 1983. Reverend Dale Engen currently serves as pastor. The church has an active membership of forty-seven, with many others actively involved in the life of the church.

Zion Lutheran

Zion Lutheran church of Ashland was organized thirty years after the Town of Ashland was originally laid out.

In 1887, Reverend W.C. Schilling of Stevens Point, came to Ashland and on the evening of his arrival held the first Lutheran service in Ashland. One can only imagine the feelings of the small group of Lutherans here, including the Martin Roehm family, who had lived here so long without a pastor. Ashland was then one of fourteen preaching or mission stations served by Pastor Schilling along the Wisconsin Central Line. He returned later that year and several times in 1878, to hold services in one of the two school houses in the small village.

Several ministers followed as missionaries to the small flock but progress was slow for the church. Ashland was discontinued as a preaching station by the Synod in 1880.

In 1883, Reverend Theodore Buenger succeeded in organizing *Deutsche Evang. Lutheran Zions Gemeinde* with eight charter members: Henry Brinker, C.W. Exchert, Fred Adermann, Fred Machmiller, William Machmiller, H.F. Clausen, Jens Nielsen and Henry Grage.

At its first regular meeting, the congregation decided to build a wooden-frame church on a site donated by the Wisconsin Central at the corner of Prentice Avenue and Fourth Street. It served the congregation until it became the school building in 1891. In 1885, E. Baese became Zion's first resident pastor.

By 1891, both Ashland and Zion were growing. In that year, the church joined the Missouri Synod and started a program to build a new church and buy a parsonage. The new church, which seated three hundred, was usually filled to overflowing and the parish school was flourishing. The Ladies Aid presented the church with its bell, which is said to have once been a cannon. The size of the bell required that the belfry be lifted about

German Evangelical Lutheran Zion Church

twelve feet. The raising was accomplished with the help of a circus elephant which happened to be in town at the time. At about the same time, the congregation purchased a new Estey Reed organ which served until the early 1940s.

In 1914, Pastor O. Hattstaedt began his twenty-two year pastorate, the longest of any at Zion. He also served congregations in Bayfield, Washburn, Iron River, Cornucopia, Benoit and Mason.

In 1937, the church was remodeled and the parsonage redone. In the 1940s, the Wicks pipe organ was purchased and two buses began to bring children to Sunday School. The memorial stained glass windows were also installed.

In the 1950s Zion, like Ashland itself, shrank. Nevertheless, many improvements were made to the church, such as the mothers' room, a new floor in the church basement, and visual education facilities. In 1959, the church celebrated its seventy-fifth anniversary.

In 1962, a resolution was passed to build a new church, but the dream of a new house of worship was not realized until 1970, when the present Zion Lutheran was constructed. Many members of the church took part in the painting, paneling and other work of building a new home for Zion.

In 1972, Zion celebrated its largest regular attendance of 447 on Easter sunday. In 1985, Reverend Roy R. Krueger was installed as pastor.

The congregation continues to grow with God's blessings and pastor's guidance. The young people take an active part in church affairs and regularly attend vacation Bible school.

First Assembly of God

The First Assembly of God of Ashland, formerly known as the Ashland Gospel Tabernacle, came into being in the 1930s largely due to the evangelistic efforts of Ruth Thompson and Betty Braidigan, who came to the area and conducted services in private homes. In 1932, Reverend Earl Cleveland came to pastor the small group of Spirit-filled believers. In 1935, Ashland Gospel Tabernacle was officially organized and affiliated with the Assemblies of God.

Reverend Earl Cleveland led the church in purchasing the former Norden Society Hall, located at 923 W. Sixth Street. This building became the church home until the spring of 1954. The pastor and his family lived in an apartment at the rear of the building.

During the ministry of Reverend Morris Hayes, who served from 1954-55, Ashland Gospel Tabernacle changed its name to First Assembly of God and purchased the former Congregational Church at 801 Fourth Avenue West. This building has been the church home up to the present time.

In 1966, during the ministry of Reverend Kenneth Wheeler, who served from 1964 to 1967, the church purchased a home located at 204 East Eighth Street for a parsonage.

In 1981, during the ministry of Reverend Jere Sherman, who served from 1976 to 1985, the church purchased over eight acres of land and a home for a parsonage located just west of Sanborn Avenue on Highway 137. The church plans to build new church facilities on this land.

In 1985, First Assembly of God celebrated its Fiftieth Anniversary as an Assembly of God Church. A special celebration was planned. Several former pastors and old friends of the church attended.

Congregational Church

The Church of Christ

The Church of Christ was established in the Ashland area in the 1950s with Robert Spears doing the preaching. In December 1965, Ronald A. Glass moved to the area to preach to the local congregation which then met on Ninth Street East. In 1967, the congregation purchased its present building at 905 Third Avenue East.

The local Church of Christ is a part of the *church* which was promised by Christ in Matthew 16:18, came into being in Acts 2 and was spoken of in Romans 16:16.

Christian Science

The Christian Science church is a branch of the First Church of Christ, Scientist, in Boston, Massachusetts. The Ashland branch was formed in 1930, with services held in a building on Ellis Avenue. In 1958, the church purchased its present structure at 410 W. Front Street.

First English Lutheran

First English Lutheran shares its centennial anniversary with the city of Ashland. Built in 1887 for the First Baptist Congregation organized in 1884, the church was moved from its first location on Third and Ellis to make room for an expanding railyard. In 1893, the *Daily Press* described it as "one of the most beautiful houses of worship in the city; it is valued at $7,500 and has 300 sittings."

In 1908, the building was vacant and St. John's Lutheran was organized as *Der Deutsch English Ev. Luth. St. Johannis*. The German Lutherans purchased the building and, in 1915, dedicated it.

In 1931, this congregation united with the predominantly Norwegian Trinity Lutheran, which worshipped in its sanctuary on Sixth Street West at Eleventh Avenue. The chancel furnishings from this church were moved to St. Johannis and installed there for use in the new home of the united congregation. This furniture had been constructed in the Scott-Taylor plant where many church members worked. Also installed at the new location was a statue of Christ purchased by the Young People's Society of the Trinity Congregation.

The architectural style of the white frame building is typical of its time and is an example of "the Akron Plan" with a corner entrance and bell tower, a slanted floor in the nave, and a chancel of reserved proportions. The gold and white, ornately panelled altar, altar-rail, pulpit and baptismal font are also typical of the period.

The name *First English Lutheran Church* came about through the eventual use of the English language in the church. The Lutherans were usually very reluctant to give up their mother-tongues. They preferred to worship in their native German, Swedish, Norwegian, Finnish and Slovakian languages. St. John's Fifteenth Anniversary booklet, published in 1923, says that, "The congregation was organized a bilingual one, employing both the English and the German languages, but in the course of its development, the English language has become the means of expression through which all of the work and most of the services are conducted."

The First English Lutheran Church edifice has been completely restored. Brightly-colored windows, a new roof, siding and furnaces, plus a paint job were part of the restoration.

Trinity Norwegian Lutheran Church

Continuing to dominate the interior for the assembled congregation and its guests is the statue of Christ above the altar in the chancel. It portrays the Lord bestowing His blessing.

Saron Lutheran

Saron Lutheran church began with three families who held their first service in 1884. The following year they built their first small wooden church building at the rear of the present church property. The church was officially organized in 1887. Charter members were: Fred Peterson, Matt Mattson, A.P. Peterson, Mr. and Mrs. Gabriel Rasmussen, Hannah Berggren, Andrew Anderson, Mr. and Mrs. Isak Anderson, Mr. and Mrs. C.J. Stark, Carl V. Stark, Frederick Ellison, Mr. and Mrs. Andrew Anderson, Olof Lindgren, Alfred Carlson. Pastor J.D. Nelsenius accepted the call to serve as Saron's first pastor.

Saron began as part of the Swedish Lutheran or Augustana Synod, which was organized in Clinton, Wisconsin, in 1860.

The congregation rapidly outgrew its first church and built a new one in 1892. Members

Swedish Evangelical Lutheran Church

contributed over two thousand dollars and 240 days of labor to complete the structure. In 1914, the church was decorated, a pipe organ installed, and a new altar and altar painting, pulpit, baptismal font, candelabrum and other furnishings acquired. The church was further remodeled and decorated in the 1920s and 30s. In 1942, a mortgage burning ceremony was held to celebrate the first time in its history that Saron was out of debt.

Three years later disaster struck. The church burned to the ground, with virtually all its furnishings and equipment. Only the altar cross and missal, the Christian and American flags and one altar candelabra were saved.

After the fire, Saron resolved to build a new church. In the interim Nidaros Lutheran, Bethesda Lutheran, Episcopal and Covenant Mission churches all offered facilities and aid. Pastor Nels Nelson reported, " . . . a decision has been reached to build a new church on the corner of Ninth Avenue West and Sixth Street. . . Construction will begin as soon as ground can be broken."

Pastor Nelson served Saron for thirty-five of its 102 years of existence. A distinguished scholar, he came to Ashland in 1923 and remained at Saron until his death in 1958. He left behind a progressive, vital church, one which had evolved from an exclusive society of Swedish immigrants to a servant church of the community.

Saron's present house of worship, built on the site of the second church destroyed by fire, is of Gothic design and patterned after some of the beautiful churches of Europe. It was completed and dedicated in 1951.

In 1967 Saron, under the direction of Pastor R. Dean Johnson, completed construction of a new parish education addition. It provides classrooms for the Sunday School, offices for the pastor and Sunday School superintendent and other facilities.

Three years earlier, Saron, as had other Augustana Synod churches, adopted the constitution and became affiliated with the Lutheran church in America.

In 1984, Pastor Dale Franson came to Saron and is currently the pastor.

St. Agnes Catholic

Ashland has a rich Catholic heritage. Father Rene Menard, a Jesuit Missionary, came to the shores of Chequamegon Bay in 1661 and in 1665, Father Claude Allouez built a small chapel within the present city limits. This was the first house of Christian worship erected in Wisconsin. The first recorded Mass in Ashland was said by Father John Chebul in 1872. He ministered to the area for about ten years.

The first St. Agnes Church was begun by Father Xaverius Pfaller in 1874. In 1877, the first class was confirmed by Bishop Michael Heiss. In 1878, the Franciscan Fathers took over at St. Agnes.

Father Casimir Vogt was the first pastor. He was followed by Fathers John Gaffron and Eustace Vollmer. Father Vollmer enlarged the church, bought an organ and pews, and built living quarters for the priests.

St. Agnes was officially incorporated as a parish in 1885. As more immigrants came to the Ashland, church membership grew. A steeple, bells, and side entrances were added to the church. A three story school, the largest in the city, was completed in 1895. It soon proved too small and the old frame school was used once again. Crowding became less of a problem after Ashland's population peaked in 1905, and the St.

Agnes school served students many more decades. The Franciscan Sisters of Perpetual Adoration, headquartered in La Crosse, staffed St. Agnes school almost from its beginning. In the 1950s, twenty-six Sisters and one layman staffed the school with its five hundred students.

In 1927, Father Peter Volz was pastor. He built De Padua High School, which had the largest gym in the city for many years. De Padua served Ashland until 1967, when its students merged into Ashland High School.

In 1956, St. Agnes experienced a great development in its ability to reach the public with the broadcast of the liturgy over WATW radio. In 1965, small portable altars were added to the sanctuary to allow the priest to say Mass facing the congregation. During the pastorate of Father Andre Schludecker a shrine was built on the north side of the St. Agnes property. The log building, according to Father Schludecker, was built in memory of "the spirit and gifts of St. Francis of Assisi." There are presently over 1,250 families registered in the parish.

St. Agnes Church

Holy Family Church

Holy Family Catholic

St. Agnes experienced a phenomenon common to many parishes in the late 1800s. She bore an offspring in the form of Holy Family. Holy Family is a Polish ethnic church located three blocks east of St. Agnes on Front Street. As early as 1884 parishioners of Polish extraction belonged to St. Agnes. They had difficulty with the language and needed their native tongue to hear the Word of God.

Father Anastasius Czech was the first minister to the Poles at St. Agnes.

In 1899, Ashland Poles received permission to build a separate Polish church. The first building they erected was a school that opened with 115 students. Ten years later three hundred children attended. In 1900, a cornerstone for the church was laid and the superstructure erected. Holy Family flourished as an independent parish until the 1970s when its school was consolidated with St. Agnes and St. Mary's in Odanah. Father Humbert Korgie served as pastor from 1960 to 1976. Holy Family currently shares its pastor, Father Vernon Olmer, and his assistant, Father Paul Gallagher, with St. Agnes. There are presently 350 families registered in the parish.

Seventh-Day Adventist

The Ashland Seventh-Day Adventist church was organized in 1894. In the early years of its organization, members met in homes, rented halls and other church buildings. For a number of years the Scandinavian members met as a separate congregation.

In 1916, the North Wisconsin Conference of Seventh-Day Adventist, comprised of the churches of northern Wisconsin and eight counties of Michigan's Upper Peninsula, was established in Ashland with Elder J.J. Irwin as president.

The church body moved to its present location at 622 Tenth Avenue West in 1919. The conference offices were then located on the second story. The English-speaking and Scandinavian congregations were united in 1921.

For several years a parochial school was maintained by the church at its present location. Some of the students who attended then have gone on to hold responsible positions in the work of the church in this country and overseas. Altogether, more than twenty members have entered the organized work of the denomination.

The Ashland church is currently served by Pastor Dennis Pumford.

Father Christmas visited the Bardon children in this 1880s photo. No lights or candles are on the tree, but plenty of presents are scattered on the floor beneath.

Ashland's Most Honorable

World War I

Edward Carl Aderman
August Bodine
William Bernard Boyle
Alex Checkie
Edward L. Cossette
Stanley Delaski
Nellie Dingley, R.N.
Axel Ellison

Robert Edward Friske
Edward Orville Gaudur
Charles Guinand
Harry Hangard
Martin Hangard
Guy Harmon Holton
Roy William Kelly
Bernard Gordon Kromer

Leon M. Lawrence
Ervin Lawrence Le Febvre
Joseph Lorbecki
Frank Mardiket
Edward John Marek
Lester Joseph McCallum
J. Parker
Max Richards

Oliver Wilson Seaton
Elmer F. Shanks
John Henry Shaw
Edwin B. Thorsen
Archie Joseph Vanark
Michael T. Wilmann
Frank Wolfe

World War II

Fred Anderson
Edward Barrett
Frank Edward Bauer
Donald J. Benson
Edmund A. Bogart
Eugene Patrick Brinker
Robert Carlin
Robert Casey
John M. Cate
Lawrence J. Craig
Vernon Crawford
Thomas H. Deragon
John Durick, Jr.
Louis Foris
David Francisco
William Sterns Fuller

Arnold E. Gilley
Paul Goeltz
Wilmer H. Goldinger
Robert C. Green
Sheldon Grey
Louis J. Heck
Donald E. Hill
Bruno A. Hmielewski
Allen Howard Johnson
Robert Johnson
Robert H. Johnson
Clayton Judd
James A. Kennedy
Wilbert T. Kleinsteiber
Felix Klimas
Lyman Lane

James E. Leith
Sigurd Lindseth
William James Maloney
Richard Andrew Masko
Charles McGeehan
Paul N. Miller
Arden Nystrom
John F. O'Donahue
Alvin E. Ohlsson
John J. Osness
William John Peterson
Lyman Plyer
Joseph Thomas Reil
Maurice Ristvedt
Robert T. Roberts
Thomas B. Robinson

Winfield Nye Robinson
Edward D. Rogers
Arthur Rose
Joseph M. Saric
Lyle P. Schroeer
John E. Sharp
William E. Skews
George William Steinmetz
Daniel Sullivan
Robert Tweet
Rolland Vocelka
Thomas D. Warner
Wesley Warvi
Charles F. Watson
Wilbur Wicks
Sherman Yankee

Korea

Wayne R. Amelung
Donald E. Anderson
Philip V. Deragon
Lawrence Ferkovich

John Ellis Laborg
Edward M. Morrison
Thomas E. Nelson
Donald D. Shaw

Jack Weister

Vietnam

Frederick A. Berweger
Marvin L. Erickson
Keith Brian Janke
Kenneth L. Strittmater

These lists of Korean and Vietnam War dead have been compiled from official United States Department of Defense rolls supplied by the Wisconsin Department of Veterans Affairs. Neither the federal or state veterans department claims that these lists are complete. If an Ashland native did not use an Ashland address when he entered the military, his name is not listed with Ashland veterans. Consequently, there are probably some names of Ashland natives missing here. We apologize if we have missed the name of any man or woman who died in service. At the same time, the State Department of Veterans Affairs and the local office in Ashland would like to set the record straight. If you know of any Ashlander who died in Korea or Vietnam and is not on this list, please contact the veterans service office in Ashland.

Admiral William D. Leahy, 1875-1957

William Leahy was born in Hampton, Iowa, the son of Michael Leahy, an Indian agent who moved his family to Ashland shortly after William's birth.

After he graduated from Ashland High School in 1892, Leahy hoped to gain appointment to West Point. When his Congressman told him there were no openings at the army academy, Leahy successfully applied to Annapolis. He graduated just in time to see action on board the battleship *Oregon* in the Spanish-American War.

He later served in the Pacific during the Philippine Insurrection and the Boxer Rebellion in China. During World War I, Leahy commanded the dispatch boat *Dolphin* in the Caribbean. His last active command was off Nicaragua, during the American occupation of that land in the 1930s.

Leahy reached the professional naval officer's highest post when he was named Chief of Naval Operations in the late 1930s. After retiring from the Navy in 1939, Leahy was appointed Governor of Puerto Rico by President Franklin Roosevelt. Prior to American entry into World War II, he served as Ambassador to the Vichy regime in France.

After the United States entered the war, Leahy came home to serve as Roosevelt's Chief of Staff and Chief of All American Forces. He accompanied the President to the crucial Casablanca Conference and helped formulate the grand strategy for victory in World War II.

Leahy was proud of his Ashland roots. He returned to the city for the 1948 Homecoming of old settlers and gave the keynote speech at the 1954 Centennial Celebration. When Leahy died in 1957, the Navy chartered an airplane to carry fifty Ashlanders to the funeral.

Ashland naval hero William Leahy at mid-career.

The City of Ashland presented this medal to soldiers for service in World War I.

Veterans of five wars met in the 1950s. (l to r, bottom) William Dormady, WW II; Albert Woolson (Duluth), Civil War; Bill Dowden, Korea; (top) Bill Provost, WW I; Oliver Dandeneau, Spanish-American War; Nate Cohodas, WW II.

Company A of the Wisconsin National Guard training in The Barrens. Hub Wallace, Howie Pearson and Dugan Pearson are in the picture here. During World Wars I and II, troops guarded the docks and Ashland Junction rail lines.

Robert J. Piff (third from left) on a patrol boat at Cat Lai in Vietnam, 1970.

The Faces of Ashland

"The people who live in Ashland own Ashland."
Ashland Daily Press, *1892*

A myriad of avenues of communication exist for an individual or an entire society to share values with others. Transmission of information can be by written or spoken word, or it may be symbolized by other means such as fashion, culture or the built world. A human structure can serve as a communication medium when it conveys—through attention to detail, embellishments, and the degree of investment in quality of materials—the elements valued by the owner and designer.

Through form and function, architecture makes a statement which summarizes the habits, attitudes and needs of a people at a specific time. It uses repetition to reinforce those beliefs. Architecture becomes art when it communicates a statement of value.

Architecture is also an historical reference for documenting the economic and social mores of past generations.

Settlers came to Ashland by the hundreds following the city's connection to the national rail system in 1877. Some came to labor, others to invest and make jobs. All required places to live and conduct business.

An 1891 issue of the *Daily Press* proclaimed, "The people who live in Ashland, own Ashland. This fact makes it the most desirable place for solid investment of capital in legitimate business enterprises, thus the substantial growth of the city is assured . . ."

Ashland's city fathers were primarily upper middle class Yankees of established wealth and position from Maine, Ohio, Pennsylvania and the cities of Detroit, Chicago and St.

Looking east on Second Street West in the early 1800s. Both street and sidewalks are raised on piers and surfaced with wooden planks. When the boards were replaced with earth fill, the original first story of many buildings was buried. Large building at left is old County Courthouse located where the Post Office now stands.

111

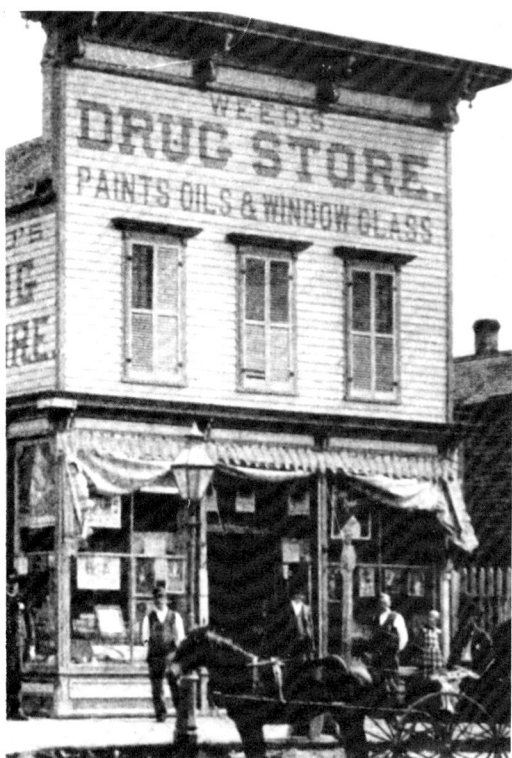

In 1888, the 400 Block of West Second Street is lined with frame structures and the streetcar is horse-drawn.

Weed's Drug and Paint store had a typical boomtown false front. Big windows provided excellent display space downstairs.

Paul. These people came to gamble on investment. They came to develop and build. They came to increase their profits. They made Ashland their home and thus, by their investment, they established a city.

These city builders came from diverse geographical locations. Each brought with him his preference in architecture and life style. They arrived with their families in a wilderness, but they insisted on having familiar elements of sophistication, luxury and comfort. Their diverse, sophisticated tastes gave newborn Ashland the image of a most modern city. By 1892, nearly every home and business in Ashland had access to city sewer and water, gas and electricity. New construction and improvements totalled two million dollars that year. In less than a decade, Ashland was transformed from boom town to an established metropolitan city.

Evidence of this transition is readily witnessed by changes in construction and style of commercial buildings. In the late 1870s and early 1880s, Second Street was lined with clapboard structures. The easy availability of lumber from local mills influenced the style of construction.

From a design point of view, the boom-town or false-front commercial building simply extended the facade so that the building appeared larger than it was. This image did not fool the citizenry, but it provided symbolic

By 1908, the storefronts are brick, sidewalks are concrete and lined with curbstones, and the streetcar is electric. Masonic Hall is at right front.

evidence of civilizing progress.

Clustered together, false-front buildings suggested an interesting profile of orderly balance because lot sizes were generally similar, while composition and design relationship were proportional. These storefronts helped to create a defined business district and gave the sense of a developing center which conveyed an image of progress and prosperity. In short, the false fronts made the buildings appear larger than they were and grander than their owners could afford.

After city incorporation, the false-front buildings were replaced by more permanent-appearing brick structures or were incorporated into buildings with brick or stone veneers. As merchants grew more prosperous they wanted more imposing buildings, and cut stone was now as available as wood once was. The 1890s saw rapid industrial and technological advances. New construction methodology, as well as implementation, and zoning and building codes led to the construction of more sophisticated, quality structures. Continuing economic success allowed for more substantial property investment.

The brick storefront was built as a single building or sometimes in groups separated by party walls. While they varied in height from two to three stories, their basic plans were quite similar. A store occupied the ground

Powers and Fosshage Grocery in the 700 Block of West Second was an excellent example of ornate corbelled brickwork.

113

In 1890, the Security Savings Bank was faced with brownstone. Thirty years later the building was remodeled with black granite stonework.

floor, with living quarters upstairs. In many areas of downtown Ashland, street grade allowed for many garden level service shops with their entrances a few steps below street level.

Brick-front organization resulted from repeated themes or rhythms—window and door openings, height. Display space was provided by large, oversized windows on the first floor. As these stores were often narrow and quite deep, these windows provided a necessary source of indirect light reflected by gloss-painted tin ceilings. Display windows also provided an excellent space for inspection of merchandise by potential customers on the street and eliminated the need for elaborate signs.

The upper levels of these storefronts allowed space for freedom of expression through decorative panels of geometric brickwork, friezes and cornices with elaborate corbeling and metal work. The commonly-used continuous lintel or sill bound the building laterally. The cornice was a cap under which other elements were arranged. The name of the owner and date of construction were often included in the design as a further statement of permanence.

Bay windows were used to bring additional interior light to stores like the Garnich and Levy building since taller buildings cast shadows on their neighbors. The increased use of stone in buildings symbolized the maturity and strength of the downtown district.

The Shores Block housed the first Northern State Bank.

An arcade or commercial block like the Wilmarth Block enforced the image of permanence. It was the symbolic marriage of commercial and residential life for a community. Residential in scale, the business block was intended to be an imposing structure which employed the latest high-style architectural design.

The Shores Block is a fine example of a corner block or arcade block. As a corner property, it was designed to be viewed from two elevations. The cantered, or corner, entrance focused attention on the union of two commercial streets. The use of rounded arches called arcades gave the style its name. In the late 1880s, the designs of architect H.H. Richardson were considered the most modern and sophisticated of American architecture. Characteristic of the so-called Richardsonian-Romanesque design were the traits of strength and solidity through a treatment of coursing stonework, contrasting surfaces, deeply recessed windows and curvilinear design. As a potential metropolis, Ashland fashioned its most substantial blocks in the Richardsonian style.

The ability of architecture to communicate values through image is recognized in the evolution of two of Ashland's major banking institutions.

Northern State Bank had its first home in the Shores Block in 1890. The interplay of brick and stone on the building's exterior

symbolized strength. The location in a corner block signified the bank's significance as the heart of the business community. Even the interior reflected an image of security for investment which the bank wished to portray to its customers. The embellishments of quality finishes conveyed an air of sophistication to investors.

In the early 1920s, the bank constructed a temple-like, Greek Revival structure which was decorated with pillars of strength. In contrast to its predecessor, the new building had clean lines to imply the image of conservative, sound banking practices. This structure was

The Wilmarth Block was one of many commercial properties that helped make Lewis Wilmarth a real estate magnate.

The Ashland National Bank building is the Security Plaza today. Its classical style represented conservative solidity in the 1920s.

Thomas Bardon's Ashland National Bank opened at 518 Second Street in 1884.

imposing but serious—as permanent and sophisticated as Greek philosophy.

Ashland National Bank, now Union National, is another example of the relationship between image and architecture. In 1884, Ashland National was housed in Thomas Bardon's building in the 500 block of West Second. It had an Italianate storefront, a style popular in the 1870s and 80s. This was one of the first successful styles of commercial storefront built from manufactured materials and was one of Ashland's first brick commercial properties. The window treatment of tall two-over-two segmented windows with corbelled surrounds and a central entrance were the primary characteristics of the Italianate style.

By 1891, the bank constructed an imposing arcade block, complete with a corner topped by a tower which rose from a recessed, cantered entrance. Romanesque in style, with arches meeting at the corner on a column of brownstone, this imposing rusticated stone and brick structure established the new heart of downtown Ashland at Ellis and Second Street. The site proclaimed the flamboyant strength of a community soon to be the giant of the northland.

The Ashland National Bank at Second and Ellis. With its arched windows, corner entrance and turret, the building was one of Ashland's most impressive structures.

By 1926, a new image for banking was established. Not to be outdone by its competitor, Ashland National also adopted an image of stability and antiquity. Classical Revival in style, the building was intended to evoke images of wisdom and permanence for investors. No longer were Ashlanders defying the elements. The community had evolved to a level of culture and high-style.

Union National's 1970s building makes a statement which reflects modern banking practice and philosophy—security, yes, embellishment, no. The current Union National Bank building makes a statement of conservative strength but with a serious, no-nonsense approach.

Ashland's commercial architectural evolution can also be seen in its schools. Before this century, only the most affluent property owners hired architects. Excepted from this rule were substantial commercial properties, government and institutional buildings. The value a society of immigrants and first generation Americans placed on education was reflected in the investment made by the public sector in its educational facilities. In Ashland, all of the educational properties were designed by well known architects and no expense was spared on their construction.

Ashland public schools presented an image of the highest style of architecture popular at the time of their construction, Richardsonian

Ashland High School

Henry Wildhagen, 1856-1920

Henry Wildhagen was Ashland's most prolific builder. He was born in Germany and emigrated to the United States. By the mid-1880s he was already a successful industrial architect who specialized in designing paper mills. He built the first sulfite paper mill in the United States in Alpena, Michigan and other mills in New Hampshire, Michigan and Wisconsin. He came to Ashland to execute just such a commission for the Menasha Paper Company in 1892 and liked the community enough to make it his home.

Between 1895 and 1905, Wildhagen designed approximately 150 buildings within a fifty-mile radius of Ashland. He built fifteen schools, including the four distinctive stone and brick schools in Ashland. He also designed Holy Family church and school and supervised construction of a major addition to St. Joseph's Hospital. Many of Wildhagen's buildings, like the Ashland schools, are on the National Register of Historic Places. Ashland's architecture is distinctive and distinguished. It owes much of its quality to Henry Wildhagen.

Romanesque. Wilmarth and Beaser schools were designed by architect Henry Wildhagen and were constructed of the finest brick and brownstone the region had to offer. The substantial dollar investment in the construction of these properties by local taxpayers reflected a philosophy which appeared to state: education can never cost too much.

The overall massing of these buildings, even their prime real estate locations, reflected the priority of education as an investment for the future. Except for the present City Hall building and the Knight Hotel, Ashland schools—especially old Ashland High (also designed by Wildhagen and built by Archie Donald and Frank Tomlinson)—were among the grandest properties in the city.

Contemporary educational facilities have adopted dollar-conservative, scaled-down

Ninth Avenue School

Ellis School

Bay City School

Beaser School

Central School

Wilmarth School

The new Ashland High School opened in the fall of 1973. Over six hundred students in grades nine through twelve take classes at the Beaser Avenue location.

design and construction. In a society where even a secondary education is an assumed, rather than a luxury, the lack of embellishment demonstrates a shift in attitude. Schools now offer educational services and curricula unheard of a century ago. In addition, changes in building design, materials and cost of personnel have made modern schools look and function very differently than their predecessors.

How Ashlanders perceived their environment has also changed in the past century. Wheeler Hall on the Northland Campus can serve as a symbol of the pioneer attitude of defiance towards the harsh northern environment. The building was erected on a then treeless bluff with its main entrance facing north. At the time of its construction, the building must have looked like a man-made mountain, a pinnacle of excellence, challenging the wilderness with its sophistication. In contrast, Northland's Sigurd Olson Institute, built eighty-five years later, presents an almost invisible image. Designed to blend with the environment, its entrance facing south to be warmed by the sun, the Institute demonstrates how Ashlanders have tried to become a part of the environment, at odds with it no longer. The permanence of the community has been realized.

North Wisconsin Academy

The City of Homes

In the last quarter of the last century the "American Dream" of individual home ownership became popular. The literature of the time is full of essays on the subject of home and house building.

"A house is the shell, the hive in which busy hands and anxious hearts combine their toil and hope, ever looking toward that impenetrable vail, behind which is concealed the future and the true ideal of *home* . . ." said one popular author in 1876. These sentiments were felt in Ashland, which had a rich climate for the fulfillment of the homebuilder's dream. The city is fortunate to have inherited much of the region's finest domestic architecture.

Homes in Ashland are of two principal sorts, vernacular or styled houses. In an architectural context, vernacular refers to buildings without a pure, recognizable style. Often fairly simple, this type was generally a scaled-down interpretation of a style, which incorporated modest elements of a more stylized structure. Vernacular types generally result from a third-hand exposure to a style modified by local resources and economics. By comparison, styled houses are true to

The Martin Juhl home on St. Claire Street was a simple Victorian vernacular home circled by a very elaborate, hand-turned cow fence.

The Dr. Joseph Madden home at 523 Chapple was a Queen Anne mansion. Striped awnings were both decorative and functional.

Stick-style houses on Prentice Avenue were painted in multi-colored finery. Even roof shingles were painted in different shades.

particular design. Ashland has many surviving examples of pure *Queen Anne, Revival, Stick, Shingle, Richardsonian Romanesque* and *Second Renaissance Revival* styles.

With more than a dozen sawmills along its shore, Ashland had at its disposal a wide variety of locally manufactured wood products. They were used to erect and enrich the finest homes, chiefly those in the *Stick, Queen Anne* and *Shingle* styles. Particularly noteworthy are surviving homes on Beaser, Ellis, Prentice, Chapple and MacArthur Avenues, as well as those on Second Avenue West and Fifield Place. They were the homes of the founding opportunists and developers who used their houses to visually express their wealth and success. These three styles were intended to express their frame construction through the use of exposed timbers, contrasting paint colors, and carved and sawcut ornaments that reinforced the significance of lumber in the community. Common design characteristics included a tall center with a vertical thrust, asymmetrical massing, projecting gables and bays, interconnected interior and exterior spaces, and a central plan with hallways circulating around a core.

The *Stick* style was perhaps Ashland's most

frequently used residential style at the turn of the century. Characteristics include tall proportions, applied stickwork as exposed framing and bracketing, steeply-pitched and ornate gables, plus a picturesque roof line often highlighted by a tower. The arrangement of the clapboard and vergeboard in a combination of horizontal and vertical patterns of various dimensions suggests the stacking of lumber, or "sticks," and emphasizes the frame construction. Often the use of as many as a dozen paint colors were used to highlight the framing.

The *Eastlake* style is a variation of the *Stick* style highlighted by a great deal of embellishment and chiseled detail of floral or geometric patterns. Charles Eastlake became a well-known artist in the 1870s. His work inspired housing styles and influenced both interior and exterior design, from furniture to wrought iron fences and stencil patterns to wall papers. Elements of *Eastlake* design are quite evident on many porch aprons, fretwork and gable brackets in Ashland.

An offshoot of the *Stick* and *Eastlake* styles were the *Picturesque* and *Queen Anne* styles. Reminiscent of French palatial cottages, *Picturesque* took Eastlake a step further in embellishment.

The *Queen Anne* style came to Ashland with some of its East Coast settlers. The style is characterized by a massive scale, complex plans, with a strong sense of centrality. Projecting wings, intersecting gables, towers or turrets, and the mixed use of clapboard and shingles for exterior cladding are part of the style.

A more subdued version of the *Queen Anne* style is called the *Princess Anne*, which embodies many of the same elements, modified and scaled down with hipped roof lines.

Shingle style is the last of the ornate woodframed Ashland styles. It differs from *Queen Anne* and *Stick* styles in that the framing is primarily hidden. It has large geometric proportions with extended roof lines, wide gambrel or gable roof, and full or partial cladding of row-set shingles.

An excellent surviving and recently restored example of *Shingle* style is found at 701 Chapple, originally the home of attorney E.F. Gleason. Typical of this style is the occurrence of a semicircular wall or porch, a horizontal flow of space and a visual line which causes the structure to appear close to the ground, i.e. heavy, rather than "spiring." Other examples of the *Shingle* style residences can be found at 221 Twelfth Avenue East, 810 MacArthur, 901 Chapple, 608 Ninth Avenue West and 600 West Third Street.

The most popular category of turn-of-the-century residential architecture is known as *Late Picturesque*. It broadly includes all the

Previous Page

The brick and stone Shores Mansion with its shingled dormers was one of Ashland's most impressive residences. However, the wrap-a-round porch had room for a hammock.

The Emeline Vaughn home was built in Eastlake style with a flair for the chateauesque.

Archie Donald, 1858-1911

As his name indicates, Archibald Donald was born in Scotland. He apprenticed as a stonecutter there, learning the trade that would become so important to his adopted city of Ashland.

Donald came to the Bay in 1887 and soon after set to work laying stone at St. Agnes Catholic Church. He also cut the brownstone used for the Northern National Bank and then for most of the other stone buildings downtown.

In 1890, Donald was in partnership with Frank Tomlinson as contractors for brick and stonework. They had a twenty-five year lease on the Washburn brownstone quarries and hauled stone across the Bay in scows pulled by tugs to build the breakwaters in Ashland.

Some of Donald's finest work was done on Wheeler Hall at Northland, St. Joseph's Hospital and the old Ashland High School. He also served as a county supervisor and was twice elected register of deeds. For many years he was the best known and most popular singer of Scots songs at Masonic Socials and birthday parties in honor of Robert Burns.

---

other styles of its time and variations thereon. It was a common practice for the affluent to refer to their homes as "cottages." They often took the designs for their cottages out of an ad in a fashionable magazine such as *Godey's Choice*, which sold plans, or they showed the illustration to a local contractor. A residence which might have been built this way is *Evergreen Cottage*, the home of Sam Fifield at One Fifield Place. Sears also specialized in catalog houses. A person could buy the plans or purchase the house pre-cut and delivered ready to assemble. The home at 715 West Sixth Street is an example of a *Victorian* pre-fab.

Several *Victorian* styles are not well represented in Ashland, although a few single examples exist. The most significant existing property is the former L.C. Wilmarth residence at 522 Chapple. Designed in the *Georgian Revival* style with classically detailed facade, pediments, columns and symmetrical facades, it was one of Ashland's most elegant homes. Its rich interior demonstrates the sophisticated level of craftsmanship available to those who could afford it.

An example of the *Jacobethan* style house for 1890 is the residence at 822 Chapple which features a shingled low gable roof with projecting dormers. This structure differs from the post-1900 *Tudor* style at 1021 Second Avenue West and 823 Ninth Avenue West in that it does not utilize the technique of half timber work with stucco.

One example of the *Italianate* style in residential construction still in good repair is 615 Vaughn Avenue. Its features include a rectangular plan, coupled with S-scroll brackets, flat hip roof and tall narrow windows.

A wide variety of vernacular residential architecture survives in Ashland. As better than fifty per cent of the residences in Ashland are more than sixty-five years old, many examples of each vernacular style, in various states of preservation, still stand. The simplest type is the two story frame house with a gabled roof and simple rectangular windows with or without porches or verandas. One story houses, with a central hip roof are also frequently found, such as those at 704 Willis, 310 East Sixth Street or 520 West Seventh Street. Another often seen vernacular style is the L-plan, commonly called a "basic old house."

The two most significant styles used in Ashland after 1900 were the *Prairie School* and the *Bungaloid*. As the century turned, public taste seemed to reject the overly-stated, showy styles of the *Late Picturesque* period. Homes were scaled down. Most popular was the *American Foursquare* house, which is typically two stories tall with a low and broad-hipped, often dormered, roof.

Prairie style was given its name because it purposely exaggerated the horizontal lines of the house to put them in harmony with the broad flat spaces of the midwestern grasslands. The basic plan is adopted from the *Foursquare*, but the strong horizontal line is transmitted by low roof, wide eaves, and a horizontal band of windows. A stucco finish gave it a monolithic quality, sometimes interrupted by wood strips for variety. A fine example of the style exists at 704 Ninth Avenue West.

The *Bungalow* is a unique American house type which borrowed its form from other

cultures but used American sensibility and materials to produce an original design. As Americans became more interested in compact living, built-in storage, simple furnishings, and a more casual life style the *Bungalow* style evolved. It was the first American style which seemed bigger inside than it appeared outside. Inexpensive plans that illustrated many variations on the one and one-and-a-half story designs were available by mail. This fact resulted in the construction of many nearly identical structures like those seen at 1011 and 1005 Ellis. Hanson and Nystrom were two local contractors who built many bungalows.

A single example of the *International* style of the 1940s exists at 1301 Vaughn Avenue. Designed by a Detroit architectural firm, it won the House of the Year Award in *The Ladies Home Journal* in the early 1940s.

Since World War II the style of homes in Ashland has become homogenous with the rest of the country. Mass communication and transportation have given access to a national market and culture. Homes with distinctive geographical styles like the wood and stone rich Ashland homes of old are built no more.

Mom and Pop on the porch of the "basic old house" that most Ashlanders called home.

Places for Gathering

"...the best commercial house in the Northwest."
1890s ad for the Colby House

The old Chequamegon Hotel stood on the present grounds of the Ashland County Courthouse. It was intended to be the centerpiece of the city for both residents and visitors.

A hotel is a gathering place for social and professional exchange, a facility for lodging and dining, a privately-owned, public building. Whether boomtown or metropolis, every nineteenth century city had a hotel or boarding house that was the visitor's first stop, a dining room and public meeting place. Ashland was no exception.

In 1871, J.M. Davis arrived in Ashland from Belmont City, Ohio. He soon opened the Colby House, Ashland's first hotel, at the corner of Vaughn and West Second Street. The Colby House was a modest ten-room frame structure which served salesmen and other travelers. A few years later, the ten-room Penoka Hotel was also providing lodging for the commercial trade.

The original Colby House burned down in 1881 and Davis built a $6,000 replacement. The new Colby could seat eighty in its dining room, and a substantial pot-belly presided over a lobby that became a gathering-place for story-swapping railroad men. By the mid-1890s, Frank Ingalls was the manager and the hotel billed itself as the "best and oldest commercial house in the Northwest." It was one of more than twenty lodging houses in the city, each one catering to a specific segment of the traveling public.

The boarding house became a home away from home for many salesmen. Each drummer had his favorite stopping place and proprietors would often reserve the room the salesman liked best. Friendships were formed and many commercial travelers would coordinate their visits and meet in Ashland for long nights of poker and cribbage.

The Leland began life as The Merchants Hotel at 213 Third Avenue West. Located near the Union Depot, the Leland offered special rates to lumber dealers and charged $1.50 for an overnight stay. The Michigan

The Colby House, Ashland's first hotel, stood at the northeast corner of Vaughn and Second Streets.

House, with its Sample Room where salesmen could display their wares, was located at 200 West Second Street and charged a reasonable rate of $1.00 a day. The Revere House, at 220 Third Avenue West, was owned by Sam Ormond and boasted of being the hotel closest to the depot. The Tremont House, next door to the opera house on Third Avenue West, catered to actors and other show people. Hotel rates at the turn-of-the-century ranged from $1.00 to $1.50 per night, with a $4.00 charge for a week's stay.

On the list of commercial hotels were: The Commercial Hotel of Mrs. Anna McNeill, which offered "first class accommodations at a reasonable rate;" the Hopkins House of J. Hopkins with its "homelike atmosphere;" the Northern, located on the second floor of the J.C. Penney store at Fourth Avenue West and Second; the Scandinavian Hotel, the White River House and the Central House.

Ashland also offered a wide selection of restaurants. The Boston Eating House of F.G. Asbach featured fresh pastry and served short orders day or night. A ticket good for twenty-four meals cost $5.00 and $3.50 would buy sixteen. Schupp's Restaurant at 307 West Second Street specialized in fish and game of the season and also featured a lunch counter. The Boston Ideal at 118 West Second Avenue had a restaurant and coffee house. Fred Smith's Greenhouse offered an ice cream and soda parlor set amongst the ferns and aquariums he had for sale.

Resort hotels were multi-purpose lodging

Peterson's Boarding House offered accommodations for working people as early as 1872.

houses offering rest in a healthful environment, opportunities for social contacts and business dealings, and amusements of all sorts. Since Colonial days, Americans who could afford the time and expense have visited resort hotels near the shore or in the unspoiled countryside.

The growth of the middle class in the nineteenth century greatly increased the number of people able and willing to travel to

The lobby of the old Chequamegon.

resorts. Railroads gave them the means to travel farther and faster than ever before. It was logical for the railroads to encourage travel by building and investing in resort hotels in attractive places like Ashland. By encouraging travel in northern Wisconsin, railroads also took the opportunity to show their extensive land holdings to prospective buyers. So it is no surprise that two months after the rail line south from Ashland was completed the Wisconsin Central opened the Chequamegon Hotel under contract to Pratt and Andress.

Originally built with sixty rooms in a large L-shape, the Chequamegon sported four hundred feet of veranda and commanded an unequalled view of the Bay. By 1885, the building was shaped like a giant **J** spreading 250 feet across. A shaded court with a pretty fountain, croquet grounds and walks to the billiard hall and bowling alley were located between the wings. The broad veranda surrounding the building was expanded to 530 feet and was referred to as the hotel's finest feature, offering as it did a splendid shaded promenade along the lakefront.

In July 1880, the Wisconsin Central hosted a tour for Associated Press reporters that included Ashland and the Chequamegon Hotel. The purpose of the junket was to publicize the northland and the reporters, in return for five days of travel, fine dining and lodging, were happy to oblige. The reporter for the Wilmington, Illinois *Advocate* enthused:

> ...The Chequamegon is a commodious structure surrounded with wide verandas commanding a fine view of the bay...The outlook—Venetian in its beauty—more than convinces the traveler that one need not go abroad to find magnificent scenery. Ashland is a little place of 700 inhabitants, aboriginal, half-breed, foreign and American. It is situated on a broad plateau sixty feet above the bay and is becoming noted as a rural retreat for invalids and sportsmen; the streams in the vicinity...being filled with trout and its large lumber interests commanding the attention of foreign shippers, one-half of the products of these mills being sent to England...
>
> Immediately after breakfast the party were invited...out in the steamer *Eva Wadsworth*, others cruised the bay in sailboats. Returning in good season the evening was passed in sociality, music, and dancing in the drawingrooms, promenading on the verandas, etc. A band of music was kept on duty in the corridors of the hotel during our entire stay; the house was decorated with mosses, ferns and evergreens, until one needed by small imaginative powers to believe we were within sylvan shadows in fairy dells...

Such editorial accounts of Ashland and the finery of the Chequamegon helped spur Ashland's growth. Six months after incorporation the city hosted a banquet celebrating its progress and the Chequamegon Hotel was the most appropriate site.

The Chequamegon was the pinnacle of sophistication and elegance in the northland for over a dozen years. Its reign ended in 1891 when John Knight built his hotel.

If the substance of a city can be illustrated by the solid character of its buildings, if they in turn denote the character and enterprise of its citizens, then the Chequamegon and Knight Hotels can be used to gauge the development of Ashland. The Chequamegon, a wooden structure, was built in Ashland's pioneer days. The Knight, built of brownstone, signalled the end of pioneer times and marked a second era of progress for the city.

The Knight was designed to be the most striking feature on the cityscape. It would not only serve the tourist and salesman, it would also be a "temple of trade" for Ashland. The ground floor was intended to house the finest stores and the second floor would accommodate business and professional offices. Several generations of Ashlanders went nowhere else but the Knight when they needed a doctor, dentist, realtor or lawyer.The entire structure was called the Knight Block to denote its status not as just a hotel but as a commercial block as well.

The Knight was billed as the first fireproof building in the city. Twelve inches of sand was placed between the joists between floors to prevent fire from spreading. The kitchen was cut off from the rest of the building and the boiler room was isolated with fireproof doors, walls and ceiling. The building also had its own power plant, with generators supplying

The Knight Hotel was a massive block of stone that served as a commercial, residential and social center for decades.

light and power for two elevators.

The Hotel had a fourth floor dining room, billiard room and a Music Hall with seating for 500 people. It was designed to attract lecturers, parties and conventions. Only the best Haviland China, silver and crystal were used on the tables in the dining room, which soon became nationally famous for its planked whitefish. Over half the guest rooms had connecting baths, and each one had a sink. Every floor in every room was of polished maple and all the carpets throughout the building were the best Wilton and Body Brussels. The lobby was one hundred feet long with a mosaic tile floor and was lined with numerous rocking chairs. The hotel's first manager was F.A. Whitney who was the former manager of the Montezuma Resort Hotel in Hot Springs, New Mexico.

When the Knight Hotel opened in time for the tourist season in 1892, a grand opening ball was attended by many dignitaries, including Governor George Peck and Senator Henry Vilas. The Knight's guest list grew to include John D. Rockefeller and Marshall Field and many others who traveled on the Northwestern's *Ashland Special* weekend train.

As the Knight gained prestige, the Chequamegon declined. A fire in the mid-1890s damaged the building and it became a workingman's lodging house. Its core was moved to the northwest corner of Second Street and Seventh Avenue West and renamed The Culver. It was later called The Menard and its dining room was noted for its fine food until it was destroyed by fire in 1957.

Means of transportation and commerce have changed greatly in this century. The automobile gave birth to the motel and the concentration of businesses into a downtown block like the Knight became less attractive. Between 1950 and 1984, 248 motel rooms were built in Ashland, and the lodging needs of tourists are met by the Aloha, Anderson's Chequamegon, Ashland, Bay Manor, Bell, Crest, Harbor, Holiday House, Lake Aire, Lakeside, L-Gene, Super 8 and Town Motels.

Just as the construction of the Knight Hotel

The new Chequamegon harkens back to the days of its namesake and hopes to be the centerpiece of a revitalized Ashland.

signalled an era of development for Ashland in 1891, it may be said that the construction of the new Hotel Chequamegon marks another era of growth and prosperity for the city. The new Chequamegon, whose design and facilities take their roots from the past giants of Ashland, has begun to reestablish the city as a point of destination for the tourist and commercial trade. The Chequamegon measures 180 x 80 feet and ascends almost 90 feet from its foundation on the lake side. Built less than one hundred yards from the site of the original Chequamegon, and fashioned in its style, the new Chequamegon sits on the disposal site for the demolished Knight. Perhaps this is a note of historic irony. It appears that the new era for Ashland, marked by this centennial of incorporation, has its roots deeply in the past.

Welcoming Sights

"No country in the world affords better facilities for gratifying the desire...to enjoy a season with Nature, than does our grand Lake Superior country..."
Ashland Daily Press, *1893*

The "Skater" was a popular excursion boat for trips to the Apostle Islands.

A shirtwaist dancing party given by the Elks in the Eagle Club at the turn of the century.

Formal balls were held in the sun room on the top floor of the Knight Hotel. Women wore lovely dresses. Men wore top hats, tails and white gloves.

The Old Faithful Spring at Prentice Park.

The Scottie Club fountain west of Ashland.

Grace Sexton and her popcorn wagon were popular fixtures at public events for many years.

An elegant visitor at the Ashland County Fair circa 1900.

The Brownstone Bowl near Bodin's Resort offered swimming, log rolling and three diving boards.

Catching the wind during a sailing race at Bay Days in 1979.

Ashland children sing "Put a Little Love in Your Heart."

Winter is never too cold for ice fishing on the Bay.

Flowers planted in the center of Ellis Avenue helped give Ashland the title of "The Garland City."

Ashland's mute swans are beautiful symbols of the city. However, if a Department of Natural Resources plan is realized, mute swans will be replaced by native American trumpeter swans.

The Competitive Spirit

"All the days in Ashland . . . that I went through, I enjoyed them all."
John Verbrocken

Judge Joseph W. Cochran, president of the Northern National Bank and friends after a successful moose hunt in 1902.

"We used to ice skate on the Bay. We'd punch holes in the ice and the tide would flood the rink," said Howie Pearson. His words make a good description of the photo.

138

Two Nimrods back from the field in the late 1800s.

Ashland defeated Superior 6-0 in this hard fought contest in which H. McRae ran seventy-eight yards for the only score. Playing for Ashland were: H. Serles, C. Nordstrand, A. Clauser, H. Sampson, S. Brace, T. Penn, R. Austin, R. Blalnik, R. French, R. Paulson, and L. Freeman.

"Ashland's Greatest Baseball Team," of 1898, included (l to r, top) R. Burns, George Vaughl, Art Armstrong, Oscar Toeppel, Reuben Tarbox, Bolton Scott. (second row) Ed Kellogg, Scott Tomkins, Eugene Kuntz. (bottom) Lyman Pool, Frank Hughes.

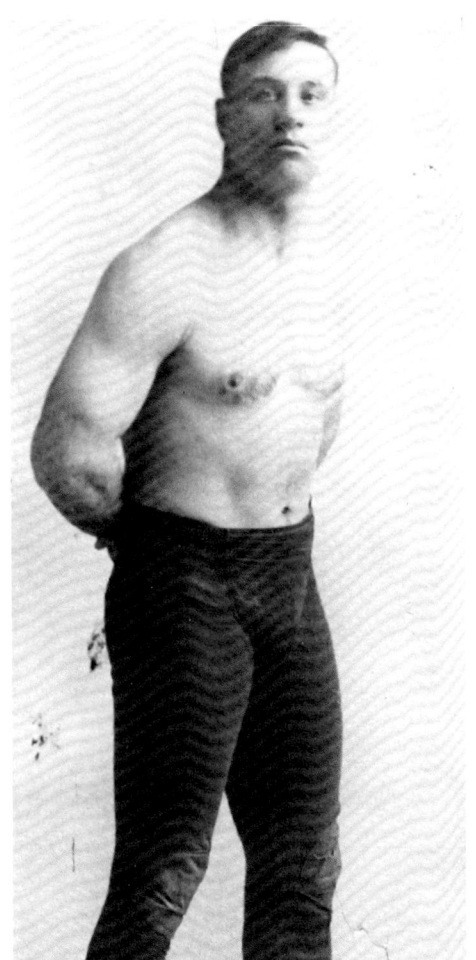

Elmer Sanders, Wisconsin heavyweight wrestling champion, at the height of his career in 1920.

Charles Yderstad in 1946. He was the first All-State footballer from Ashland and was named All-Big Ten at the University of Wisconsin. Yderstad is currently working as a civil engineer in Minneapolis.

The 1946 Michigan-Wisconsin Conference Champions. (l to r, front) Skip Skjeir, Myron Anderson, Clare Goldsmith, Rodney Asplund, Robert Olson, Allen Zar, Fill Ottman, Jerry Hines, Tom Ziolkowski, David Westby, Dave Siminski, Charles Yderstad, Roy Klein, Stan Kivela, Ken Tidstrom. (second row) Coach Harold Nielson, Coach Roy Melvin, John Carlson, Frank Sidel, Dick Magnuson, Don Larson, Bob Lindholm, Kelley Douglas, Bob Bond, Pete Peterson, Elwood Leren, Ed Ziolkowski, Bob Howard, Fred Tidstrom, Harry Jozawiz, Stu Melviny. (third row) Wilcox La Plavey, Bill Chase, Bill White, Jeff Wattson, Dave Penn, Bundy Peterson, unidentified, unidentified, Larry Hines, unidentified, Bob Sky, unindentified, Bob Larson, unidentified, Erv Larson.

The 1945 basketball team placed third in Wisconsin. (l to r) Coach Roy Melvin, Bob Howard, Bruce Fossum, Bob Hanson, Charley Nelson, Ken Tidstrom, Dick Axnes, Vern Fryklund, Duane Ruth, Harvey Johnson, George Papadakis. (inset) Jake Knokol and Kelly Butterworth.

Lt. Governor Sam Fifield and Charles Carlston show off a string of lunkers after a day on the Bay aboard the "Sam Fifield."

Roy Prince and a big one from the Bay in the 1920s.

A fine catch of Bay trout by Sam Veda in 1987.

Crack skiers from all over the country competed at the National Ski Tournament at the White River Hill in 1907. Ashland's Aksel Holter was instrumental in making the city the ski center of the United States in the early 1900s. The Holter Ski, the first factory-made skis in America, were made here.

Six young men ready to try out their new Holter skis.

Aksel Holter was one of the first four inductees into the National Ski Association's Hall of Fame at Ishpeming, Michigan in 1965. Holter was one of the founders of the Association and a pioneer-builder of the sport.

1983 Baseball Sectional Champs. (l to r, front) Craig Roberts, Craig Gast, Rob Melin, John Reimer, Ralph Hall, Jerry Yachinich, Rod Stibbe, Coach Fran Hicks. (back) Brian Stolarzyk, Dave Roberts, Dan Ante, Fred Tidstrom, Mike Mestelle, Dave Martinson, Todd Cabe, Chris Barnes, Brian Chingo, Bill Mestelle.

1984 runner-up WPAA Girls Softball Team. (l to r, front) Linda Beiersdorff, Amy Nuutinen, Kim Sellung, Jeanne Martino, Joanne Becksma, Julie Gregoire, Annette Vandeventer, Mary Lynch. (back) Coach Donna Brown, Gigi Cloud, Wally Bressette, Jodi Vandeventer, Marilyn Puig, Ann Bretting, Janeen Beiersdorff, Pam Gordon, Asst. Coach Karen O'Malley.

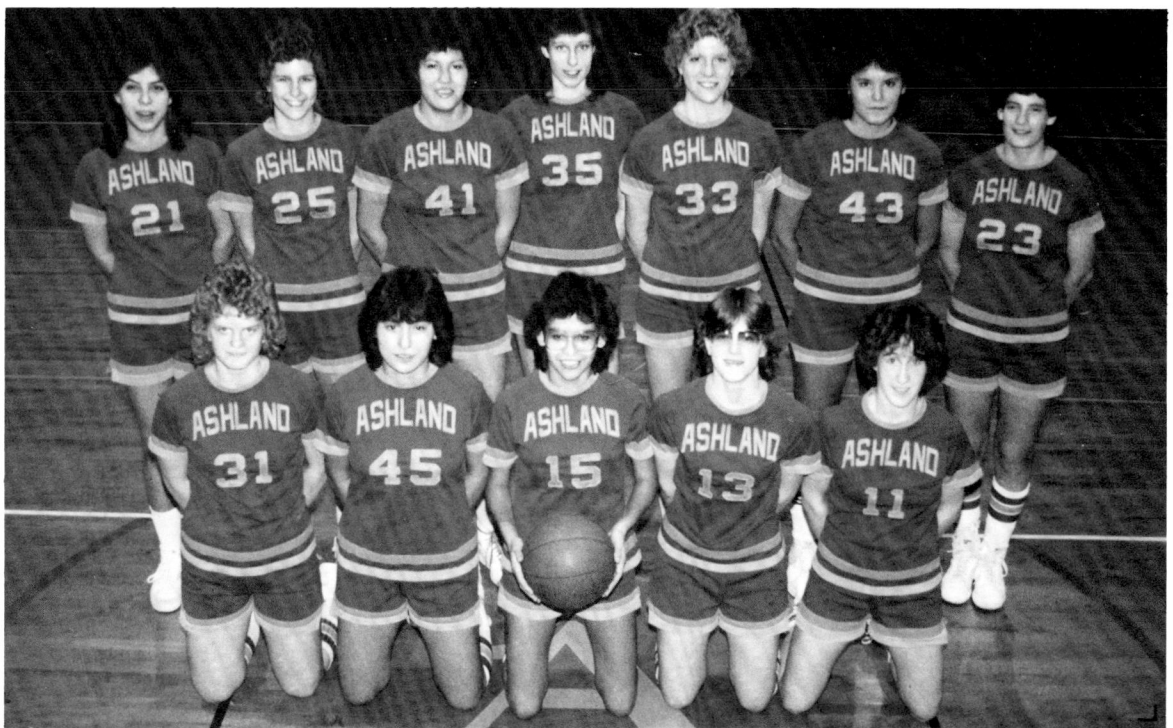

1984 Girls Basketball Team which swept first place in the Lumberjack Conference, took the regionals and sectionals, and placed second in the class B state tournament. (l to r, back) Georgiana Cloud, Jody Zipperer, Marth Tyson, Julie Raarup, Wendy Tolliver, Julie Bressette, Julie Gregoire. (front) Marilyn Puig, Jodie Vandeventer, Annette Vandeventer, Michelle Stone, Mary Martino. Coach was Tom Mestelle.

Oredocker 1984 Division II State Champion Football Team. (l to r, bottom) J. Nelson, E. Neumann, S. Renz, R. Sherman, T. Gast, M. Dormady, K.J. Pufall. (2nd row) T. Vyskocil, B. Slavik, R. Stibbe, B. Olson, M. Leplavy, T. Brown, M. Hudack, K. Polich, E. Hanson. (3rd row) B. Mikkonen, L. Griffiths, T. Louko, J. Shubat, P. Cross, K. Nemec, M. Watson, D. Tarasewicz, J. Ciran, M. Bochler. (4th row) E. Croteau, K. Munson, J. Reardon, R. Mestelle, B. Chingo, B. Mestelle, J. Witcpalek, B. Zepczyk, B. Hendrick. (5th row) M. Kurilla, F. Frost, J. Habas, B. Pralle, B. Mikkonen, T. Brown. Coached by Tom Mestelle.

Creative Expressions

"The music teachers would come to your house. Miss Hobin told my Father he was wasting his money."
Martha Donald Welker

Community theater in the 1800 s.

Ashland's first artists were homespun crafts people who brightened their daily lives with works of imagination and skill. Carvers, painters, seamstresses, embroiderers, weavers, potters, music makers, dramatists and others drew on both European and American roots to develop a rich heritage of folk art that, although often unheralded, still enhances the city.

Ashland's first commercial artists were sign and wagon painters who used their skills to advertise local businesses. The first artist mentioned in the *Press* was Thomas Nast, "a successful delineator," who also happened to share his name with the most famous American political cartoonist of his day. C.M. Dunbar and Ed Snow were known as successful sign and ornament painters. Among the few surviving works of local painters of a century or more ago is an original storefront sign panel done in black and gold leaf above the door of Bardon's Building at 518 Second Street West and the decoratively painted landscape on the door of the old Security Bank vault at 212 Second Street West.

Ashland's early building boom seems to have attracted a sizable number of artists who embellished city structures with both stone and wood carvings. The stone worker's ability is most easily seen on Richardsonian Romanesque-style facades and in the brownstone arches, foliated capitals, and gargoyles of today's City Hall, Masonic Temple and Northern States Power buildings.

Herman Kruschke and the craftsmen who worked in his furniture factory are the best remembered of Ashland's wood carvers. A Bible stand in the form of an eagle at St. Andrew's Episcopal Church and a carving of *The Lord's Supper* at St. Ambrose Catholic Church in Ironwood are two excellent examples of Kruschke's work. The most famous wood carving in Ashland is Kruschke's Chief Sitting Bull. It stood for many years in front of Parson's Cigar Store and is now located in City Hall.

City directories of the 1890s list only a handful of artists—Bige Buchanan, A.C. Baker, P. Buntman, G.S. Carey. They do report up to eight stores carrying art supplies, which suggests that many other artists were at work. By the end of the century Martin J. Hekking was billing himself as a portrait artist and three photographers—S.W. Bailey, Henry Johnson, and Whitesides and Irvin—competed with him. In 1903, Christian Raven opened the Palm Art Studio across the street from the current post office.

Eugenia DeFersia Prince Durfee, wife of mayor and mill owner William Durfee, was a writer and painter of note. Her works in gouache and watercolor are owned by many Ashlanders today. Her account of the Indian legend *The Creation of the Apostles*, included in Guy Burnham's *Lake Superior History*, and other selections from her regular *Chequamegon Column* in the *Daily Press*, gives her a strong claim to the title of Ashland's first creative writer. She lived in Ashland until 1928.

Dave Murray was once heralded as Ashland's Poet Laureate. A printer by trade, he was known for his poetic greetings to friends and his inspirational philosophy and humor. Guy Burnham was also one of Ashland's most distinguished men of letters. A long time reporter and editor of the *Press*, historian and civic leader, Burnham was

Music was so popular in the Garland City at the turn of the century that Ashlanders purchased 864 pianos for their homes in 1905.

The Windmill Gallery opened in October 1983. The gallery, owned by Peg Sandin, presently represents eighty artists in northern Wisconsin. (l to r) Nikki Cadwell, Jennae Giles, Don Albrecht, Kelly Randolph, Karlyn Holman, Donna Lanni, Ruth Campbell, Arlene Peterson, Lizabeth Sockness and Sam, Peter Sockness, Diana Randolph, Jo Suderman, Dorothy Morrow, James Pellman, Sheryl Tetzner.

known throughout Wisconsin as one of Ashland's leading voices. No Ashland writer was more popular than John C. Chapple. The famous "Squibber" personified and wrote of a wise decency that spoke directly to the best sentiments of his readers.

In the first third of this century Ashland's professional artists were often also photographers as well. Joseph Hitchinson painted in the early 1900s, but left little trace of his work. Clara and Andrew Delaney combined painting and photography until they left the city in the late 1930s. M.V. Moore, Jean Wilkins, J.A. Irvin, Georgianna Wilkinson and Katherine Bertram all had studios in these years.

Artists of the period 1930-50 are not well documented and little evidence of their presence exists. One surviving work, dated 1934, is a mural found today at Ed's Safari Tavern on East Second Street. Painted by a drifter named Jim McGillan, it depicts a northern Wisconsin evening landscape scene that required considerable effort and skill. It was all done, as the story goes, "for a bottle of wine."

It is difficult to determine the public attitude toward artists in this period. It has been suggested that artists seeking to establish themselves in the area were less than welcome. The role of the artist in relation to society in a difficult time of war and depression may have been less appreciated than in the grand days of pioneer Ashland. The unconventional, sometimes controversial, ways of artists as social commentators may

not have been understood.

Art Bloomquist is an exception to this rule. Born in Ashland in 1906, he started in watercolors and oils at the age of fourteen. He and his wife Anne first opened their Browser Book and Art Shop on Seventh Avenue West in 1934. In the 1940s they moved down to Second Street. While operating the store Art studied art books, experimented with various art products and eventually developed his own technique and style. He painted at night and sold his works in his store by day.

After 1959 he painted mostly watercolors of local scenery and became famous for his glowing portrayals of birch trees. He won awards at the University of Wisconsin and had a sell-out show at Doth Galleries in Minneapolis. The Bloomquists have lived and kept a gallery just south of Washburn since their retirement in 1972, where they've been joined by their artist-son David.

In 1955, Northland College hired Robert Eckels to expand the Student Industrial Program begun by Louis Collanco and "Than" Dexter. Students in this program made items of wood and metal and were paid on a piecework basis to help fund their education.

Eckels recalls that when he arrived in Ashland the only well known artists in the area were John Black, a farmer by trade and primitive style artist by inclination; "Snowball" Vanderventer of Red Cliff; and Art Bloomquist. In time Eckels also got to know state fair prizewinner Ruth Olson and Frieda Norlin, as well as sign painter Desmond "Bud"

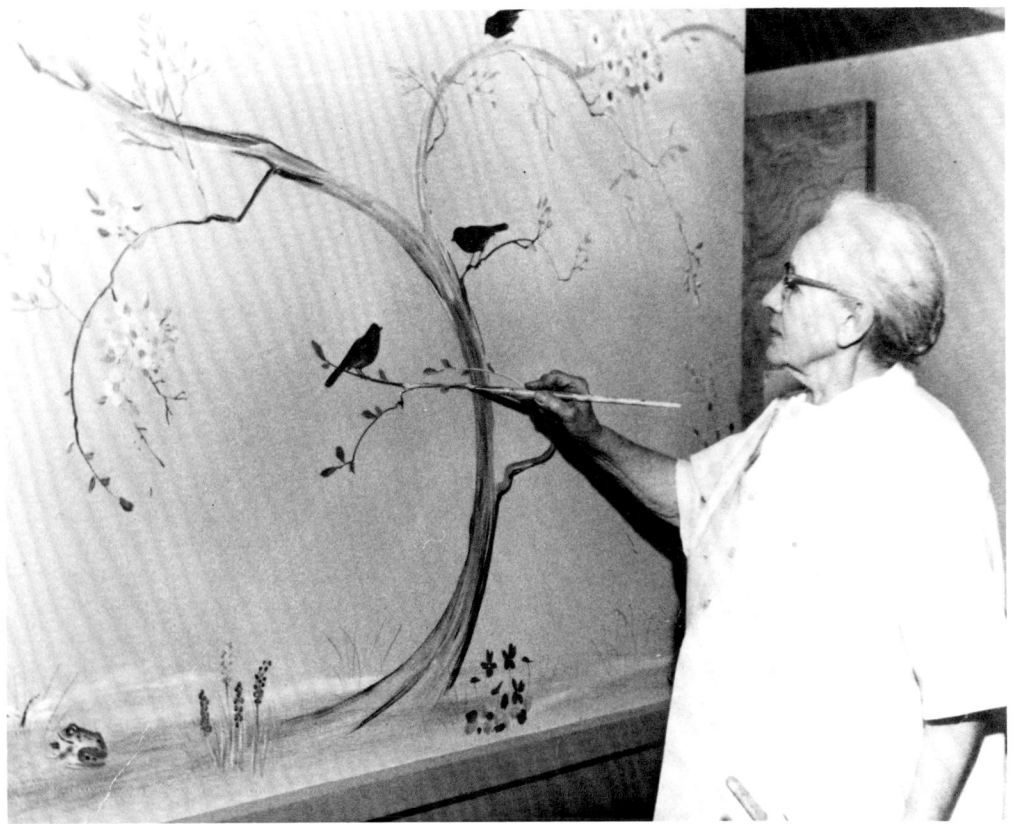

Douglas.

As had other ceramic artists and brickmakers before him, Eckels tried to use local clay in his work. When fired in the kiln, however, the limey earth exploded or crumbled. The artist continued to teach drawing design, painting, metal work, jewelry and print making at Northland. He also formed a partnership with Glenn Nelson and opened the Pot Shop. It was located on Highway 2 until construction of the Holiday House Motel prompted a move to Bayfield. Since he opened the shop, Eckels has trained no less than fifty apprentices.

His first apprentice was Washburn native Karlyn T. Holman who, after studying at the University of Wisconsin, joined Eckels on the Northland teaching staff. Paul Hubinsky arrived at Northland in 1969. Five years later he and several students designed and painted a colorful landscape mural on a barn outside of Washburn. Sponsored by a grant from the National Endowment for the Arts, the mural was featured in a *Time Magazine* article in 1977. Hubinsky continues to teach at Northland today.

The influence of Eckels, Holman, and Hubinsky on contemporary northern artists cannot be understated. Their teaching at Northland and WITI, along with printmaker Sheryl Tetzner Budnik, spread knowledge and appreciation of fine arts and helped draw many other artists to the area.

One of the early art instructors at Northland was Ashland native John Szarkowski. He became a leading authority on photography and a well-known photographer, critic and artist. His works have been displayed in many museums and galleries, including the Museum of Modern Art in New York, the Art Institute of Chicago, the George Eastman House in Rochester, the Walker Art Center in Minneapolis, and the Museum of Modern Art in Tokyo. In the late 1960s he was director of photography at the Museum of Modern Art and a consultant to President Lyndon Johnson. He has written several books, most notably a study of architectural genius Louis Sullivan.

David Genszler moved to Ashland in 1979. Seven years later he unveiled a large painted steel sculpture on the Ashland lakefront. In early 1987, he composed an ice sculpture called *Ice Blink* made of one hundred pyramids of ice, each one lit with an auto headlight. A record warm spell melted all the pyramids before the scheduled opening. Genszler then rebuilt the project with large blocks of ice from Lake Superior.

Ashland's first contemporary art show was held at Northland in the late 1960s. This show has since been succeeded by the Tri-

Lucia Hokansan, 1888-1974. Born in Sweden and trained as a decorative designer at New York's Cooper Union, she moved to Ashland in 1958 at age seventy. She painted murals for Trinity Hospital and the Ashland Nursing Home and produced countless canvases, painted driftwood and rocks.

Through grants from the Wisconsin Arts Board, Dorothy Morrow has in recent years pursued her artistic career by sketching Ashland elementary school children. Another project involved a group portrait of workers at the James River Paper Mill.

State Fair in Bayfield and the Bay Days Art Fair held in Ashland since 1980. The Union National Bank's yearly art show began in 1977. Upon the initiative of Assistant Cashier Grace Wangen, the community room in the lower level of the bank was opened for exhibits. It is now an annual event coordinated by Eleanor Gengelbach and supported by Larson Picture Frame as well as the bank. An average of one hundred artists from northern Wisconsin and Upper Michigan exhibit their work there. The Union National Bank has also sponsored an artist of the month, displaying examples of the featured artist's work in the lobby.

Other outlets for area artists to display their work include Peg Sandin's Windmill Gallery and the Memorial Medical Center. MMC has one of the largest collections of local art in Ashland. Over 350 works of art in nearly every medium comprise the collection which is the result of the efforts of the Friends of MMC.

Organized in 1972, the Friends raised over $13,000 to fund the collection and commission the painting of Paul Hubinsky's lakefront mural for the front lobby. In 1983, the Hospital Auxiliary assumed the Friends role and, under the direction of Patti Skoraczewski, continued to expand the collection. Local artist Dorothy Morrow had been honored by MMC for her commitment to the Friends.

The same clear northern light, blue waters, and forest greens that attracted artists to Chequamegon Bay a century ago still bring thoughtful, creative people to its shores in 1987. Ashland and environs has more artists than ever, and their work makes the city a richer place in which to live.

Music

The formal history of music in Ashland begins with the arrival of Martin Beaser's Chickering piano in 1859. The instrument spent more than a month on the lakes as it traveled from Buffalo to Ashland. Since the Soo Locks had yet to be constructed and large ships could not enter Lake Superior from Lake Huron, the piano was carried up the St. Mary's river via Indian canoe. The old piano remained in the Beaser family until 1925, when Anna Beaser presented it to the Old Settler's Club. It now resides in the Ashland Historical Museum, as ready to play as it was 130 years ago.

Although not every Ashland pioneer could afford to ship a piano from Buffalo, New York, nearly all of them brought an affection for music to the Bay. Church choirs, ethnic singing and dance groups, and military bands were much in vogue in the city's early days.

The George A. Custer Drum Corps mustered twenty pieces for parades and played every Friday night for a number of years at the Ashland Theater. They sported blue and gold uniforms and "U.S. Regulation helmets."

Bige Buchanan led the fifteen piece Chequamegon Brass Band with its gold and white uniforms and Franz Winninger organized the Harmonia Band at about the same time. A Scandinavian Band followed a few years later, along with the Ashland City Band, the Opera House Orchestra and Joseph Marek's Orchestra.

Shortly after the turn of the century the Hibernian Drum Corps had charge of St. Patrick's Day events. The thirteen member Corps specialized in Irish music, but the list of members included a few suspiciously non-Irish names.

Nels Yderstad, organist at Nidaros Lutheran Church, directed a strictly teetotaling men and women's singing group called the Good Templars of Sweden. Northern European music was also sung by the Swedish Glee Club and two German societies, the *Maennerchor* and *Liederkranz*. Emeline

The Ashland City Band circa 1910.

Vaughn organized the Yankees into her Vaughn Choral Society in 1896.

These groups were joined by uncountable numbers of singing groups, ethnic bands, and dance groups that made Ashland a United Nations of popular culture. On just about any given weekend until the 1950s, a willing music lover could find Finnish, Lithuanian, Swedish, Norwegian, Danish, Russian, Polish, Czech, German, Slovakian, Hungarian, Italian, French, Irish, English and American song performed within the city.

Prior to World War I up to ten music teachers resided in Ashland. Among the most notable was Ruth E. Hoppin, who taught "piano, singing, harmony and history of music," at her studio in the Wilmarth Block. For a short time, Ashland also had a Conservatory of Music where Emil Liebling, Edgar Brazelton, Mary Gleason and Rosemond Lamoreux taught piano and Mary Sage Brazelton specialized in voice.

The Cable Piano Company sold "many brand of pianos, cottage organs and Victrolas" in the first twenty-five years of this century. In 1905, when Ashland reached its peak population, Manager Pelle Larson placed 864 pianos in Ashland area homes. In 1917, the McDonald sisters opened The Garland City Music and Gift Shop. They sold and serviced musical instruments until 1956.

From its beginning in 1908, Northland College has been the musical center of Ashland. The principal organization was the choir, which, from its earliest days under the direction of Sigurd Steen, traveled widely. The Congregational Church sponsored regular tours throughout the middle and eastern states. In 1950, a Northland choir led by director Kathryn Church, performed at Orchestra Hall in Chicago. Twenty years later, the instructor William Otis organized the *Voyageurs*, who specialize in French Canadian music and lore.

Northland has also given Ashland a jazz band that has been improvising since 1951. It is currently directed by Joel Glickman. The Chequamegon Symphony, a college and community orchestra, was founded in 1965 by Donald Jackson and Jay Winking and has continued under the direction of Roland Stycos and Joel Glickman.

The first Ashland High School Band was assembled in 1913. Its members were Charles Lodle, Terry Bigelow, Ed Aldrich, Lawrence Lamoreaux, Charles Archibald, Warren

Ted Mesang, Ashland High School band director and nationally renowned author of over two hundred original band compositions.

Mayor John Dodd and Band Director Ted Mesang pose with the Ashland Band in the Bandshell newly constructed by the WPA.

French and Martin Lamoreux. Three years later this group and a few others played a formal concert in the new Royal Theater, opening with John Philip Sousa's *Stars and Stripes Forever*.

In 1924, the Ashland City Council appropriated $3,000 to establish a city band under the direction of Theodore Steinmetz. This group was also known as the 32th Division Band and, with 263 members, the "World's Biggest Boys' Band."

In 1930, Ted Mesang became director of the Ashland High School Band and made it one of the finest bands in the country. It marched and played for every civic occasion, as well as state, regional and national events. Mesang himself was one of America's outstanding band composers, author of over two hundred compositions and several band books. He was one of the first experts in marching band formations at a time when elaborate football half-time entertainments were in their infancy. He left Ashland in 1948 to compose full time but instead accepted the directorship of the Oregon State University Band and led its performance at the Rose Bowl. In 1952, Mesang was elected to the American Society of Composers, Authors and Publishers.

Pre-dating Ted Mesang's efforts on behalf of music in Ashland are those of Myrta Chapple. An accomplished pianist and member of the Presbyterian Church, she began organizing Christmas choir concerts in 1918. Each year,

Virgil and Mary Crozier and John Chapple play for a group at the VFW/American Legion in the 1980s. They also make regular performances at nursing homes.

she invited all local churches, including the Jewish Temple, to send a choir to sing in the concert. Her philosophy was that people of all faiths should have the opportunity to join in singing. Though nearly seventy years have passed since the first combined concert was held, crowds continue to more than fill the Presbyterian-Congregational Church to sing and listen on the traditional first Sunday of December.

The Ashland tradition of fine choral music is also maintained by the Chequamegon Area Choir, which includes members from all over the Chequamegon region. The group has been active since 1972 and presents at least two concerts a year. Charter members still singing with the group are organizers Vernelle Mercer and Carolyn Sneed, as well as Carole Anderson, Rosemary Bodin, Gary Holman, Rose Hovey, John Kramolis, Harold Moe, Isabelle Moe, Pat Olson, Arlene Peterson, Betty Hansen and Mary Kay Ortman.

Performing Arts

The performing arts were popular in Ashland and events took place year round at several theaters in the business district. In the optimistic 1890s construction of an elaborate Opera House with a "full-fledged three tier theatre, complete in every detail," was proposed but never built. In 1914, the old Royal Theater was opened on the Opera House site.

A large dance-hall was built in the Kuhn Block of 500 West Second Street at the turn of the century. It was popular with the Elks and for large balls sponsored by the Knights of Columbus.

The Grand Opera House at 208 Third Avenue West was designed by Chicago Architect Oscar Cobbin and opened in 1893. By 1917, it was supplanted by the Royal which offered "road attractions, high class photo play features, concert orchestra and features of quality." In the 1920s the Royal played both live acts and motion pictures. Featured on the bill were Madame Leginska, Thomas L. Thomas, Maria Galla-Curci, Mischa Elman, Florence MacBeth, Arthur Shetluck, Reinald Warranrath, the Flonzale Quartet, Madame Schumann-Heink and John McCormack.

By the end of the 1930s, the live acts were

This 1962 movie entitled "Adventures of a Young Man" was based on the stories of Ernest Hemingway. It was set in Upper Michigan but filmed in Mellen and Ashland. The movie starred Richard Bremer, Paul Newman, Dan Dailey, Arthur Kennedy and Susan Strasberg. Local engineer John Kotny is at right.

gone and only "high class movies" played. In 1938, a "mammoth air conditioned cooling system" drew patrons to the theater for evening and matinee showings with adult tickets costing twenty-five cents. By 1956, television put the Royal out of business and the building was no longer used as a theater.

Other Ashland theaters no longer in operation were the Bijou at 310 West Second Street, the Princess at 403 West Second Street and the Majestic at 309 West Second Street.

In 1937, the Bay theater at 420 West Second Street was built in the Art Deco style popular in those days. Fifty years later the Bay still displays its distinctive neon-lit marquee. Murals depicting life on Chequamegon Bay decorate the lobby and the art deco style is carried through the building.

Another Art Deco building in Ashland was the Rocket Cafe and Cocktail Lounge at 410 West Second Street. Harold and Billie Holvick managed the Rocket from 1947 until 1956. The beautifully lit Art Deco bar, with its royal blue pillars and typically deco painting of a stylized male figure on a futuristic background of planets can be seen today at Mr. John's at 717 Second Street West. In its day the Rocket attracted live entertainment from Chicago and was Ashland's leading night spot.

Amateur theatrics have always been a part of life in Ashland. Perhaps the most notable performer and director of the past was William "Bill" Dormady, who is said to have produced the greatest home talent shows known in the area. He produced at least several hundred shows in the late 1940s and early 1950s, and took them on the road to Mellen, Phillips and Ironwood. He organized, produced and directed the shows as well as performed as a solist. They were considered great community events, in part because of their high quality. Dormady expected perfection and he often accomplished it.

The ladies of the Macabee Lodge rode in this float in the 1913 Labor Day parade. Raymond Johnson drove the team.

Fellowship and Service

Ashlanders have joined clubs and groups for special purposes since before the city was founded. A community's organizations tell much about how its people think and what they care about.

A city of immigrants like the Ashland of a century ago had literally dozens of ethnic societies dedicated to helping the newcomers survive in their new environment. In addition to providing practical help in daily life, ethnic societies boosted the morale of immigrants. They could meet with others from their homeland, speak their native tongue, reminisce about the old country, and share their experiences in the new land. Many ethnic clubs took an active interest in the politics of their own land, and debates about independence for Ireland, Poland or Slovakia or discussions about the German Kaiser or the Norwegian king kept club meetings lively. It is a measure of the success of the melting pot that, as the immigrants and their children came to feel at home in their new land, they no longer needed ethnic societies. Nearly all of them have disappeared.

Many societies were organized to provide aid and comfort to those who had lost their loved ones. Nearly every fraternal group offered low cost burial or life insurance to its members, an important benefit to blue collar workers who worked for low pay and no fringe benefits.

Religious societies were important, of course. They still are today. Patriotic and commercial organizations still thrive, as do clubs whose main purpose is fellowship and community service. These needs do not change with the times.

Gone, however are the temperance groups that organized to prevent alcohol abuse in the last century. They've been replaced by professional and governmental services.

Recreational clubs were rare a century ago; so were sporting and conservation groups. There are more art, music and theatrical groups today. Some of these clubs fill in the spaces left by the demise of the old ethnic clubs, others reflect the fact that people with leisure time seek each other out to have fun together.

The list below is loosely organized according to type of clubs. Space limitations require that only a brief listing be granted to each group. To detail the complete history of many listed organizations and truly recognize all that they have done for the community would require more pages that this book contains. Still, this brief rundown of Ashland's community groups paints a picture of the city, past and present. How we've organized tells how we've lived.

Past Organizations

Native Sons and Daughters of the Badger State—1924

Danish Brotherhood of America 146—1907
O.H. Berg, N.P. Anderson.

Scandinavian Lodge Norden 60—1889
Ole Jackson. 105 members.

Order of Owls, Ashland Nest 1353—1913
Joseph Suess, J.A. Johnson.

Order of Vasa, George A. Custer Post 140—1926

Order of Vasa, Scandia Lodge—1924
Ellen Nelson.

Order of Vasa—1928
Olga Schedin.

Scandinavian H and EF of America, Lodge 7
Martin Higgen, Ole Valsted, Henry Siferson.

Scandia Lodge—1907
Louis Berg, Arvid Hedlof, John Olson, J.A. Hall and N.S. Hedin.

Scandia Sick Benefit Society—1926
J.C. Engholm.

Scandinavian American Fraternity—1917
Alf Thorson, Ole Hammer.

Scandinavian Sisters of America, Thelma Lodge 4—1939
Adeline L. Oien.

Sons of Norway—1907
C. Rood, T. Bjorndahl, James Moe, S. Lunde, P. Hallen.

Svea Society—1901
Martin Nordin, Fred Laborg, John R. Anderson, John Sundstrom. 35 members.

Soter Lodge 35—1937
Ingrid Olsen.

St. Casimir Society
M. Kurszewski, Aug Gersewski, John Wierkus, Alexander Kluczikowski.

Polish National Alliance Gmina 40, ZNP—880
A.F. Piniachowski, A. Sobolewski. 540 members.

St. Joseph Society, Branch of Polish National Alliance—1907
John Szumal, Louis Lewandowski.

Kosciusko Society, Branch 104, Polish National Alliance
Anton F. Piniachowski, Alexander Hroscichowski.

Independent Order of B'Nai Brith—1924
Joseph Cohen.

St. George Lithuanian Society—1905
John Ludkewicz.

Ancient Order of Hibernians, Division 1—1892
Dr. T.W. O'Brien, Patrick Keenan, Jeremiah Sullivan, Frank L. Matthews, John Mahoney, William B. Brown, Reverend Fabian Rechitene, OSF.

German Harmonia Society—1884
Emil Gerth, Herman Herberg, William Gerth.

Ashland *Maennerchor*—1887
Emil O. Auster, Carl Schindler, John Raetz, Mrs. W.G. Nohl, A.A. Zipperer.

The Ashland Printers Union posed outside the print shop with apprentices dressed as printer's devils.

Ashland *Liederkranz* German singing society in 1909.

Ashland *Liederkranz*—1903
Emil O. Auster, Mrs. H. Goeltz, Carl Schindler, John Raetz, Mrs. H. Vogel.

Sunshine Society—1926
Mollie Cole.

Royal Neighbors of America, Goldenrod Camp 902—1937
Mary Lucas.

Royal Arcanum, La Pointe Council 1113
B.S. Lucas, R.C. Murray.

United Order of Americans, Court Madeline 95—1924
Amanda Kelly.

United Order of Foresters, Court Madeline 95—1903
Burton Barnham, Bernice Griffith, Mrs. J.T. Wells.

Woman's Catholic Foresters, St. Mary's Court 683—1907
Mrs. J.J. McDonald, Mrs. A.J. Houle, Mrs. Dan Burk, Mrs. George W. Stenz, Mrs. William Garvin.

Catholic Order of Foresters—1895
George Stenz.

Catholic Order of Foresters Ladies Auxiliary—1924
Mrs. Joseph Mauch, Mrs. Homer Lesperance, Mrs. George Stenz, Mrs. Edward Butler, Mrs. William Stenz.

Independent Order of Foresters—1924
J.W. Sharp.

Grand Army of the Republic, William Chapple Circle—1911
Mrs. Henry Fessler.

Grand Army of the Republic, George A. Custer Post 140—1884
C.L. Judd, F.B. Waterbury, J.W. House, O.H. Premo, J. Hill.

United Spanish War Veterans (United States War Veterans), John T. Kingston Camp 34—1922
William E. Otis, F.J. Palmquist, William Upthegrove.

John T. Kingston Auxiliary 15—1922
Amanda Kelly, Cecilia Seiferman.

Wisconsin National Guard, Company D, 128th Infantry—1920
Thorwald Thorsen, Milton Gardner, Roy Robertson.

Ashland County Bible Society
J.W. Clarke's Depository.

Wisconsin Congregational Association, Northern Division—1915
Reverend F.N. Dexter

Women's Christian Temperance Union—1886
Belle Dufur, Mrs. E.A. Shores, Mrs. E.J. Lewis, Thomas Edwards. 40 members. Promoted temperance.

Frances Willards Women's Christian Temperance Union
Mrs. J.F. Scott, Mrs. J.C. Haskins. 100 members.

Independent Order of Good Templars, Swedish Lodge Ny Strid 53—1900
Evar Kraft, Martha Erickson, John Olson, Axel Strom, Louis Newquist, Andrew Nelson. 25 members.

Independent Order of Good Templars, Norwegian Lodge 50—1889
John Sannes, Annie Severson, Ole Mazness, Margido Lerstad, Ingeborg Olson, P.O. Unseth. 70 members.

Independent Order of Good Templars 211—1887
Miss Eva Banks. 125 members.

Young Men's Christian Association—1886
Dr. R.L. Nourse, D.L. Wiggins, T.C. Schutt, C.E. Street, Louis N. Larson. "Any person of good moral character can become an associate member upon payment of $5.00."

Elegance and comfort abounded at the old Elks Club located where the New China Cafe now stands.

A crowd gathered in 1912 for the grand opening of the Bohemian Hall.

YMCA Ladies Auxiliary—1889
Mrs. S. Boynton, Mrs. C.M.E. McClintock, Mrs. W.G. Bancroft, Mrs. E.B. Baldwin, Mrs. L.E. Harper, Mrs. John Bannatyne.

Ladies' Benevolent Society of Ashland—1886
Mrs. W.G. Bancroft, Mrs. J.S. Paul, Mrs. J.L. Brown, Mrs. Thomas Bardon. 40 members. "To relieve the needy and the poor."

Ladies' Hebrew Benevolent Society—1888
Mrs. C. Cohen. 13 members. "To relieve the needy and the poor."

Sacred Heart League—1905
Louis Zak, Anna Kursevvski.

Holy Rosary Society for Married Ladies—1913
Reverend Rembrant Stanowski. 65 members.

Catholic Knights of Wisconsin—1885
A.A. McDonald, Ed Freeman, Adams Stenz, P. Keenan, Joseph Mauch.

Chequamegon Club—1909
L.K. Baker, R.B. Prince, C.A. Rudquist. 40 members.

Brotherhood of American Yeoman 6771—1928
Charles Hieber.

Bear Lake Club—1899
W.G. Nohl, K.K. Kennon, T.R. Yankee.

Parent Teachers Association, Beaser School—1924
W.S. Cate.

Ashland Humane Society
D.L. Wiggins.

Ashland County Production and Marketing Administrations—1947

North Wisconsin Sportsmen's League—1903
A.A. Miller, John H. Gardner, W.G. Nohl, J.V. Woodhead. Organized for the protection of fish and game.

Ashland Baseball Association
Henry C. Donnelly, James McCully, W.D. Kuhn, A.P. McDonald, William T. Gardner.

Trades and Labor Council—1926
Viggo Sommers.

Ashland County Bar Association—1888
E.J. Dockery, W.L. Windom. 35 members.

Yourself and Ladies are respectfully invited to attend the
SECOND ANNUAL BALL
given by
Chequamegon Lodge, No. 303, B. of R.R.T.
At the Ashland Theatre,
Ashland, Wis.,
Thursday Evening, Oct. 23rd, 1890.

CARDS OF ADMISSION, $1.00.

Ashland County Medical Association—1892
J.A. Marchessault, J.M. Dodd, A.J. Hosmer.

Ashland-Bayfield-Iron County Medical Society—1913
Dr. W.T. Rinehart, Dr. C.J. Smiles.

Wisconsin Anti-Tuberculosis Association—1947

Improved Order of Red Men
John McRae, David Cochran, William McDonald.

Fraternal Reserve Association—1903
V.T. Pierrelee, O.A. Metzdorf.

Equitable Fraternal Union—1900
A.P. Tompkins, H.P. Sorenson, H. Munkwitz.

United Commercial Travelers, Chequamegon Council 24—1915; Council 245—1928
O.H. Simmerling, H.R. Cady.

Ancient Order of United Workmen—1899

Arbutus Lodge 20
Mrs. J. Ducett, Mrs. L.F. Wells, Richard Pike, Mrs. Ida Kettinger.

Columbia Lodge 19—1899
Mrs. E.W. Shatto, Julia Harder.

Ashland Lodge 115—1885
P.J. Raarup. 66 members.

Peerless Lodge 94—1889
George Hill. 57 members.

Independent Scandinavian Workingmen's Association

Morgenistjernen Branch 12
J.B. Nordby, Hans Thorson, Andrew Martinson, G.N. Risjord, Dr. N.N. Glim, Nels Stensland, Harold Hanson.

Ashland Branch 12
Harold Hanson, Louis Palm, W. Stark, Ole Hammer, Andrew Lien, Charles Ellison.

International Order of Odd Fellows

Encampment 71—1883
John Waltman. 85 members.

Lodge 63—1881
Miles Semple. 140 Members.

Brownstone Lodge 219—1894
Matthew J. Hart. 85 members.

Canton Ashland Lodge 6
J.H. Murray. 28 members.

Prosperity Lodge 37—1890
Mrs. Marcia Van Orman. 84 members. Became Daughters of Rebecca in 1913.

Knights of Maccabee—1892
Michael Cannon, M.H. Hanson. 60 members.

Knights of Pythias—1888

George B. Shaw Division 9
M.J. Hart, T.C. Smith, H.H. Ginsburg. 30 members.

The Ashland Hiking and Ski Club was organized in 1927 by Aksel Holter. These girls were no "lollypop" organization, skiing and hiking from Ashland to Washburn and beyond. The club encouraged physical, moral and spiritual fitness.

Uncle Sam (Rudy Dickert) took center stage at a 1964 VFW meeting. (l to r, back) Howard Garvin, Ray Casey, Ted Nohl, I. Ivanson, Hub Perrin, Andrew Thone, Lyle Reynolds, John Haugan, Joe Nemec, Connie Rydmark. (front) Chas. Lodle, Gus Brienfeld, Bill Snyder, John Kruschwitz, Rudy Dickert, Wis. State Comm., Dist. Comm., Post Comm., Bob Uecke, Wallace Ringham,...

Ashland Lodge 184 — 1924
A.R. Kuhn. 59 members.

Northern Lodge 55 — 1886
F. Georgen, F.W. French.

Chequamegon Lodge 184 — 1924
A.R. Kuhn.

Ashland Commandery 22, KT Masons — 1888
C.A. Lamoreaux, H.F. Higbee. 94 members.

Ancient Landmark Lodge 210, AF and AM Masons — 1878
James Firth, F.S. Struble. 146 members.

Ashland Chapter 58, Royal Arch Masons — 1890
S.D. Wood, G.H. Downie. 110 members.

Eastern Star Chapter
A.F. Wright, Mrs. S.W. Bailey. 100 members.

Ashland Council 30, R and SM Masons — 1901
Frank S. Struble, M. Kerwin, F.B. Warner, Fred W. French.

Ashland Council 58, R and SM Masons — 1899
Frank S. Struble, M. Kerwin.

Ashland Council 24, R and SM Masons — 1915
T.C. Ryerson, C.W. Hahl.

Chequamegon Chapter 696, Order of DeMolay — 1937
H.G. Sollie.

Modern Brotherhood of America Lodge 1001 — 1917
Victoria Konkol.

Modern Samaritans, Camp 96 — 1909
Alf Taylor, H.A. Cress, W.G. Nohl. 30 members.

Modern Woodmen of America

   Camp 1109 — 1889
   George Waterman, John Fosshag.

   Golden Rod Camp
   Mrs. J.H. DuMez, Mrs. L.A. LaFlamboy, G.E. Cole, Mrs. G. Ward, Mrs. P. Donahue.

Mystic Workers of the World Lodge 938
Raymond Martin, Joseph Suess. 70 members.

National Fraternal League Lodge 7 — 1902
A.M. Thoreson, Minnie Pugsley, J.G. Upthegrove. 400 members.

Knights of St. Michael 93
John Pufall, Michael Zasada, Simon Brzsciezak, V. Rrotek, Leo Fons, M. Kurszewski.

Current Organizations

Salvation Army—1888
Fdng. Off: Captain Costley, Lieutenant Woodie, Cadet Blackman. Cur. Off: Jerry Nemec, Ken Provost. Community work and help to needy families.

The Monday Club—1891
Fdng. Off: Mrs. E. Vaughn, Mrs. Wilson, Mrs. H. Sampson, Mrs. W. Merrill. Cur. Off: Sharon Roberts, Mary Jean Anno, Margaret Ritchie, Jane Sizer, Gloria Tardiff. One of oldest Women's Clubs in Wisconsin. Youth work and social club.

United Commercial Travelers of America—1903
Fdng. Off: Edgar W. Brown, E.H. Olds, Fred Van De Water, Fred Colby, Frank Dingee, M.R. Cady. Cur. Off: Clifford Barry, Terry Welty, Harold Main, Howard Tardiff. Programs for the retarded.

Ashland Wednesday Music Club—1913
Fdng. Off: Mrs. Walter J. Hodgkins, Mrs. Ione Palladeaux, Mrs. F.T. Beers. Cur. Off: Lyla Clow, Florence Brenseke, Jean Smart, Marian Penn, Lois Lightner, Jean Forsberg, Vina Penn, Lynn Adams. Works to inspire musical activity and culture. Organized its first annual Christmas Concert in 1918.

American Red Cross—1924
Fdng. Off: A.T. Pray, Mrs. W. Buckley, R.B. Prince. Cur. Off: Don Cameron, Linda Fisher, Marge Walworth. Service to military families and during community emergencies.

Pearce Peppers 4-H—1928
Fdng. Off: Linnea Johnson, Sylvia Hunt, Marie Flaherty. Cur. Off: Jill Nagro, Hedda Klatt, Anna Klatt. Spring road clean-up and fair projects.

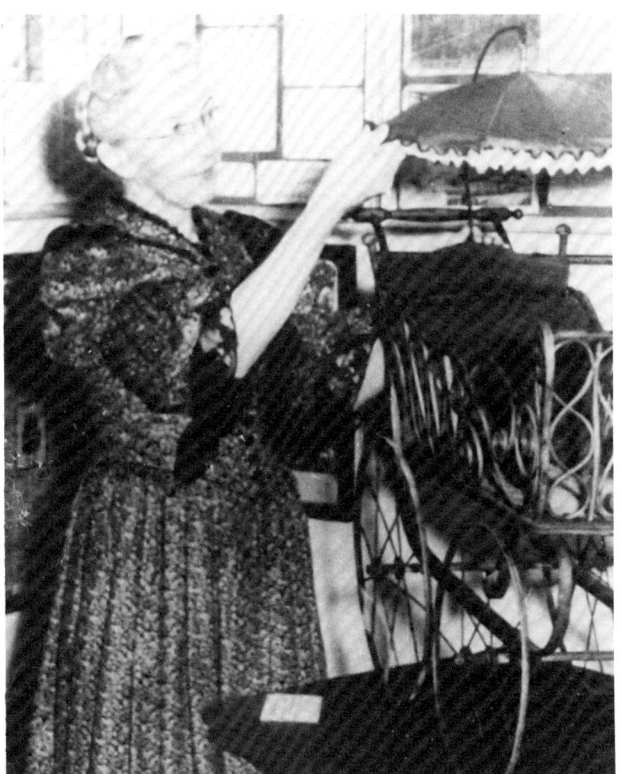

Cora Angvick, founder of the Ashland Museum and second generation of Angvick's store.

THE MONDAY CLUB

This song is all about the club of which you must have heard
Its fame has spread both far and wide so I'll just add a word
Its aim is high, its purpose good—you'll see before I'm through
Tho' of the so called weaker sex we've strength and back-bone too.
In 1891 we're told the club was organized
A few congenial spirits met and they were not surprised
To find that others fell in line to aid the work begun
And they have still kept up the pace and been excelled by none
Here we laud to the skies—Our members wondrous wise.

CHORUS
Here's to the Club with its faith ever new
Heedful of Duty's call
Sometimes I think 'tis a dream come true
There's a club in the world for us all.
It is opposed to all malice and strife
'Tis cultured through and through
I hope I may be a member for life
And what better could I wish for you.

Operation K.I.S.S.—1981
Fdng. Off: Eleanor Halverson, Elaine Kopp, Karin Pierce, Dorothy Scholl, Suzanne Smiles, Christine Sutton, Susan Vlasaty. Cur. Off: Susan Vlasaty, Karin Pierce, Christine Sutton. Informs parents of the need of child safety restraints and rents car seats for children and toddlers.

The Jaycees—1955
Cur. Off: Rex Koenamann. Community service, individual development, Halloween Haunted House. Runs Voyageur Games at Bay Days, Tree Planting Project and erects sandboxes (sand donated by Roffers Construction) for children.

Lion's Club—1986
Fdng. Off: Warren Knowles, Darryl Zak, Tom Malinowski, Richard Barringer, George Skogen. Cur. Off: Richard Barringer, Darryl Zak, Tom Malinowski, George Skogen, John Ensign. Programs for the blind, hearing impaired, mentally handicapped.

The R.S.V.P.—1973
Fdng. Off: Nellie Heffner-Beilkie. Cur. Off: Jan Washnieski, Marge Pascale. Sponsored by Northwest Community Service Agency. Enlists 600 senior citizen volunteers in community work.

Chequamegon Bay Area Retired Teachers Association—1974
Fdng. Off: Harriet Broman. Cur. Off: Leona Schraufnagel, Cora Johnson, Mildred Ledin, Ann Justice. Concerned with education and retired persons.

Friends of the Vaughn Library—1982
Fdng. Off: Jane Smith. Cur. Off: Doris Askue, Joyce Neumann, Marilyn Twining. Fund raising and volunteer work for the library.

Wisconsin Right-To-Life—1978
Cur. Off: Jane Schraufnagel, Kathy Heybrecht, Theresa Lachecki. Anti-abortion.

Ashland Historical Society—1980
Fdng. Off: Keith Dallenbach, Allan Cate, Jean Kreher, Randy Wassgren, Sue Van Hoof, Marge Longstreth, Howard Pearson. Cur. Off: Ann Moran, Jane Tolliver, Jean Kreher, Connie Cogger, James Klatt, Howie Pearson, Pat Parent, Sue McCue.

Cele Carnahan's Kitchen Belles played and sang the "good old songs" at community events in 1962.

Dutch elm disease in the 1970 s and 80 s robbed Ashland of hundreds of its beautiful elm trees. The Jaycees annual spring tree planting efforts have attempted to recapture the Garland City atmosphere. (l to r) George Lawver, Paul Bertucci.

Compassionate Friends, Chequamegon Bay Area Chapter—1981
Fdng. Off: Jenny Strzok, Pat Vernier, Mary Maller. Cur. Off: Esther Pufall, Gordon Hillsman, Pat Vernier. A support group for parents who have experienced the death of a child through miscarriage, stillbirth, infant death, accident and illness.

Chequamegon Audubon Society—1984
Fdng. Off: Tom Syverud, Jim Bussey, Daniel Schell, Ron Lockwood. Cur. Off: Jim Bussey, Lee Gehrke, Paul Strong, Jean Kreher. Environmental educational and social organization.

Chequamegon Theatre Association—1972
Fdng. Off: Mr. & Mrs. David Trudeau, Mr. & Mrs. Norman Glovsky. Cur. Off: Linda Fish, Jim Solberg, Faye Christensen, Lynn Adams, Warren Kehn, Tim Colglazier, Sue Theno, Donna Kramolis, Deb Neuheisal Smith. Brings live theater to the area.

Chequamegon Animal League—1980
Fdng. Off: Allen Kettinger, Peggy Nieland, Fran Ante, Jill Gallant. Cur. Off: Fred Brown, Fran Ante, Arlene Slais, Tordis Yderstad, Marion Zinnacker, Rachel Strom. Operates an animal shelter that serves three counties.

American Cancer Society—1960
Fdng. Off: Amy Sollie. Cur. Off: Hildegard Morris, Kyle Tidstrom, Eileen Schraufnagel, Elna Hanson, Jeanne Beirl. Public education and assistance to cancer patients.

League of Women Voters—1955
Fdng. Off: Caroline Sandin, Jean Kreher, Joyce Clark, Alice Boalind, Marj Lockard. Cur. Off: Leslie Hamp, Beth Oujiri, Linda Hmielewski, Marjory Longstreth, Linda Larson. Promotes the active and informed participation of citizens in government.

It just wouldn't be Christmas in Ashland without the Children's Theater annual presentation of the "Nutcracker Suite" under the direction of Sue Theno.

Chequamegon Theater Association presented "Carousel" in October 1986. (l to r, back) Michelle Larson, Pam Noble, Gena McNutt, Sandy Larsen (front) Sally Durand, Shelley Hicks, Nancy Nelson.

Children's Theater production of "Tom Sawyer" under the direction of Sue Theno. (l to r) Gina Monroe, Jessica Webner, Ben Sandin, Scott Theno, Mike Miller.

The Ashland Foundation—1930
Fdng. Off: Helen Baker. Cur. Off: Walter Larson, H. Lyman Bretting, Norman Warren, Darrell Robertson, Matthew Anich, David Pauli, Mary Taggett, Mayor Dan Theno. Grants to local non-profit groups.

The Little League—1960
Fdng. Off: Ed Kernan, Bob Lindsey, Bill Carnahan, George Hennell, Norman Warren, John Peterson, Robert Eley, Pete Hanson, Bert Strom, Gil Paulson, Ronald Harrison, John Harrison, Marius Berg, Tad Bretting, Duane Jensen, Howard Sampson, Jr., Peter Sherfinski, Hank Martinson, James Trelford, Ted Thomas, Fran Hicks, John Burke, Myron Brose, LeRoy Ming. Cur. Off: Mark Van Vlack, George Stolarzyk, Mike Masterson, Gene Martino.

Bay Area Clergy—1970
Cur. Off: Reverend Steve Foster, Sister Margaret Halaska, Father Robert Kozarek. Crop Walk for Hunger, Annual Prayer for Christian Unity, Co-Pace.

American Business Women's Association—1983
Fdng. Off: Carol Laudenbach Cur. Off: Mary Ganzel. Thirty-six area members dedicated to bringing together business women of diverse backgrounds and providing opportunities for them to help themselves.

American Association of Retired Persons—1974
Fdng. Off: Ron Harrison, Lloyd Amundson, Hazel Roy, Nellie Heffner, Kurt C. Johnson, Fred Smith, Elmer Rothing, Lillian Morander, Helen Magneson, Verner Sandstrom. Cur. Off: Lyla Clow, Jerry Delvux, Evelyn Oestricher, Bernice Brinker, Bert Anderson, Katherine Anich, Henry Zeck. Concerned with legislative, social, medical and financial concerns of the elderly.

Hospital Auxiliary of Memorial Medical Center—1972
Fdng. Off: Betty Jauquet, Joan Kramer, Bertha Dunn, Mary Jean Schafer, Nelle Hagstrom. Cur. Off: Barbara Barry, Patricia Stromberg, Marcia Kraft, Betty Chambers. Fund raisers for Memorial Medical Center.

Lakeshore Art Association—1974
Fdng. Off: Lucele Gadda, Toine Gildersleeve, Evelyn Durocher, Eileen Carlson, Kay Chapin, Lee Schmidt. Encourages area artists through workshops and exhibitions.

Rotary Club—1920
Fdng. Off: W. Sanborn, R. Bretting, M. Seaman, D. Murry. Cur. Off: A. Wilhelm, P. Erickson, M. Wallschlaeger. J. Bay, J. Langford, H. Martinsen, B. Evenson, J. Audetat. Youth work, exchange students, Northland scholarship and international health and education programs.

New Day Shelter, Northwoods Women Inc.—1983
Cur. Off: Barbara Hansen, Robin Trinko-Russel, Kathy Carlson, Anne Wickman, David Siegler, Candy Jackson, Nancy Wagner, Donna Lapp, Judith Lokken-Strom. Shelter for victims of domestic abuse.

Friendship Card Club—1968
Fdng. Off: Mildred Smith, Della Oien, Clara Veno. Cur. Off: Lillian Marander, Astrid Bertheaume, Elizabeth Hubbard. Social club.

Kiwanis—1944
Fdng. Off: Hans Christiansen, B.H. Metternich, Ervin Kam, John Voss, Ardath Garnich. Cur. Off: John Goossen, Jack Anderson, William Eggert, Wayne Reed. Numerous youth and community service projects.

Girl Scouts—1918
Fdng. Off: Mrs. C.L. Koons. Cur. Off: Carol Melin, Sharon Manthei, Rosie Ochsner, Kathy Budreau, Jane Asbach, Carol Pauli, Sarah Cinker, Lori Hoffman, Wendy Dufek, Carol Root, Anne Nelson, Stephanie Spealman, Eileen Van Pernis.

Western Fraternal Life Association (Z.C.B.J. Lodge)—1902
Fdng. Off: Joseph Suess, Joseph Ludack, Joseph Dufek, Frank Vocelka, Jacob Konop, Joseph Borecky, John Jilek, Frank Mateofsky, Joseph Chvala. Cur. Off: James McGraw, Harold Martin, Fran Holvick, Clara Sveda, Betty Drolson, Joseph Bradle, Sr., Roxann Sutarik.

Knights of Columbus—1903
Fdng. Off: T.E. Sullivan, M.H. Shrank, J. Egan, J. O'Brien, J.J. Sullivan, E.A. Myott, E.J. Hoppenyan. Cur. Off: Pat Flynn, John Doane, John Donahue, Ken Secord.

Fraternal Order of Eagles—1901
Fdng. Off: William Heim, V.T. Pierrelee, Tony Huotte, Thomas Kenneally. Cur. Off: Bill Erickson, Myron Anderson, Jerry Nemec, Martin Eder. Community service.

Eagles Auxiliary—1953
Fdng. Off: Erma Anderson, Leona Pentony, Laura Pearson, Loretta Kupczyk, Sylvia Zar, Agnes Cadotte, Ethel Jacka, Barbara Wiberg, Dorothy Johnson, Fran Armstrong, Emma Mathiowitz, Lorraine Anderson, Belle Bellile. "People Helping People" is their motto.

Moose Lodge—1973
Fdng. Off: Bill Mertig, Dick Emmert. Cur. Off: John Carli, Harry Hultman. Support for child city of Mooseheart and Moosehaven for senior citizens in Florida.

Women of the Moose—1975
Fdng. Off: Carol Ante, Barbara McLennon, Barbara Tomlinson, Frances Holvick, Kathleen Mertig, Mary Emmert. Cur. Off: Beverly Hall, Lori Mahnke, Charlene Chidsey, Kathleen Carli, Ruth Nordin, Jeanne Hultman. Objective is to assist in all charitable activities of the Moose and the community.

The *Voyageurs* under the direction of Bill Otis perform French Canadian music and lore throughout the Northland.

Lac La Belle Chapter 24, Order of the Eastern Star—1892
Fdng. Off: Emeline Vaughn Mackinnon, G.W. Carrington, Sarah Bancroft, Effie Heydlauff. Cur. Off: Jean Stenberg, Alex Mathey, Lillian Ketchem. Charitable and social organization.

United Transportation Union—1970
(Began as Brotherhood of Railroad Trainmen, Chequamegon Bay Lodge 213 in 1901). Cur. Off: Dorothy Leciejewski, Gloria Tardiff, Viola Roetig, Laura Pearson, Ceil MacDonald, Elaine Burke, Janet Fossum, Peg Howard, Dorothy Cameron, Josephine Mason, Elaine Welty.

St. Agnes-Holy Family Post 1667, Catholic War Veterans—1950
Fdng. Off: Fr. Ladislas Siekaniec. Cur. Off: Eric Blancfeld, Frank Szumal, Pius Schafer. A social club.

Prosperity Rebekah Lodge 37—1890
Cur. Off: Anita Lindberg, Laura Deeth, Grace Grehn, Charlotte Kettinger, Lorraine Johnson. A community service and social club.

Elks 137—1900
Fdng. Off: M.E. Dillon, E.E. Tennant, D.E. Cartier, E.F. Gleason, R.C. Murray, W.S.Cate, A.A. Habbs, F. Brennan, C. Clark, W.B. Rae. Cur. Off: Allan T. Anderson, Gerald Gurske, Scott Sprague, Thomas Marincel, Francis Hicks, Jeffrey Beirl, Lawrence Fischer,Sr., Ralph Anderson, Richard Wallace, Joseph Kegel, Roger O'Malley. For all forward thinking men who seek association with their fellows in an atmosphere of freedom from mercenary motives, political or religious controversy.

Chequamegon Memorial Post 690, Veterans of Foreign Wars—1945
Fdng. Off: Edwin Quistorff, Thomas E. Anderson, Claude Cooper, Clayton Wallin. Cur. Off: Harris L. Woodard, Allan T. Anderson, Donald Roethig, Kenneth Somppi, Ellerd Beesley, Russell Willoughby. Takes care of veterans's needs.

Chequamegon Memorial Auxiliary to Post 690—1946
Fdng. Off: Catherine Gay, Celia Sieferman, Minnie Meagher, Mary Baranby, Mary Quistorff, Caroline Beil, Theresa Rosenfield. Cur. Off: Judy Pospychalla, Elaine Jaskowiak, Bettie Parent. Helps veterans and their families in times of need.

Kelly-Johnson Post 90, American Legion—1919
Fdng. Off: James McCully, Lyman Pool, Walker Sanborn, Thorwald Thoresen, Wesley Wilman, Jake Olsen, George Harrison. Cur. Off:Pat Pospychalla, Steve Flanders, Allan T. Anderson, Ron Lockwood, Les Pufall. Work in youth, community and veterans' programs.

Lake Superior C.B. Club—1975
Fdng. Off: Carl Ledin, Tom Massen, Bill Carlson. Cur. Off: Deanne Tannenberg, Joyce Erickson, John Puska. For the mutual benefit of all interested in C.B. Radio.

Fidelis Gamma Chapter—1984
Fdng. Off: Carmen Griffiths, Jane Sizer, Dorothy Kangas, Daisy Johnson, Louise Shubat, Katherine Anich, Esther Thayer, Bernes Butterworth. Cur. Off: Jane Sizer, Louise Shubat, Katherine Anich, Esther Thayer, Faye Hnath, Dorothy Kangas, Marie Van Guilder, Virginia Tarter. Gives scholarships to students majoring in education.

Pythian Sisters, Chequamegon Temple 40—1921
Fdng. Off: Isabelle Lamoreux, Lulabelle Eva, Mayme Bessey, Mabel Thorsen, Nell Gaarder, Effie Stensland, Hazel Larson, Emma Gahlaar, Harriet Anderson. Cur. Off: Helen Mehalik, Arlene Sveda, Lillian Marander, Laura Pearson, Thelma Gadda, Dorothy Plizka, Gladys Eckholm, Martha Jonovic, Dorothy Nettleton. Helps crippled children who have heart and other birth defects.

B.P.O. Does #882—1964
Fdng. Off: Darlene Dulitz. Cur. Off: Karen Dickerhoff. Charitable organization.

Ashland Women's Bowling Association—1947
Fdng. Off: Leora Strom, Agnes Benedict, Harriet Borowick, Agnes Berglin, Agnes Coffey. Cur. Off: Marlene Parkhurst, Joyce Pufall, Jeanne Oksiuta, Paula Cuffle, Marge Provost. Promotes women's bowling in Ashland area.

Northland College Student Association—1970
Fdng. Off: Drew Olim, Jim Miller, Patricia Ortman, Devon Dutra. Cur. Off: Tony Williams, Star Rice, David Livingston, Charlie Schmalz, Sharon Kindon, Troy Juntenen, Chris Strom. Legislative power of Northland college students.

Ashland Gun Club—1944
Fdng. Off: Roy Malmberg, Ray Casey. Cur. Off: Jeff Johnson, Jon Berg. Promotes trap shooting and runs trap shooting leagues.

Industrial Men's Bowling League—1929
Cur. Off: Garfield Carlson, Ozzie Morrison. Tony Rogalski has bowled in the League every year since it was formed.

Women's Volleyball—1969
Fdng. Off: Joan Nelson. Cur. Off: Carol Ante, Denise Lampson, Nancy Carlson. Recreation for women out of high school.

Men's Softball Association
Cur. Off: Gary Kaiser, Gene Cichon, John Marincel, Dan Kucinski. Promotes men's softball.

Women's Softball Association—1972
Fdng. Off: Kathy Culligan, Lynn Toman, Michele Kegel. Cur. Off: Carol Ante, Sue Schanadore, Denise Lampson. Promotes softball for any female over the age of twelve.

Karate Club—1977
Fdng. Off: Bruce Prentice, Brian Kerr, Paul Susienka. Teaches karate and martial arts to all ages of men, women and youngsters.

Lake Superior Chapter, Ducks Unlimited—1971
Fdng. Off: Jack Price, Sarg Havner, Jerry Huhn. Cur. Off: Jerry Huhn, Carl Bauer, Robert Fiegle, Tom Hubbard. Raises funds for preserving wetland breeding grounds for waterfowl.

Chequamegon Bay Birders—1976
Fdng. Off: Dick Verch, Doris Leppla. Cur. Off: Dick Mihalek, Joanna Mihalek. Observes and studies birds.

Chequamegon E.Z. Riders—1971
Fdng. Off: Charlotte Nye, Ron Nye, Bob Wadzinski, Carol Wadzinski, Nancy Peck, Lisa Boness, Mr. & Mrs. Mike Gregor, Pete Bartol, Evelyn Bartol, John Bloomquist. Cur. Off: Sandy Kubarek, John Pearson, Barb Bitzer, Evelyn Bartol, Nancy Beckman. Sponsors horsemanship clinics and promotes interest in equines.

Bay Area Gymnastic Club—1981
Fdng. Off: Laura Metcalf. A member of United States Gymnastics Federation, the club competes on state and regional levels and with Canadian teams.

Men's Senior League Hockey—1987
Fdng. Off: Tom Hubbard. Promotes adult ice hockey.

Bay Area Runners Club—1979
Fdng. Off: Arnold Lumberg, John Hogan, James Scott. Cur. Off: Arnold Lumberg, Pete Viator, George Grosjean, Donna Austin. Promotes running.

Elk Ladies Social Bowling League—1953
Fdng. Off: Irene Hansen, Margret Erickson. Cur. Off: Vicki Joyal, A. Pero. Social club.

Bay Area Rod and Customs—1977
Fdng. Off: Bob Schwiesow, Jon DeMars, Ed Karaba, Bob Karaba. Cur. Off: Al Piff, Jr., Les Lampson, Trudy Mashlan, Ed Karaba. Promotes and helps people restore and show antique cars.

Bay Area Women's Volleyball—1980
Fdng. Off: Jan Kupczyk, Cathy Sunie, Jan Kontny. Cur. Off: Sherry Lehto, Lois Belanger, Donna Tarasewicz. Created so teams can have more playing time and be more competitive.

North Wisconsin Rod and Gun Club—1915
Fdng. Off: W.G. Nohl, Gust Larson, Ted Nohl. Cur. Off: Bud Williams, Malcolm Traaholt, Robert Belsky, Dean Westlund, John Kirklewski, Paul Ratliff, Tom Pingel, Dave Pero, Gilbert Westman, Gerald Carlson, Mike Bietka, Mike Delasky. One of the oldest conservation clubs in Wisconsin. Supports wise use of fish, game and other natural resources.

Ashland Booster Club—1982
Fdng. Off: Don Blazek, Ed Pufall, Gary Kaiser, Kay Minten. Cur. Off: Ed Pufall, Tim Pralle, Gary Kaiser, Ann Roffers. Supports and encourages high school athletes.

Northwood's Cyclists—1980
Fdng. Off: Joe Agostine, Sandy Agostine, Shelly Viator, Barb Hennell. Cur. Off: Pete Viator. Promotes cycling. Organizes 40 Mile Race and 100 Mile Run.

Ashland Snowmobile Association—1977
Cur. Off: Tom Marincel, Larry Miller, Julie Marincel, Lori Schmidt. Fund raising for local causes. Maintains snowmobile trails.

Chequamegon Outboard Boating Club, Inc.—1952
Fdng. Off: Gilbert Westman, Glen Paulson, Manard Holtz, Paul Solberg. Cur. Off: Allan Smiles, Emil Erickson, Ken Fossum, Frank Kucinski, Garfield Carlson, James Tomczak. Provides a focal point for boating enthusiasm on Chequamegon Bay. Cooperatively maintains a public boat landing.

Ashland Youth Hockey—1969
Fdng. Off: Harvey Haukaas. Cur. Off: Jerry Huhn, Robert Ford, Barb Bochler, Les Whiteaker, Don Neste, Jan Kupczyk, Mel Maday, Joey Ford. Promotes and supports youth hockey.

1987 Youth Hockey. (l to r, front) Scott Theno, Chris Hogan, Ben Sandin, Kelly Jensen, Allan Kupczyk. (2nd row) Eric Mirwald, Mike Brown, Shawn O'Connell, Ricky Ogle, Ryan Goetz, Danny Van Hoof, Jason Root, Shawn Watland, Shawn Lund. (3rd row) Cory Ford, Aaron Larson, Matthew Van Hoof, Paul Halbe. (4th row) Jay Meierotto, Chris Vernier, Chris Wilmot, Paul Wickman, Jeff Brown, Paul Knowles, Chris Houle, Chad Gauthier. (5th row) Brian Louko, Scott Bochler, Barry Stromberg, Don Wilmot, Steve Wotruba, David Johnson. (6th row) Scott Mirwald, Paul Cross, Nate Schraufnagel, Ryan Swanson, Garit Pederson, Jeff Culligan. (top) Brian Lee, Paul Neste, Todd Culligan, Davy Pratt, Danny Leciejewski, Tim Dietman, Bill O'Connell.

Boy Scout Anniversary

Boy Scout Trout #1 organized in Ashland in 1912. Pictured are the 1916-1917 Boys Scouts. (l to r) Martin Juhl, Maurice Otis, Harold Thines, Bud Koons, Stewart Hosmer, Paul Bloomquist, Jimmy Good, Henry Anderson, Murry Wilson, Walter Smith, Leslie Koons, Rodney Osborn.

The year 1987 marks the Seventy-Fifth Anniversary of the oldest continually active Boy Scout Troop in Wisconsin—and that troop is sponsored by the United Presbyterian-Congregational Church, Ashland.

Not only is Troop Number 331 the oldest in the state, but one of the oldest in the nation. In May, the troop celebrated its birthday in grand style. It's quite a feat to have operated a troop every year since May 12, 1912, when the troop was chartered as Troop Number 1. Leading the boys as the first Scoutmaster was the Reverend Carlton L. Koons, pastor of First Presbyterian.

The troop began the current year with only one member. There are now seven Scouts and Number 331 is looking for more.

Members of the Troop are Ryan Skoraczewski, Dallas Roberts, Nathan Pierce, Ryan Pierce, Joshua Kramer, Mike Haukaas and Garrette Baird.

Scoutmaster is Floyd Hovarter and Tom Cogger and Eric Adams are Assistant Scoutmaster. The Troop Committee consists of Harvey Haukaas, Eric Lipke, Tom Cogger, Sue Robinson and Eric Adams, who is also Scouting Coordinator for the church.

Two of the oldest Scouts in the state, who began their Scouting adventures in Ashland, still live in the city: Alec Paton, 88, was a member of the first Ashland Boy Scout Troop when it was associated with the Congregational Church in 1911; and Lyle Reynolds, 90, who still sings in the church choir, was a member of the Presbyterian Church Scout Troop when it was organized in 1912.

Scouting in Ashland began only one year after the Boy Scout movement became active in the United States. A great tradition lives on in Ashland as the city marks its Centennial.

Bibliography

Aikens, Andrew J. and Proctor, Lewis A. (ED), *Men of Progress, Wisconsin, A Selected List of Biographical Sketches of the Leaders in Business, Professional and Official Life,* Milwaukee: The Evening Wisconsin Company, 1897.

Album of Wisconsin Railroad Scenery (no other info provided).

"Articles of Incorporation" The Ashland Foundation, 1930

Ashland City Directories, Ashland, Wisconsin and St. Paul, Minnesota: R.L. Polk & Co., 1890, 1892, 1895, 1897, 1899, 1901, 1903, 1905, 1909, 1911, 1915, 1917, 1922.

The Ashland Daily Press Vol. IV, No. 259, published in Ashland, Wisconsin, January 15, 1892, by Joe. M. Chapple.

The Ashland Daily Press Annual Edition, 1893.

The Ashland Daily Press, Special Edition, "Garland City of the Inland Sea", September, 1905.

Ashland Daily Press, Chequamegon Region Who's Who Edition, 1929.

Ashland Daily Press, History and World War II Edition, December 31, 1945.

Ashland Daily Press, Memorial Edition, May 1, 1947.

Ashland Daily Press, December 31, 1948.

Ashland Daily Press Historic 1951 Chippewa Indian Edition, March 26, 1951.

Ashland Daily Press, Centennial Progress Edition, July, 1954.

Ashland Daily Press, 125th Ashland Anniversary Edition, July 14, 1979.

Ashland Gateway to the Apostle Islands Ashland: Chamber of Commerce, 1925.

Ashland and Environs: The Chequamegon Region, Parts 1-8. Neenah, Wisconsin: Art Publishing Co., 1888.

Ashland Salutes 100 Years of Progress, Official Souvenir Program and Historical Booklet of the Ashland Centennial Celebration, Ashland: Ashland Centennial Corporation, 1954.

Ashland, Wisconsin, Illustrated, Milwaukee: The Art Gravure & Etching Co., 1891.

Benton, Marjorie F. (ED). *The Golden Days of LaPointe, Bayfield, Ashland, Washburn: Historical Study of Chequamegon Bay Area,* Ashland: The American Association of University Women, Chequamegon Branch, 1972.

Burnham, Guy M., *The First House Built by White Men in Wisconsin.* Ashland: Ashland Daily Press, 1931.

Burnham, Guy M., *The Lake Superior Country in History and in Story,* Boston: Chapple Publishing Company Limited, 1930.

Chapple, John B. (compiler) *History of Ashland, Wisconsin, and Our Region.* Ashland: Ashland Daily Press, 1947.

Chequamegon Chronicle, Supplement to The Daily Press, Chequamegon Area Bicentennial Edition, Ashland, July, 1976.

Chequamegon: *A Pictorial History of the Lake Superior Region of Ashland and Bayfield Counties,* Ashland: Ashland-Bayfield Bicentennial Committee, 1976.

City Charter of the City of Ashland, Ashland: Daily News Print, 1889.

Commemorative Biographical Record of the Upper Lake Region, Chicago: J.H. Beers and Co., 1905.

Culver, Edith Dodd, *610 Ellis and the Hospital Children.* Ashland: Browser Books, 1978.

Dictionary of Wisconsin Biography, Madison: The State Historical Society of Wisconsin, 1960.

Dodd, John Morris, *Autobiography of a Surgeon,* New York, Walter Neal, 1928.

Duluth Sunday News-Tribune Feature Section, June 27, 1954.

Harris, Walt, *The Chequamegon Country, 1659-1976.* Fayetteville, Arkansas: Walter J. Harris, 1976.

Historical Atlas of Wisconsin, Compiled and published by Snyder, VanVechten & Co., Milwaukee, Wisconsin 1878.

History of Northern Wisconsin, Chicago: The Western Historical Company, 1881.

Illustrated Souvenir: Chequamegon Bay and Its Surroundings, Ashland: J.M. Turner & Company, circa 1890 (no actual date given).

Insurance Maps of Ashland, Ashland County, Wisconsin, New York: Sanborn-Perris, 1901 and 1890.

MacDonald, Flora J. and the Social Problems Class of Ashland High School, *The History of the Public Schools of the City of Ashland,* Ashland: Board of Education, 1940.

Minutes of the Meetings of the Ashland City Council, 1887-1987, Ordinance Books of the Ashland City Council, 1887-1987.

Ruth, Harry S, *Ashland County, Wisconsin in the World War 1917-1919,* Boston: Chapple Publishing Company, Ltd., 1928.

Sennott, Steve, with Tolliver, Jane, *City of Ashland Historic-Architectural Intensive Survey Report,* Ashland: Northwest Wisconsin Regional Planning Commission in connection with the City of Ashland and the Ashland Historical Society and the State Historical Society of the State of Wisconsin, 1983.

A Souvenir of Ashland County, Wisconsin, Iron Mountain, Michigan: C.O. Stiles, 1904.

Official Program of the Twentieth Annual Convention of the Department of Wisconsin American Legion Convention, held on August 13-16, 1938 in Ashland, Wisconsin.

Lewis, Catherine Whittier. "Women's Lib-Ashland Style," *Wisconsin Sampler,* Edited by Sue E. McCoy, Madison: Northword, 1983.

Hyde, Charles K, *The Northern Lights,* Lansing, Michigan: Two Peninsula Press, 1986.

Assorted Unpublished Articles, Manuscripts and Papers Located In The Genealogy Research Room, Second Floor, Vaughn Library.